WOMEN, MEN & U.S. POLITICS: TEN BIG QUESTIONS

WOMEN, MEN & U.S. POLITICS: TEN BIG QUESTIONS

JENNIFER L. LAWLESS
AMERICAN UNIVERSITY

RICHARD L. FOX
LOYOLA MARYMOUNT UNIVERSITY

W. W. NORTON & COMPANY
NEW YORK • LONDON

W. W. Norton & Company has been independent since its founding in 1923, when William Warder Norton and Mary D. Herter Norton first published lectures delivered at the People's Institute, the adult education division of New York City's Cooper Union. The firm soon expanded its program beyond the Institute, publishing books by celebrated academics from America and abroad. By midcentury, the two major pillars of Norton's publishing program—trade books and college texts—were firmly established. In the 1950s, the Norton family transferred control of the company to its employees, and today—with a staff of four hundred and a comparable number of trade, college, and professional titles published each year—W. W. Norton & Company stands as the largest and oldest publishing house owned wholly by its employees.

Editor: Peter Lesser
Project Editor: Linda Feldman
Associate Editor: Samantha Held
Managing Editor, College: Marian Johnson
Managing Editor, College Digital Media: Kim Yi
Production Manager, College: Eric Pier-Hocking
Media Editor: Spencer Richardson-Jones
Associate Media Editor: Michael Jaoui
Media Editorial Assistant: Ariel Eaton
Marketing Manager, Political Science, Erin Brown
Design Director: Hope Miller-Goodell
Designer: Debby Dutton
Photo Editor: Stephanie Romeo
Permissions Manager: Megan Schindel
Composition: Graphic World
Manufacturing: Sheridan

Permission to use copyrighted material is included on page 201.

ISBN 978-0-393-60254-8 (pbk.)

W. W. Norton & Company, Inc., 500 Fifth Avenue, New York, NY 10110-0017
wwnorton.com
W. W. Norton & Company Ltd., Castle House, 75/76 Wells Street, London W1T 3QT

1 2 3 4 5 6 7 8 9 0

BRIEF CONTENTS

CONTENTS

CHAPTER 3: GIRL POWER ISN'T POLITICAL POWER: THE GENDER GAP IN POLITICAL AMBITION

KEY QUESTION: WILL THE NEXT GENERATION OF ELECTED LEADERS CONTINUE TO BE DOMINATED BY MEN?

CHAPTER 4: INTO THE FRYING PAN: WOMEN'S EXPERIENCES RUNNING FOR OFFICE

KEY QUESTION: DO WOMEN HAVE A TOUGHER TIME GETTING ELECTED THAN MEN?

CHAPTER 5: SHOW ME THE MONEY: THE MALE-DOMINATED WORLD OF CAMPAIGN FINANCE

KEY QUESTION: ARE WOMEN AND MEN EQUALLY LIKELY TO USE MONEY TO GREASE THE WHEELS OF THE POLITICAL SYSTEM?

ABOUT THE AUTHORS

JENNIFER L. LAWLESS is professor of government at American University, where she is also the director of the Women & Politics Institute. She received her Ph.D. in political science from Stanford University and her B.A. from Union College. Professor Lawless's research, which has been supported by the National Science Foundation, focuses on representation, political ambition, and gender in the electoral process. She is the author of *Becoming a Candidate: Political Ambition and the Decision to Run for Office* (Cambridge University Press, 2012) and the coauthor of *Women on the Run: Gender, Media, and Political Campaigns in a Polarized Era* (Cambridge University Press, 2016), *Running from Office: Why Young Americans Are Turned Off to Politics* (Oxford University Press, 2015), and *It Still Takes a Candidate: Why Women Don't Run for Office* (Cambridge University Press, 2010). Her work has appeared in academic journals, including the *American Political Science Review, American Journal of Political Science, Perspectives on Politics, Journal of Politics, Political Research Quarterly, Legislative Studies Quarterly,* and *Politics & Gender* (of which she served as editor from 2010 through 2013). She is also a nationally recognized speaker on electoral politics. Her scholarly analysis and political commentary have been quoted in numerous newspapers, magazines, television news programs, and radio shows. For the 2012 and 2016 presidential elections, she was part of NBC's *Decision Night in America* programming. In 2006, she sought the Democratic nomination to the U.S. House of Representatives in Rhode Island's second congressional district.

RICHARD L. FOX is professor of political science at Loyola Marymount University. He earned his Ph.D. from the University of California, Santa Barbara, and his B.A. from Claremont McKenna College. His research, which has been funded by the National Science Foundation, and teaching focus on the U.S. Congress, elections, media and politics, and gender politics. He is the coeditor of *iPolitics: Citizens, Elections, and Governing in the New Media Era* (Cambridge University Press, 2011) and *Gender and Elections: Shaping the Future of American Politics* (Cambridge University Press, 2013). He is also the coauthor of *Running from Office: Why Young Americans Are Turned Off to Politics* (Oxford University Press, 2015), *It Still Takes a Candidate: Why Women Don't Run for Office* (Cambridge University Press, 2010) and *Tabloid Justice: The Criminal Justice System in the Age of Media Frenzy* (Lynne Rienner, 2007). His work has appeared in *American Political Science Review, Journal of Politics, American Journal of Political Science, Political Psychology, PS,* and *Politics & Gender*. He has also published op-eds in the *Washington Post, New York Times,* and *Wall Street Journal*. Prior to coming to Loyola Marymount University, he was professor and chair of the political science department at Union College in Schenectady, NY.

PREFACE AND ACKNOWLEDGMENTS

It seems that no matter where you look, sex and gender shape the political landscape. The 2016 presidential election is a case in point. Donald Trump's comments on the campaign trail, coupled with revelations about his previous personal behavior toward women, sparked a national conversation about sexism. Hillary Clinton's historic candidacy raised questions about whether women have a tougher time running for office than men do, and why the United States has never elected a female president. And exit polls revealed stark differences between male and female voters. If only women had voted in 2016, Clinton would have entered the Oval Office with a Democratic majority in Congress to help push forward her agenda.

Of course, the relevance of sex and gender in U.S. politics is about more than campaigns and elections. It's also about political representation. After all, women are significantly underrepresented numerically in all political institutions throughout the country. Men serve as governor in 44 of the 50 states. They run city hall in 90 percent of the nation's largest cities. They hold three-quarters of state legislative and statewide positions. In the 115th Congress, they occupy more than 80 percent of the seats. And as this book goes to press, the United States lags more than 100 other nations in the percentage of women serving in the national legislature. Given that women comprise half the population but only 20 percent of the nation's elected officials, pundits, politicians, and political scientists regularly assess why so few women run for office and how government would function differently if more women had political power.

When we turn to public policy, gender dynamics are also front and center in discussions, deliberations, and legislation. The debate over equal pay for women and men is one example. Barack Obama signed the Lilly Ledbetter Fair Pay Act in January 2009, which strengthened laws allowing workers to challenge instances of pay discrimination on the basis of sex, race, age, religion, or national origin. Yet when the Department of Labor released its annual statistics on gender and wages in 2015, the data revealed that, among full-time workers, women still earned only about 80 cents for every dollar earned by men. The political fight over abortion rights is another example. From state governments trying to restrict abortion access, to presidential candidates campaigning on the issue, to U.S. senators grilling Supreme Court nominees about whether they'd uphold *Roe v. Wade*, the debate over reproductive rights is among the most contentious in U.S. politics. Pay equity and reproductive freedom are just two examples of the many policy issues where sex and gender are pivotal. They are also central when it comes to child care, poverty, health care, foreign affairs—you name it.

It should come as no surprise that we feel strongly that citizens must understand how women and men navigate, respond to, and shape the various facets of U.S. politics. Whether we're talking about political behavior of citizens or candidates, political institutions, or public policies, students of U.S. government need to see the importance and relevance of gender in the day-to-day functioning of the political system. In fact, Donald Trump's victory, the policy changes his administration pursues, and how women and men across the country and throughout the world react to his presidency heighten the importance of studying how gender shapes political life.

For many years—as we have studied, written, and taught courses about women and politics, campaigns and elections, media and politics, and public opinion—we've had in the back of our minds a desire to write a series of short, timely, focused pieces about how sex and gender play a role in U.S. politics. That's what we hope we've created here: an accessible book that identifies and answers some of the most critical and contemporary questions in the study of women, men, and politics in the United States—one that can be used in women and politics classes as well as courses about U.S. political behavior and political institutions. In this vein, we had several goals:

- **Frame each chapter around a critical, current, yet enduring question** about sex, gender, and U.S. politics. The topics are wide-ranging: Are young women interested in running for office? Did feminism die with the 2016 presidential election? Is a woman's right to have an abortion secure? These are just a few of the 10 questions we investigate in the book.

- **Include only brief historical or scholarly background** for each question. Many excellent books already offer a rich history of the topics we cover. Our goal is to answer the central questions with short, provocative chapters that will engage students.

- **Use original data** to shed light on the questions that frame each chapter. We didn't want the chapters to offer mere summaries of what we already know. Rather, we wanted to provide fresh insights with new, or newly compiled, data. Several chapters include results from our original national survey of high school and college students. Others include original data analysis that hasn't been published elsewhere.

- **Offer an intersectional approach** that recognizes that all women and all men are not the same. Whether we're talking about pay equity, the gender gap in party affiliation, or views about feminism, it is important to examine and understand how race and sex interact to shape attitudes and experiences.

- **Push readers to think about topics in new ways.** Several chapters present findings that refute the conventional wisdom about sex and gender in U.S. politics. Others encourage readers to disentangle myths from realities about women and men as voters, campaign donors, political candidates, and elected officials.

- **In every chapter, forecast what the future might hold,** especially in light of the 2016 elections. In some cases, we argue that the status quo is here to stay. In others, we outline specific scenarios that might lead to change.

Put simply, a book about sex and gender in U.S. politics should be engaging, timely, and informative. We hope this book is just that.

If it is, then it's only because of the many people who provided helpful and thoughtful feedback as we drafted the book. Erin Beck, Kathy Dolan, Brian Frederick, Sally Friedman, Mary Nugent, Zoe Oxley, Kathryn Pearson, Jessica Preece, Monica Schneider, Elizabeth Sherman, Janie Steckenrider, Michele Swers, Mackenzie Israel Trummel, and Christina Wolbrecht all commented on the proposal or various draft chapters. Danny Hayes and Sean Theriault were instrumental in the data collection and analyses in Chapters 4 and 7. They were also both very understanding when one of us (Jen) was constantly running behind on other projects because she became obsessed with completing this book before the due date. (This obsession, incidentally, caused the other one of us—Richard—considerable stress and anxiety.) Samantha Guthrie and Rae McBean searched for obscure facts and figures, always without a map and often with little direction, that would make the prose more interesting and the narrative more compelling. And Jen's Spring 2017 Women and Political Leadership class "tested" all of the chapters, offered helpful suggestions, and caught a couple of pretty egregious typos.

W. W. Norton & Company provided us with a crack production and editorial team that published this book in a high-quality, timely way. Theresa Kay provided thorough and helpful copyedits, project editor Linda Feldman helped to ensure the book's consistency and continuity, Eric Pier-Hocking executed a strong production plan, Stephanie Romeo tracked down compelling photos, and associate editor Samantha Held made sure that we stayed on top of all aspects of the process.

Our most important thanks go to Norton editor in political science Peter Lesser, without whom there'd be no book. When Pete approached us in the summer of 2014 and asked if we'd be interested in writing a women and politics textbook, our initial reaction was, "Absolutely not." We explained that the women and politics book we would want to write isn't like anything out there. We wanted short chapters, provocative questions, empirical analyses, a casual tone, and fresh anecdotes. We didn't think we were the right people to write a traditional book about the many facets of women's political incorporation, inclusion, and influence in the U.S. political system. Pete said, "Let's do your kind of book, then." And so the project began. Throughout the process, Pete was as creative, careful, effective, and efficient as we ever could have asked. In fact, Pete might suffer from the same obsessive-compulsive disorder we do. His feedback was instantaneous, even on Thanksgiving and Christmas Eve. Because of Pete, this book was smooth sailing, something that is really important when the authors aren't exactly calm, cool, and collected.

As for our families, pets, and friends, they are sick of being thanked. And anyway, they never read anything we write. So we are not thanking them.

Jen and Richard

WOMEN, MEN & U.S. POLITICS: TEN BIG QUESTIONS

Donald Trump's win—and Hillary Clinton's loss—in the 2016 presidential election raised important questions about the state of feminism in the United States and why Trump's treatment of women didn't cost him the White House. Here, Trump and Clinton take part in a town hall–style debate in St. Louis.

CHAPTER 1

TRIUMPH AND DEFEAT: ELECTION 2016 AND THE STATE OF CONTEMPORARY FEMINISM

Key Question: Did feminism die with the 2016 presidential election?

Hillary Clinton made history in 2016. Beating back four male challengers in an open Democratic primary, she became the first woman to win a major party's nomination for president of the United States. Nomination in hand, she continued to break glass ceilings that no woman before had ever shattered. She raised more money than any of her opponents. She received a greater percentage of newspaper endorsements than any presidential candidate in modern history. And given her experience as First Lady, U.S. senator, and secretary of state, she was widely considered exceptionally qualified to occupy the Oval Office. President Obama said that there had "never been a man or a woman—not me, not Bill [Clinton], nobody—more qualified than Hillary Clinton to serve as president of the United States of America."[1] Even Republicans acknowledged that if voters judged the candidates on their resumes alone, Clinton would win the race.[2] Journalists spent the week leading up to Election Day putting the finishing touches on stories they'd already drafted about America electing its first female president.

Perhaps no one was more excited by the prospects of a Clinton presidency than generations of feminist activists who had spent their lives fighting to ensure that women and men were treated equally in all walks of life. They had waited long enough to see a woman achieve the ultimate position of political power. The march to women's equality, after all, had been an arduous struggle. As early as 1776, Abigail Adams wrote a letter to her husband, John, who was a member of the Continental Congress in Philadelphia. She implored him to "remember the ladies" as he drafted the documents that would govern the nation:

> Be more generous and favorable to them than your ancestors. Do not put such unlimited power into the hands of the husbands. . . . If particular care and attention is not paid to the ladies, we are determined to foment a rebellion, and will not hold ourselves bound by any laws in which we have no voice, or representation.[3]

John didn't listen. Despite Abigail's plea, the Constitution made no mention of women and conferred no rights to them. It took another 133 years—many of them filled with marches, picket lines, hunger strikes, and imprisonment—for women even to win the right to vote.[4]

Major advances in gender equality beyond the ballot box took even longer. Women finally began to enter the workforce in large numbers in the early 1940s. Their employment, however, had little to do with women's economic autonomy. Rather, it was a way to keep the economy afloat while men fought in World War II. But that began to change in 1963. With the publication of Betty Friedan's *The Feminine Mystique,* the fight for women's equality took on broader meaning. Friedan challenged the assumption that women were content in their domestic roles and argued, instead, that they wanted to pursue professional and personal identities beyond wife and mother. One of the women Friedan quoted in the book captured the argument poignantly: "I'm desperate . . . I have no personality. I'm a server of food and a putter-on of pants and a bedmaker, somebody who can be called on when you want something. But who am I?"[5] These sentiments resonated with millions of women across the country.

The modern women's movement gained traction and the feminist agenda continued to expand as women heeded Friedan's call to arms and began working outside the home. Women confronted unfair hiring practices, wage discrimination, and sexual harassment in the workplace. So legal protections and political rights became instrumental in addressing gender bias. Feminists created the National Organization for Women (NOW) in 1966, whose mission included pushing for better enforcement of antidiscrimination laws. Friedan served as the organization's first president. Women's rights activists also began to coalesce around the importance of passing an Equal Rights Amendment (ERA). Amending the Constitution to state that "Equality of Rights under the law shall not be denied or abridged by the United States or any state on account of sex" would ensure that women and men were treated as social, economic, and political equals.[6] Congress passed the amendment in 1972 and sent it to the states for ratification. In a major setback for the feminist movement, the ERA failed to muster sufficient support and was never adopted.[7] It's safe to say that the fight for gender equality has been difficult and the progress incremental.

That's why the prospect of a woman winning the White House was so meaningful. It would represent a crowning achievement for the feminist movement. Women, of course, had been making electoral strides for some time. In 1964, Maine Republican Margaret Chase became the first woman to launch a major bid for the presidency. Eight years later, New York Democrat Shirley Chisholm not only broke that barrier for her party, but also emerged as the first African American woman to seek the office. Geraldine Ferraro was Democratic presidential candidate Walter Mondale's running mate in 1984. And Sarah Palin became the first female Republican vice presidential candidate in 2008.

A female president, however, would be something else altogether. Teresa Younger, CEO of the Ms. Foundation for Women, made this point as she reflected on the historic arc that culminated in Clinton's candidacy: "My great-grandmother grew up in a time when women didn't have the right to vote—and now the country is ready to vote the first woman into the White House." Planned Parenthood Federation of America president Cecile Richards echoed the sentiment: "My generation was present at the creation of the modern feminist movement. I read Betty Friedan . . . fought sexism at work, and challenged society's assumptions that held women back. So of course I feel the tectonic plates of history shifting all around me." Terry O'Neill, the president of NOW, told a reporter in August 2016 that she was "moved that we actually got here in [her] lifetime."[8] You didn't have to be the president of a women's organization to recognize the significance of the moment. More than two million women around the country wore pantsuits—Clinton's signature outfit—to the polls as a way to mark their historic vote for the first female president.[9]

But something happened on the way to the White House. Donald Trump shocked the political establishment, the pollsters, and the pundits when he defeated Clinton in the Electoral College. (Clinton won the popular vote with a margin of close to 3 million.) The loss would have been demoralizing in its own right for people excited by the possibility of breaking through that highest, hardest glass ceiling. But that the defeat came at the hands of the most explicitly sexist presidential candidate in contemporary times poured salt into the wound. The result of the election left many asking whether feminism was dead.

That's the question we take up in this chapter, and the answer is complicated. Public opinion data reveal that attitudes toward feminism have always been only lukewarm. There's no evidence of a marked decline since Donald Trump hit the political scene. Public attitudes toward feminist public policies also provide little evidence of feminism's demise. A majority of citizens hold many views that are consistent with feminist policy preferences, and that was no less true on the day Trump was elected than in the years preceding it. When we focus on the dynamics of the 2016 election, though, the death knell for feminism can be heard loud and clear. Many voters simply didn't think that Trump's long history of sexist statements and behavior disqualified him from being president. And even many of those who were troubled by Trump's remarks and actions turned a blind eye as they cast their ballots. If the campaign is any indication, then the long-term implications of a Trump presidency could leave the future of feminism on precarious footing.

FEMINISM AND WOMEN'S RIGHTS: ALIVE AND WELL OR AT DEATH'S DOORSTEP?

From the moment it became clear early on the morning of Wednesday, November 9, 2016, that Donald Trump won the presidential election, many news outlets across the country asked the same question: What did the outcome say about feminism and the status of women in the United States? And many arrived at the same answer: Trump's victory represented a major setback for the women's movement. One of *Newsweek*'s post–Election Day headlines concluded, "Feminism Takes Massive Hit as Donald Trump Celebrates Election Victory."[10] At MSNBC, *The 11th Hour with Brian Williams* aired a segment in which female voters reacted to Trump's win by explaining that they felt scared and vulnerable.[11] *Buzzfeed* and the *Chicago Tribune* ran stories that included interviews with women who felt betrayed by the election results.[12] In an interview with *Fortune* magazine, feminist icon Gloria Steinem warned that, for women, a Trump presidency will bring about "a time of maximum danger in this country and we need to look out for each other."[13] These conclusions are understandable given the campaign that had just transpired, but they're not based on a systematic analysis. Only by taking a step back and examining public attitudes toward feminism, support for feminist public policies, and the dynamics of the 2016 election can we gain a full handle on where we stand as a country when it comes to the status of women and support for women's rights.

A Nation of Feminists? Never Were, Probably Never Will Be

Determining whether feminism died with the 2016 election requires assessing how alive and well it was before Donald Trump defeated Hillary Clinton. One way to do this is to examine the public's attitudes toward feminism over time. If perceptions of feminism and the women's movement didn't look terribly different heading into the 2016 election than they did in previous election cycles, then evidence for the argument that antifeminist sentiment spurred and sustained Trump's candidacy is pretty thin.

For decades, political scientists have asked national samples of Americans to rate the women's movement and feminism on a "feeling thermometer." The thermometer ranges from 0 to 100 degrees. The higher the number, the "warmer" or more positive the assessment. Lower numbers indicate "cooler" or more negative reactions. Figure 1.1 tracks the average thermometer ratings from the first time the question was asked (in 1970) until its most recent iteration (during the 2016 campaign).

Consider attitudes toward the women's movement. Citizens were leery at its outset, but by the middle of the 1970s, the average rating hit 50. And in the decade that followed, it inched up to around 60. Three decades' worth of data

FIGURE 1.1   THE PUBLIC'S ATTITUDES TOWARD THE WOMEN'S MOVEMENT AND FEMINISM

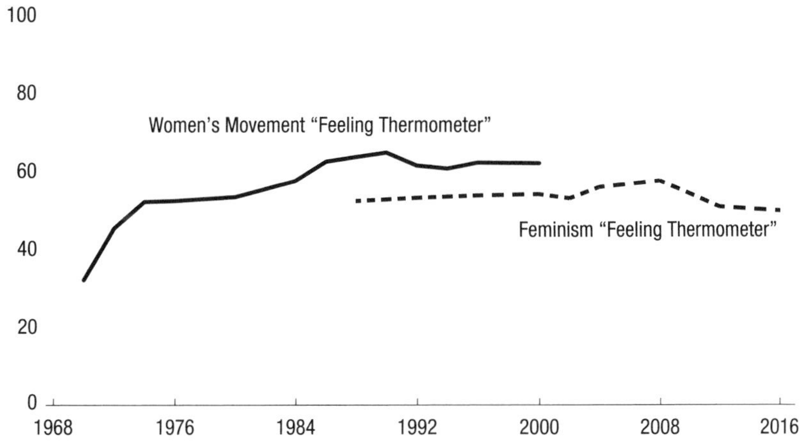

Data come from the American National Election Studies. Respondents are asked to rate each term on a "feeling thermometer" that ranges from 0 to 100. Lower numbers represent "cooler" feelings, and higher numbers represent "warmer" feelings. The figure displays the mean rating for each term every year the question was asked.

about attitudes toward feminism aren't that different. Since the question was first introduced in the mid-1980s, the average feeling thermometer rating has hovered at 50. The overall population, then, is rather ambivalent when it comes to rating the feminist movement.[14] More important for our purposes, however, is that the tepid rating for feminism has generally held steady over time. Nothing leading up to or during the 2016 election sent shockwaves through the system and fundamentally changed citizens' general assessments.

Citizens' evaluations of feminism may never have been sky high, but their propensity to consider themselves feminists is even lower. A 2014 *Economist/YouGov* poll found that only one in four people self-identified as a feminist (see Figure 1.2). Other recent polls indicate the same thing: Far fewer citizens identify with the feminist label than distance themselves from it. In March 2015, for example, a *Vox*/PerryUndem poll found that 18 percent of people said they were feminists, compared to 52 percent who said they weren't (the remaining 26 percent were unsure). A 2013 *HuffPost*/YouGov poll reported that 20 percent of people considered themselves feminists, and 71 percent did not.[15]

For some subgroups, levels of feminist self-identification are markedly higher. Women, Whites, Democrats, and millennials are most likely to embrace the feminist label. Men, Blacks, and Republicans are the least likely to do so.

FIGURE 1.2   WHO IDENTIFIES AS A FEMINIST?

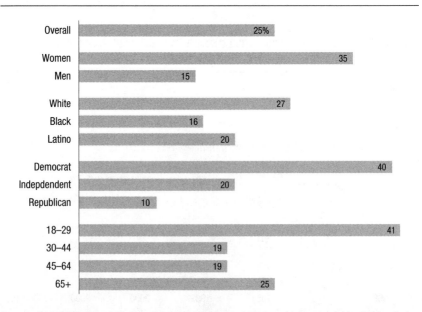

Data come from a 2014 *Economist*/YouGov poll. Bars indicate the percentage of people who responded "yes" when asked, "Do you consider yourself a feminist?"

None of this variation is too surprising. Republicans, the majority of whom are men, often have more traditional views of gender roles than Democrats, most of whom are women. The race-based differences are part of the historic and sometimes conflictual intersection between gender and race when it comes to support for the women's movement.[16] From suffrage right through the era of Betty Friedan, upper-class, White women dominated the movement and set the agenda. Although it is more diverse today, vestiges from the early days likely still affect who identifies as a feminist.[17]

No matter what demographic group we consider, though, feminist identification never crosses the 41 percent threshold. In fact, that same 2014 *Economist*/YouGov poll found that people are almost twice as likely to think that being called a feminist is an insult rather than a compliment. Based on these public opinion data, feminism didn't die with the 2016 election. It was only barely alive when Clinton and Trump entered the arena.

A Nation of Feminists? Seems Like We Are and Will Continue to Be

A second way to gauge support for feminism is by examining people's attitudes toward feminist public policies. That is, what do they think about issues pertaining to women's rights and opportunities? Here, feminism is on quite solid footing.

First, consider people's views on four feminist policies: paid family leave, insurance coverage for birth control, equal pay for equal work, and a woman's right to choose to terminate a pregnancy. On all four issues, a majority of citizens holds a position consistent with the feminist view (see Figure 1.3). In some cases, that majority is overwhelming. More than nine out of 10 women

FIGURE 1.3   CITIZENS' SUPPORT FOR FEMINIST POLICIES

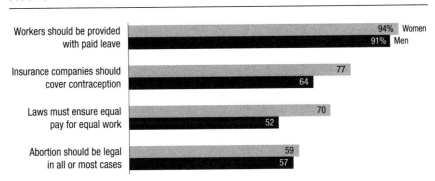

Data come from a 2016 *Washington Post*/Kaiser Family Foundation poll. Bars indicate the percentage of people who agree with each policy statement.

and men believe, for example, that employers should provide paid time off when an employee has a child or has to deal with a personal or family member's illness. Support for the other three issues isn't as universal. And when it comes to insurance coverage for contraception and pay equity, women are significantly more likely than men to adopt a feminist perspective. On all four policies, though, the key takeaway is that women and men are more likely than not to share the feminist viewpoint.

Second, citizens believe that implementing feminist policies is an important component for elevating the status of women and securing equal rights. When asked whether a series of issues should be a "top priority" for "improving women's lives," large majorities of people believe that many of the policies feminists have long advocated for should be at the top of the list. They consider reducing domestic violence, fighting for pay equity, combatting sexual harassment, providing affordable child care, reducing discrimination against women of color, and improving women's health care important components of elevating women's status in society (see Figure 1.4). Even feminist policies that generate less support—such as increasing women's presence in STEM fields (science, technology, engineering, and math) or providing paid leave or

FIGURE 1.4 TOP PRIORITIES FOR IMPROVING WOMEN'S LIVES

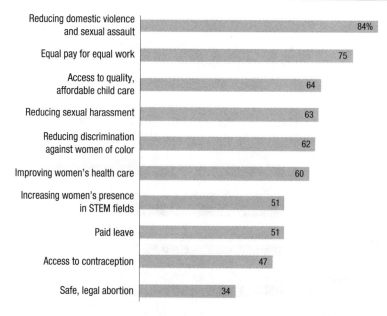

Data come from a 2016 *Washington Post*/Kaiser Family Foundation poll. Bars indicate the percentage of people who believe that each policy should be a "top priority" when it comes to improving women's lives.

access to contraception—are still seen by roughly half the population as vital for improving women's lives. Protecting abortion rights is the only exception, likely because it is such a deeply divisive, partisan issue (see Chapter 9).

Third, when provided with a definition of what feminism is, people's willingness to self-identify with the term increases substantially. Remember the 2014 poll that found that only 25 percent of citizens consider themselves feminists? Well, that same poll found that when people were told that a feminist is "someone who believes in the social, political, and economic equality of the sexes," self-identification climbed to 60 percent.[18] This effect can be seen across all demographic groups and political parties. In fact, as the bars in Figure 1.5 illustrate, once given the definition, Republicans are the only group for whom self-identification as a feminist doesn't cross the 50 percent threshold. Still, Republicans' self-identification more than quadruples when they're told what feminists actually believe.

The disconnect between identifying with the feminist label and embracing feminist ideals likely has to do with how the mass media often characterize feminists: humorless, aggressive, man-hating, and unattractive.[19] Television

FIGURE 1.5   WHO IDENTIFIES AS A FEMINIST WHEN GIVEN A DEFINITION?

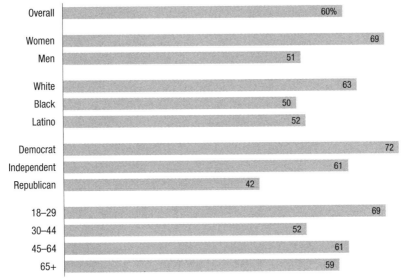

Data come from a 2014 *Economist*/YouGov poll. Bars indicate the percentage of people who responded "yes" when asked, "One dictionary definition of a feminist is someone who believes in the social, political, and economic equality of the sexes. As you think about that definition, do you think of yourself as a feminist?"

and print news often portray the women's movement as embodying an unappealing, narrow agenda—one focused primarily on reproductive rights.[20] And popular culture routinely perpetuates reasons to reject the label. Pop singer Lady Gaga said she's not a feminist because she "loves men." Actress Shailene Woodley distanced herself from the term because she believes in "sisterhood more than feminism." Mega-star Taylor Swift doesn't consider herself a feminist because she doesn't "think about things as guys versus girls."[21] Sarah Jessica Parker, Susan Sarandon, and Juliette Binoche have all made similar statements. When we look beyond the word and turn to its substance, however, there's no question that a majority of citizens—and all of these celebrities—support feminist public policies. This was true in the years leading up to the 2016 presidential election, and it continued to be the case as Trump and Clinton battled it out on the campaign trail.

A Nation of Feminists? No Way! America Elected Donald Trump President

The third way to assess claims that feminism died in 2016 is by analyzing the dynamics of the presidential election. We have already established that Clinton was a candidate like no other. She was the first woman to win a major party nomination, and her background and credentials established her as very well qualified to seek the Oval Office. But Donald Trump was also like no other. When the well-known real estate tycoon and reality television star announced his candidacy on June 16, 2015, most analysts didn't take him seriously. He had always been regarded as a master self-promoter, so the campaign was initially perceived as a vanity exercise, a gambit to promote his business interests and the Trump brand. After all, he had no political experience, and he spoke in a simple, blunt, fantastical way that might attract attention but was certainly not presidential. Just consider his remarks launching the campaign. In that one speech alone, Trump noted that he was "really rich"; said that he would "build a great, great wall on our southern border" because the Mexicans coming to the United States are "bringing drugs. They're bringing crime. They're rapists"; told the audience that he would be "the greatest jobs president God ever created"; and bragged that he "beats China all the time."[22]

Beyond the lack of experience and rhetorical bluster, one of the main reasons Trump was dismissed at the outset was his long, public record of crude and sexist statements. In 1999, Trump wrote off any ambition to run for president one day because even he didn't think he could survive his past: "Can you imagine how controversial I'd be?" he asked Chris Matthews, the host of *Hardball*. "How about me with the women? Can you imagine?"[23] His three marriages and highly publicized extramarital affairs were regular fodder for the New York tabloids. It wasn't just tabloid-style reporting that would be an albatross around Trump's neck when it came to women, though. He routinely appeared on Howard Stern's bawdy radio program, where he commented that "a person who is very flat-chested is very hard to be a 10"; described his second wife, Marla Maples, as "nice tits, no brains"; and said that he'd be willing to have sex with Mariah Carey, Cindy Crawford, and Princess Diana. In one interview, when Stern asked Trump if it was okay to refer to his daughter Ivanka as a "piece of ass," Trump smiled, nodded, and replied, "Yeah."[24]

American voters have a long history of forgiving candidates with questionable pasts, but Trump's record seemed beyond the pale. What's more, throughout the campaign, a steady stream of previously unreported examples of his sexism and sexual misconduct came to light. Most notably, a month before Election Day, NBC released unaired *Access Hollywood* footage from 2005. Speaking off-camera, Trump bragged cavalierly to the show's host about grabbing and kissing women whenever and wherever he feels like it. After the tape aired, more than 10 women came forward as victims of Trump's unwanted sexual advances. (Trump apologized for the "locker room talk" but emphatically denied inappropriately touching anyone.) Voters, of course, didn't need to look only to the past. Trump disparaged and demeaned in explicitly sexist terms his female primary opponent, female general election rival, and a female debate moderator. (See Table 1.1 for a list of some of the most notable sexist statements Trump made in the last 25 years.)

Keep in mind, too, that these are just the outright sexist statements. Trump's behavior in the presidential debates revealed his proclivity to launch subtler gender-based attacks, too. In the first debate, for example, he opened his remarks by questioning Clinton's title, asking if it was fine to call her Secretary Clinton: "Is that OK? Good. I want you to be very happy. It's very important to me." Later in the debate, he criticized Clinton's appearance and energy level: "She doesn't have the look. She doesn't have the stamina" to be president. As evidence for his claim, Trump spoke directly to Clinton and demeaned her decision to stay off the campaign trail for a few days so that she could prepare for the debate: "You've seen me, I've been all over the place. You decided to stay home." He also made it difficult for Clinton to finish a sentence. Trump interrupted her 51 times, three times more than she interrupted him.[25]

To many citizens, it was simply stunning that a presidential candidate could speak and behave this way and still win a major-party's presidential nomination. But that a country committed to feminist principles and women's

TABLE 1.1   DONALD TRUMP'S MOST NOTABLE SEXIST COMMENTS

PRIOR TO ENTERING THE RACE	
New York Magazine November 1992	Wonderful looking while on the ice, but up close and personal, she could only be described as attractive if you like a woman with a bad complexion who is built like a linebacker. *—Commenting on Olympic figure skating champion Katerina Witt's appearance*
ABC News Prime Time Live 1994	I have days where, if I come home—and I don't want to sound too much like a chauvinist, but when I come home and dinner's not ready, I go through the roof. *—He also noted that "putting a wife to work is a very dangerous thing"*
Howard Stern show 1997	I'm going to get the bathing suits to be smaller and the heels to be higher. *—On purchasing the Miss USA pageant*
Howard Stern show 2005	If you're looking for a rocket scientist, don't tune in tonight, but if you're looking for a really beautiful woman, you should watch. *—Promoting the Miss USA pageant*
Retweet April 16, 2015	If Hillary Clinton can't satisfy her husband, what makes her think she can satisfy America? *—Shared a fan's tweet, just prior to announcing his candidacy*

DURING THE PRIMARY	
Retweet August 7, 2015	Fox viewers give low marks to bimbo @MegynKelly. *—Shared an assessment of Megyn Kelly's performance as a GOP primary debate moderator*
CNN August 8, 2015	You could see there was blood coming out of her eyes. Coming out of her wherever. *—Commenting on Fox News debate moderator Megyn Kelly's tough questions*
Rolling Stone September 9, 2015	Look at that face. Would anyone vote for that? Can you imagine that, the face of our next president? I mean, she's a woman, and I'm not supposed to say bad things, but really, folks, come on. Are we serious? *—When asked about his Republican primary opponent, Carly Fiorina*

DURING THE GENERAL ELECTION	
Fox and Friends September 27, 2016	I know that person and she was a Miss Universe person, and she was the worst we ever had. . . . She was the winner, and you know she gained a massive amount of weight and it was a real problem. *—On Hillary Clinton's allegations that Trump called a former Miss Universe "Miss Piggy"*
Washington Post October 7, 2015	You know, I'm automatically attracted to beautiful [women]—I just start kissing them. It's like a magnet. Just kiss. I don't even wait. And when you're a star, they let you do it. You can do anything. . . . Grab 'em by the pussy. You can do anything. *—The release of an unedited tape of Donald Trump speaking to* Access Hollywood
Presidential Debate October 9, 2016	This was locker room talk. *—Referring to the* Access Hollywood *tapes*
Campaign Rally in North Carolina October 14, 2016	I'm standing at my podium and she walks in front of me, right? She walks in front of me, you know, and when she walked in front of me, believe me, I wasn't impressed. *—Referring to Hillary Clinton walking toward an audience member at a town hall–style debate*

equality would elect Donald Trump president of the United States was perhaps the most significant disappointment the women's movement experienced in decades.

Feminists might take solace in knowing that, according to exit polls, two-thirds of voters acknowledged that Trump did not have the temperament to be president. An even greater share of the electorate was bothered by his treatment of women (see Table 1.2). Yet nearly a third of these voters—people who willingly admitted that Trump was temperamentally unfit to serve and treated women poorly—still pulled the lever for him. Voters' tolerance for sexism also becomes apparent when we examine when people decided on a candidate. Trump beat Clinton by eight points among voters who decided their vote in the last month of the campaign—this was after the *Access Hollywood* tape came out. Trump and Clinton tied among voters who said the debates affected their vote, even though many believe the debates showcased Trump's sexism.

TABLE 1.2   THE 2016 PRESIDENTIAL ELECTION EXIT POLLS

	SHARE OF THE ELECTORATE	PERCENT VOTING FOR CLINTON	PERCENT VOTING FOR TRUMP
When did you decide your vote?			
In the last month	26%	40%	48%
Before that	73	51	45
Does Trump have the temperament to be president?			
Yes	35	5	94
No	63	72	19
Does Trump's treatment of women bother you?			
Yes	70	65	29
No	29	10	87
Were the debates a factor in your vote?			
Yes	82	47	48
No	11	41	49

Data are from CNN's exit polls of 24,558 voters taken as they left their polling places on November 8, 2016.

For a sizeable portion of the population, there was no need to overlook Trump's record with women; it just wasn't a big deal. Several Trump voters in Michigan who defended Trump's sexist rhetoric to the *Huffington Post* serve as a case in point. One noted, for instance, "He's all-inclusive. He will offend everybody equally. He just seems genuine." Another said, "I think he's very transparent. He isn't a phony. I think they take a lot of stuff out of context. I don't care. I like his honesty." To another voter, Trump's language was "just words." She concluded, "I think he'd be fair to women, pretty much."[26] Republican Party National Committee Chair Reince Priebus turned out to be right when he deflected a question about sexism and told *Fox News* in May 2016, "I don't think Donald Trump and his personal life is something that people are looking at and saying, 'Wow, I'm surprised that he's had girlfriends.' That's not what people look at."[27] Actually, it's not clear from the outcome of the race that Trump's behavior cost him anything. Trump received just less than 90 percent of the Republican vote, which is similar to the share that GOP nominees Mitt Romney and John McCain garnered in 2012 and 2008. Trump also performed similarly to, and in some cases better than, his predecessors among Whites, men, and senior citizens.

The election wasn't only about Donald Trump. Hillary Clinton, despite her qualifications, was not a perfect candidate. And in many rustbelt states, which ultimately swung from supporting Obama in 2012 to Trump in 2016, rural voters hadn't experienced the economic recovery the Democrats had promised. The political landscape was well suited for a blunt-speaking outsider with unconventional proposals. Prior to 2016, though, we might have assumed that this outsider couldn't also be a card-carrying sexist. But we would have been wrong. Indeed, some post-election analyses suggest that people's sexist attitudes correlated more closely with support for Trump than their economic dissatisfaction.[28] At the very least, explicit sexism wasn't a disqualifying factor in the race to the White House. People who hoped to smash the political glass ceiling instead found themselves in an America where voters elected the most sexist candidate in modern history.

WHERE DO WE GO FROM HERE?

Just as the question of whether feminism is dead or alive depends on your vantage point, so does the likely future of the women's movement. On one hand, several signs suggest that the Trump administration will marginalize women from the political sphere and jeopardize women's rights. On the other hand, these setbacks might serve to catalyze and heighten feminists' levels of political activity. Overall, it's probably safe to conclude that the glass for feminism going forward is about three-quarters empty and one-quarter full.

Let's begin with the empty part. From the outset, President Trump's Cabinet is among the least diverse in modern history. Whereas Presidents Bill Clinton, George W. Bush, and Barack Obama named women to at least one of the four most prominent cabinet posts (Secretary of State, Treasury, Defense, and Attorney General), Donald Trump appointed only White men. This marks the first time since George H. W. Bush's Cabinet in 1989 that men hold all these positions.[29] In fact, of Trump's top 22 appointments, only four are women.[30]

But it's more than the optics of an almost all-male Cabinet that have feminists worried. On the campaign trail, many of Trump's policy statements were antithetical to what women's rights advocates support. He promised to appoint justices who will overturn *Roe v. Wade* and suggested (but then recanted) that women should be subject to "some form of punishment" if they have an abortion when the procedure is banned.[31] He expressed concerns about paid family leave, explaining, "I think we have to keep our country very competitive, so you have to be careful of it."[32] And on child care? He told a town hall gathering that business, not the government, should provide child care because it's neither difficult nor expensive to do so: "You need one person or two people, and you need some blocks and you need some swings and some toys."[33] Trump's policy goals aren't necessarily different from those of most recent Republican presidential candidates, although it's hard to imagine that they'd articulate positions on "women's" issues in such a dismissive fashion. But Trump has done more than make campaign-trail promises. He has assembled a very conservative administration that shows little interest in pushing for equal pay legislation or affordable child care and one that does not support enforcing antidiscrimination laws, expanding access to health care, or maintaining constitutionally protected reproductive rights (see Chapter 9).

Beyond the policy implications, women's rights advocates fear that Trump's win gives license to citizens to use sexist language. Feminist author Jill Filipovic, in a column for the *Washington Post*, went so far as to argue that Trump's victory represents the triumph of misogyny: "A vote for Trump is a vote against women. He has bragged on video about committing sexual assault. . . . He evaluates women not on their intelligence or good characters, but on a physical attribute scale of one to 10. Women he doesn't like are 'pigs' and 'dogs.'"[34] Myriad journalists have also chronicled an uptick in school bullying, often directed at female and gay students, or religious and racial minorities.[35] If a candidate can say offensive things and be elected president of the United States, then students wonder why limits should be placed on them. As educator and author Glenn Singleton explains, "Politicians are unusually important voices of authority in our social fabric." Norms are at risk when "children are punished for the very transgressions which they see those seeking the nation's highest office being rewarded."[36]

The reason that some feminists don't consider the glass entirely empty is that a Trump presidency might jumpstart political activity among people who care about women's rights. Within hours of the election results, political organizers took to Facebook to create momentum for a women's march on Washington, scheduled to take place the day after the inauguration. One of the organizers summed up the mission of the march this way: "The marginalized groups you attacked during your campaign? We are here and we are watching."[37] And they were: Hundreds of thousands of women and men traveled to Washington, DC, on January 21, 2017 and took to the streets to show Donald Trump that they supported women's rights. Similar marches, protests, and rallies occurred on the same day in 550 cities and towns throughout the United States, drawing an estimated 3 million participants nationwide.[38] Marching isn't the only way that feminists are speaking out. Nonprofit organizations opposed to Trump's agenda have seen a surge in donations.[39] And organizations that recruit and train women to run for office report a record number of applicants.[40] As one woman who decided she wants to run for a county or state legislative seat in New Jersey said, "The election was a kick in the pants that I had to step up and be more involved."[41]

The reason we consider the glass only one-quarter full is because, despite bouts of passion, political activity around feminist issues is rarely sustained. The results of a 2016 *Washington Post*/Kaiser Family Foundation poll indicate that most women and men have never even voted for a candidate because of his or her position on women's rights, let alone become politically active beyond the ballot box. Indeed, only one in four people has ever expressed views about women's rights on social media sites (and that includes views that aren't consistent with a feminist agenda). When it comes to contacting elected officials to express positions on women's rights, we're down to 14 percent of women and 8 percent of men. Research also indicates that women's reluctance to get involved in politics and even consider running for office is driven, at least in part, by the perception that they'd confront widespread sexism if they entered the ring (see Chapter 4). The 2016 election may have heightened those concerns.[42]

That's not to say that Trump couldn't be an exception. The stakes might be unusually high and the pendulum might have swung sufficiently far enough in the antifeminist direction to motivate political activity.[43] How the Trump presidency unfolds, the extent to which its tone and substance mirror his campaign, and whether it is regarded as a success, failure, or somewhere in between will determine the trajectory of feminism and feminist public policies for years to come.

QUESTIONS FOR REFLECTION AND DISCUSSION

1. A post-election survey of New York voters found that 30 percent voted for Trump and also believe in gender equality.[44] How can you reconcile these two beliefs? Do you think it is possible to be a feminist and support Donald Trump? Why or why not?

2. Most people don't identify as feminists. Yet most people do support the central goal of feminism: the equal treatment of women and men in all realms of life. Is this disconnect evident in your own life? To arrive at your answer, ask 10 friends or family members whether they consider themselves feminists. Then ask them why they do or don't. Next, offer them the definition of feminism we provide in this chapter and see whether their answers change. Compile the responses to determine whether your findings are similar to the results presented in Figures 1.2 and 1.5.

3. In 2012, female voters favored Barack Obama over Mitt Romney by 11 percentage points. In 2016, they favored Hillary Clinton over Donald Trump by only a slightly larger margin (13 percentage points). Given that Clinton would have been the first female president, and in light of everything that Trump said and did, why do you think the margin wasn't larger?

4. In the aftermath of the election, there has been a lot of discussion in feminist communities about how Trump won over enough voters to become president. Which groups of voters were especially receptive to Trump's message? Go online and look at CNN's 2016 and 2012 exit polls as you craft your response. Are there any groups of voters that surprise you? Any differences between 2016 and 2012 that strike you?

5. Choose a feminist public policy listed in Figure 1.3 or 1.4 and assess what a Trump presidency will likely mean for it. What did Trump say about the issue on the campaign trail? What has he said or done since taking office? What have Republicans in Congress said or done about it more broadly?

FOR FURTHER EXPLORATION

Barakso, Maryann. 2004. *Governing NOW: Grassroots Activism in the National Organization for Women*. Ithaca: Cornell University Press.

Filipovic, Jill. 2014, July. "Why Don't More People Call Themselves Feminists?" *Cosmopolitan,* www.cosmopolitan.com/politics/news/a28510/misconceptions-about-feminism/ (accessed 2/19/17).

Freidan, Betty. 1963. *The Feminine Mystique*. New York: W. W. Norton & Company.

Gay, Roxane. 2014. *Bad Feminist*. New York: HarperPerennial.

Iron Jawed Angels. 2004. Directed by Katja von Garnier. Richmond, VA: HBO.

Mansbridge, Jane J. 1986. *Why We Lost the ERA*. Chicago: University of Chicago Press.

Smith, Barbara. 2000. *Home Girls: A Black Feminist Anthology*. New Brunswick, NJ: Rutgers University Press.

Suffragette. 2015. Directed by Sarah Gavron. Chatham, UK: Ruby Films.

Thelma and Louise. 1991. Directed by Ridley Scott. Bakersfield, CA: Pathe Entertainment.

Comparing the Rwandan Chapter of Deputies (top) and the U.S. Senate (bottom) illustrates the variation in the proportion of women in politics worldwide. What factors contribute to these differences?

CHAPTER 2

FALLING FURTHER BEHIND: WOMEN'S UNDERREPRESENTATION IN U.S. POLITICS

Key Question: Why do more than 100 nations outrank the United States when it comes to electing women?

As recently as the 1970s, women held almost no major elected positions in the United States. Ella Grasso, a Democrat from Connecticut, and Dixie Lee Ray, a Democrat from Washington, were the only two female governors throughout the entire decade. In 1978, when Kansas Republican Nancy Kassebaum was elected to the U.S. Senate, she became the first woman—ever—to win a seat in her own right. (The handful of women who had previously served had either been appointed for a brief period of time or had taken over their deceased husbands' seats.) As the decade wrapped up in 1979, women occupied fewer than 5 percent of the seats in the U.S. House of Representatives.

Almost four decades later, women's presence in U.S. politics has certainly improved. When you scan the Internet, check your smartphone, turn on the TV, or read the newspaper, you're likely to stumble upon several high-profile women in politics. Hillary Clinton was the 2016 Democratic nominee for president. Nancy Pelosi, the first female Speaker of the House of Representatives (from 2007–2011), currently serves as minority leader. Senators

Patty Murray and Debbie Stabenow hold two of the top four Democratic leadership posts in the Senate. Carly Fiorina, a Republican presidential candidate in 2016, and Sarah Palin, the 2008 Republican vice presidential nominee, remain prominent political figures. And Ronna Romney McDaniel chairs the Republican National Committee.

These well-known names and famous faces, however, obscure the fact that women continue to be significantly underrepresented in national politics. Sure, things have gotten better since the 1970s. But how much better, really? Four out of every five members of Congress are men. Women chair just a tiny fraction of the committees in both chambers. And little suggests that we should expect marked improvement anytime soon. Whereas the 1980s saw gradual but steady increases in the percentage of women running for Congress, and the early 1990s experienced a sharper surge, the last several election cycles can best be characterized as a plateau. In fact, the 2010 congressional elections resulted in the first net decrease in the percentage of women serving in the U.S. House of Representatives since the 1970s.[1] The 2016 elections produced a net gain of zero women in Congress.

Perhaps even more damning is that 100 countries have a greater proportion of women in their national legislature than the United States does. This wasn't always the case. In the last 20 years, the United States has fallen from 53rd to 104th worldwide when it comes to the percentage of women in the national government (see Table 2.1). Meanwhile, dozens of other nations—with varied political systems and political cultures—have continued to rise. This means that even though women's representation in the U.S. Congress has increased throughout the last couple of decades, the gains have not kept pace with growth around the world. In 1997, the United States was very close to the global average. By 2017, the United States trailed the global average (which had nearly doubled) by roughly 20 percent.

The United States' stunning global ranking and the relative stagnation we've seen in the number of female members of Congress present a major paradox. On one hand, the number of women in office has increased so slowly in the last several election cycles that countries in Europe, Asia, Africa, and Latin America have easily passed the United States. On the other hand, when they do run, female congressional candidates do just as well as men. They raise just as much money, garner just as many votes, and are just as likely to win their races (see Chapter 4).[2]

In this chapter, we argue that the U.S. political system does not place a premium on women's numeric representation. The lack of any formal mechanism to promote women's emergence as candidates, such as electoral gender quotas, ensures that the United States will continue to lag behind. Moreover, the tenacious gender gap in political ambition—and specific aspects of U.S. electoral politics that exacerbate it—shed light on why women's numeric representation often seems as though it has ground to a near halt. Ultimately, without a fundamental jolt to the political system, the United States will likely never fare as well as much of the world in electing women to top national offices.

TABLE 2.1 GLOBAL RANKINGS OF WOMEN IN NATIONAL LEGISLATURES

1997		2007		2017	
1. Sweden	40.4%	1. Rwanda	48.8%	1. Rwanda	61.3%
2. Norway	39.4	2. Sweden	47.3	2. Bolivia	53.1
3. Denmark	33.5	3. Costa Rica	38.6	3. Cuba	48.9
4. Finland	33.0	4. Finland	38.0	4. Iceland	47.6
5. Netherlands	31.3	5. Norway	37.9	5. Nicaragua	45.7
6. New Zealand	29.2	6. Denmark	36.9	6. Sweden	43.6
7. Seychelles	27.3	7. Netherlands	36.7	7. Senegal	42.7
8. Austria	26.8	8. Cuba	36.0	8. Mexico	42.4
9. Germany	26.2	Spain	36.0	9. Finland	42.0
10. Iceland	25.4	10. Argentina	35.0	10. South Africa	42.0
11. Argentina	25.3	11. Mozambique	34.8	11. Ecuador	41.6
12. Mozambique	25.2	12. Belgium	34.7	12. Namibia	41.3
13. South Africa	25.0	13. Iceland	33.3	13. Mozambique	39.6
14. Spain	24.6	14. South Africa	32.8	Norway	39.6
15. Cuba	22.8	15. Austria	32.2	15. Spain	39.1
16. China	21.0	New Zealand	32.2	16. Argentina	38.9
Eritrea	21.0	17. Germany	31.6	17. Ethiopia	38.8
Switzerland	21.0	18. Burundi	30.5	18. Timor-Leste	38.5
19. Korea	20.1	19. Tanzania	30.4	19. Angola	38.2
Grenada	20.1	20. Uganda	29.8	20. Belgium	38.0
53. United States	**11.7**	**82. United States**	**16.3**	**104. United States**	**19.1**
GLOBAL AVERAGE	**12.0**	**GLOBAL AVERAGE**	**17.1**	**GLOBAL AVERAGE**	**23.4**

Data compiled from the Inter-Parliamentary Union's "Women in National Parliaments" listings (as of January 1, 1997; January 31, 2007; and March 1, 2017). Percentages reflect women's representation in the lower house of each legislature.

NOT IN THE TOP 100? HOW CAN THAT BE?
REASON ONE: ELECTORAL RULES OF THE GAME

Why do countries as different as Rwanda, Bolivia, and Belgium all have two or three times as many women in the national legislature as the United States? Why does the United States trail virtually every Western democracy on this front? Why do many nations with more patriarchal histories than the United States see a greater proportion of women in politics? Why have fledgling democracies managed to elect more women in just a few short years than the United States has managed in many decades? One answer to these questions is clear: governing systems that rely on gender quotas and proportional representation.

Electoral gender quotas set a minimum threshold for female candidates or elected officials. Countries adopt them for various reasons. In some cases, quotas are the result of political pressure from local women's organizations that want to diversify the legislature. In other cases, the electoral mandate is a result of pressure from the international community. The United Nations, for example, may want a nation to signal that it has genuinely adopted an inclusive form of democratic governance. Quotas can also emerge as a "fix" for cultural attitudes that lead citizens to favor men's leadership. Once women hold electoral office, they can demonstrate that they too are capable and well-suited to politics. Because of the varied reasons they come into being, some quotas have existed since the inception of a country's constitution, others have been around for decades, and some have been adopted recently as a way to increase women's representation.

Just as quotas are adopted for many different reasons, they take many different forms as well. Some are constitutionally mandated, others result from legislation, and some are voluntarily adopted by particular political parties. Some apply to the proportion of female candidates a party nominates (such as Brazil, Kenya, and Ireland). Others reserve a certain number of seats in the legislature for women (like Pakistan, Tanzania, and Haiti). And some are mere targets (as is the case in Australia, Canada, and Sweden). But regardless of the form they take, quotas make it clear that a government acknowledges the importance of women's political inclusion and representation.

Half of all the countries in the world today have some form of an electoral gender quota. Table 2.2 lists the 76 countries that, just since 1991, have implemented the strictest types of quotas: legislative mandates for a minimum percentage or number of female candidates or elected officials at the national level, with sanctions typically imposed on political parties that violate the requirement. Quotas that demand a specific percentage of female candidates

TABLE 2.2 GENDER QUOTAS FOR NATIONAL OFFICES

QUOTAS FOR PERCENTAGE OF FEMALE CANDIDATES							
Bolivia	50	Chile	40	Portugal	33	Peru	30
Congo	50	Honduras	40	Uruguay	33	Rwanda	30
Costa Rica	50	Mexico	40	Albania	30	Serbia	30
Croatia	50	Spain	40	Angola	30	South Korea	30
Ecuador	50	Poland	35	Argentina	30	Uzbekistan	30
Lesotho	50	Slovenia	35	Brazil	30	Afghanistan	27
Libya	50	Belgium	33	Burkina Faso	30	Burundi	25
Nicaragua	50	Dominican Republic	33	Colombia	30	Algeria	20
Senegal	50	East Timor	33	El Salvador	30	Armenia	20
Taiwan	50	Greece	33	Indonesia	30	Mongolia	20
Togo	50	Guyana	33	Ireland	30	Palestine	20
Tunisia	50	Kenya	33	Kosovo	30	Paraguay	20
France	48	Macedonia	33	Kyrgyzstan	30		
Bosnia and Herzegovina	40	Nepal	33	Montenegro	30		

QUOTAS FOR PERCENTAGE OF FEMALE RESERVED SEATS							
Uganda	33	Tanzania	30	Saudi Arabia	20	Niger	10
Eritrea	30	Iraq	25	Pakistan	17	Samoa	10
Haiti	30	South Sudan	25	Bangladesh	14		
Somalia	30	Sudan	25	Egypt	14		
Swaziland	30	China	22	Djibouti	10		

QUOTAS FOR NUMBER OF FEMALE RESERVED SEATS							
Morocco	60 seats	Zimbabwe	60 seats	Mauritania	20 seats	Jordan	15 seats

Entries reflect the most recent gender quota for the lowest house of the federal government.

range from 10–50 percent; the average quota sits at 35 percent. Among the 21 countries that actually set aside a proportion of parliamentary seats for women, the average quota is 22.5 percent.[3]

For the most part, quotas operate in countries with parliamentary systems that rely on proportional representation. Basically, political parties compile lists of candidates. The people placed on the list are typically men and women who are active in the party, or whom the party wants to reward. On Election Day, citizens vote for one party's list. How well a party performs at the ballot box then determines the proportion of seats it is allocated (each party's list has more candidates than seats it will be asked to fill). In "closed list" systems, the occupants of the seats a party wins are chosen in order from the top of the list down. The order of the list is predetermined by party leaders. In "open list" systems, voters typically choose just one candidate on the list. After the votes are counted, the list is ordered and the seats are allocated based on the total number of votes each candidate receives.

To increase the number of women in elective office, countries that rely on a party list system often integrate a gender quota into the list itself—either in terms of the minimum proportion of women who must appear on the list, or the rules that govern how the list is ordered. In addition to the 75 countries listed in Table 2.2, 30 nations have at least one political party (and often multiple parties) that has adopted a voluntary gender quota of 20, 30, or even 40 percent. Not surprisingly, 15 of the top 20 countries for women's representation in 2016 (listed in Table 2.1) have instituted some type of quota.[4]

While much of the world has pushed ahead with efforts to integrate women into the national legislature, the U.S. electoral system does not include party lists or quotas. Rather, members of the U.S. Congress are elected in a winner-take-all, single-member district system. In each congressional district, candidates engage in a two-step process. First, they compete in a primary. In most states, these are partisan races, where Republicans compete against Republicans and Democrats compete against Democrats.[5] The United States has relatively weak political parties that exert only minimal influence over which candidate wins the primary.[6] Basically, anyone can run for office and affiliate with the party of his or her choice. The top vote-getter from each party's primary then competes in the second stage of the process: the general election. The person who wins the most votes is elected to represent the district. Here, too, the parties tend to play only a limited role. With the exception of the most competitive races, they provide little, if any, financial or logistical support to candidates. Put simply, in the United States, candidates—not parties—dominate and structure electoral competition.

This weak party apparatus bears directly on women's candidate emergence. Congressional candidates in the United States are, for the most part, left to their own devices. To compete for almost all top offices, candidates must do more than be politically active. They must raise money, build coalitions of support, create campaign organizations, and develop campaign strategies. In competitive electoral races, they often must engage in these endeavors twice—at the primary stage and in the general election. Explicit connections to political party organizations and platforms, as well as other support networks, are entirely at the candidates' discretion and are their responsibility to cultivate. In short, candidates must be ambitious entrepreneurs to make it in electoral politics. As we'll demonstrate in the next section, women are significantly less likely than men to fall into this category.

Although the electoral system in the United States lacks features that are well-suited to promote women's numeric representation, it is important to recognize that quotas and party lists aren't always a surefire way to do so either. There is, without a doubt, a strong relationship between systems with quotas and party lists and the percentage of women serving in the national legislature. But there have also been plenty of instances in which quotas and party lists haven't worked particularly well. In France, for example, the penalty for failing to comply with the quota is so weak that parties sometimes choose to pay a fine as opposed to include the required number of women on its list.[7] In other cases—such as Costa Rica's first quota law—the quota doesn't include a "placement mandate." This means that it doesn't specify where women's names must fall on the list, so parties often just stick them at the bottom. Because seats are allocated from the top down, the party might technically meet the quota requirement but still not actually elect many women. And then there was Brazil's 2009 quota law, which required that parties reserve seats for women. The only problem was that the law didn't require that those seats ever be filled.[8]

All of this is to say that quotas and party list systems don't guarantee increased women's representation. But when designed and implemented in a particular manner, they can facilitate the election of women in a way that single-member, winner-take-all districts simply cannot.

NOT IN THE TOP 100? HOW CAN THAT BE?
REASON TWO: THE ENDURING GENDER GAP IN POLITICAL AMBITION

In a candidate-centered electoral environment, citizens' ambition to run for office, and their comfort and familiarity engaging in entrepreneurial campaign activities, are vital. But deeply embedded patterns of traditional gender socialization make it far less likely, even today, for women than men to emerge as candidates. By "patterns of traditional gender socialization," we mean that the primary institutions of social and cultural life in the United States continue to impress on women and men—from an early age—conventional gender roles and expectations. Not only do women continue to bear responsibility for a majority of household tasks and child care, but they also face a more complicated balancing of these responsibilities with their professions than men do.[9] A masculinized ethos in many public and private institutional settings reinforces traditional gender roles. That is, political organizations and institutions that have always been controlled by men continue to promote men's participation in the political arena.[10] Further, whereas men are taught to be confident, assertive, and self-promoting, cultural attitudes toward women as political leaders leave an imprint suggesting to women that it can be inappropriate or undesirable to possess these characteristics.[11] Traditional gender socialization, in short, creates a set of circumstances in which the greater complexities of women's lives, both in terms of how society perceives them and how they perceive themselves, may depress their political ambition.

This isn't just an abstract argument. Throughout the last 15 years, we've conducted a series of surveys and interviews with thousands of women and men in the pool of "potential candidates" to determine how gender affects ambition to run for office. In these studies of lawyers, business leaders, educators, and political activists, the women and men are similar in race, region, education, household income, profession, and interest in politics. So we can determine whether women and men—all else equal—have similar ambition to run for office.[12]

Long story short: They don't. Men are significantly more likely than women to consider seeking elective office, and the gender gap has held steady throughout the last 15 years. In our first survey—conducted in the summer of 2001—more than half of the respondents (51 percent) stated that the idea of running for an elective position had at least "crossed their mind." But as we show in the leftmost bars of Figure 2.1, men were 16 percentage points more likely than women to have considered it. Because men might be more cavalier than women when assessing whether they ever thought about pursuing an elective position, we also asked whether they ever investigated how to place their name on the ballot or ever discussed running for office with potential donors, party or community leaders, family members, or friends. Men were significantly more likely than women to have engaged in each of these fundamental campaign steps as well.

The political environment certainly changed in the decade after we conducted the 2001 survey. The attacks of September 11, wars in Iraq and Afghanistan, Barack Obama's election, and the Tea Party movement are only a handful of the most significant political events in recent history. Yet the middle and rightmost bars of Figure 2.1 demonstrate that the gender gap

FIGURE 2.1   WHO CONSIDERS RUNNING FOR OFFICE?

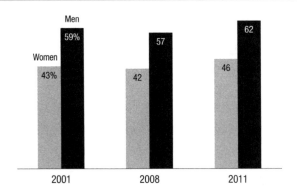

Bars represent the percentage of male and female "potential candidates" who reported they had "seriously considered" or "considered" running for office. This includes people who actually ran for office. The gender gap is statistically significant in all three comparisons.

in political ambition did not change. In both 2008 and 2011, it was the same size as it was in 2001. That's right; across this 10-year period, the gender gap didn't change at all. And this was the case across all types of women and men: Democrat and Republican, rich and poor, political activist and educator alike. In all comparisons, the gender gap was striking—and strikingly similar in magnitude—at all three points in time.

In fact, the gender gap in interest in running for office at some point in the future has actually grown over time. While men's interest in becoming a candidate remained virtually unchanged across the 10-year period, women's interest dropped; 18 percent of women in 2001, compared to 14 percent in 2011, reported interest in running for office in the future. Moreover, disparate levels of interest were greatest for high-level office. Men were approximately 40 percent more likely than women to consider running for the state legislature. The gap was even larger when we asked about Congress. Men were roughly twice as likely as women to express interest in running for the U.S. House or Senate.

As persistent as the gender gap in political ambition may be, its magnitude does vary across racial categories. Figure 2.2 presents the percentage of women and men who have considered running for office broken down by whether they self-identified as White, Black, or Latino/a. Notice that although men of all races are significantly more likely than women to have thought about running for office, the gender gap among Whites is about 40 percent larger than it is among Blacks and Latinos/as. We don't want to make too

FIGURE 2.2   SEX, RACE, AND CONSIDERING A CANDIDACY

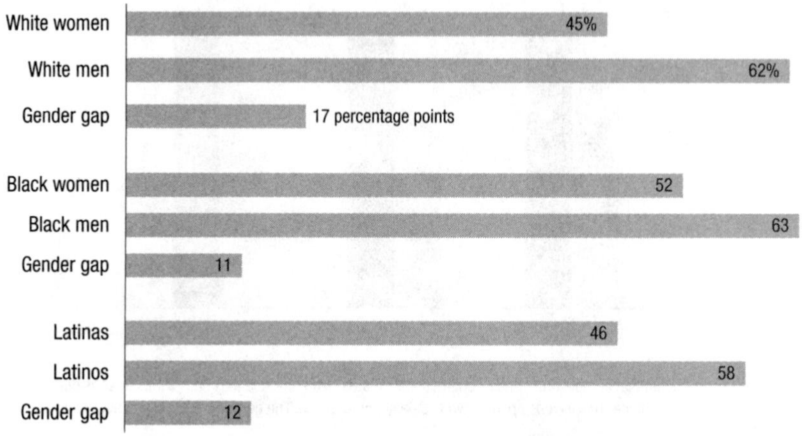

Data are based on the 2011 wave of the Citizen Political Ambition Study, which includes 2,971 White respondents, 232 Black respondents, and 249 Latino/a respondents. Bars represent the percentage of people within each group who have considered running for office. The gender gap is statistically significant in all comparisons.

much of the different size gender gaps across races because the gender differences within each race are far more substantial than the differences across them. But the data suggest that women of color are at least as likely as their White counterparts to consider running for office.[13]

That women are less likely than men to envision themselves as candidates certainly accounts for much of the stagnation in women's numbers in Congress. But two additional aspects of congressional politics exacerbate the consequences of the gender gap in political ambition. First, incumbency confers overwhelming advantages to members of Congress who seek reelection, making it incredibly difficult for any traditionally excluded group to make significant headway. In 2016, for example, only 41 (out of 435) House incumbents chose not to seek reelection. Of those who ran, just 13 lost their races. And keep in mind, this was an election cycle that was pretty hostile to incumbents. On Election Day, less than 20 percent of citizens approved of the job Congress was doing. The numbers were similar in 2014, when 95 percent of incumbents seeking reelection won their races. And heading into that election cycle, a poll showed that citizens rated root canals, traffic jams, cockroaches, and used car salesmen higher than they did members of the House and Senate.[14] Overall, in the last 10 election cycles, 95 percent of House incumbents who wanted to keep their jobs were re-elected. The reelection rates in state legislatures are even higher (see Figure 2.3).

FIGURE 2.3   REELECTION RATES IN CONGRESS AND STATE LEGISLATURES

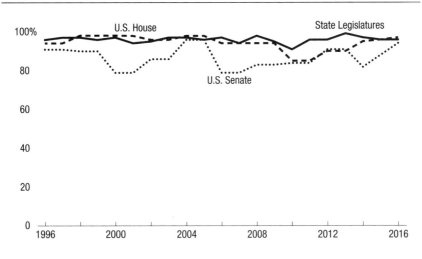

Lines indicate the percentage of incumbents winning reelection (of those who sought reelection) and come from the Center for Responsive Politics.

Because of the incumbency advantage, open seats present the best opportunities for new legislators to enter Congress. Yet in most cycles, they amount to just a few dozen opportunities. If women are less likely than men to express ambition to run for office in the first place, then passing on any of these opportunities limits the gains women can make.

The second aspect of contemporary U.S. politics that aggravates the gender gap in political ambition is the lopsided ratio of Democratic to Republican female candidates and elected officials. Seventy-eight Democratic and 26 Republican women hold seats in the 115th U.S. Congress. In other words, 75 percent of the women in the U.S. House and Senate are Democrats. Furthermore, whereas Democrats have experienced steady increases in the number of women in most elective offices throughout the last three decades, Republicans have not. If women are less likely than men to enter the electoral arena, then providing them with only one party through which to express that ambition nearly guarantees only sluggish gains in their numeric representation.

WHERE DO WE GO FROM HERE?

Will the United States ever catch up with other nations, or one day become a world leader when it comes to electing women? Certainly not anytime soon. Although some women's organizations are devoted to the cause, little else exists in the way of systematic effort or public will. In 2014, the Pew Research Center asked citizens whether they "personally hoped that the United States elected a female president in their lifetime." One woman. Any woman. Only 38 percent of people responded affirmatively. Fifty-seven percent said it made no difference to them.[15] When gender quotas have, on occasion, come up at the local or state level as a way to increase women's representation, they've never gained traction. In 2014, for example, a former legislator in Montana proposed a constitutional amendment that would mandate gender parity in the state legislature. The few proponents of the initiative failed even to collect the necessary number of signatures required to put the issue up for a vote.[16] Electing more women just isn't a priority for the vast majority of Americans.

Beyond general apathy toward women's representation in the United States, the political system makes big changes unlikely. Even if, at some point, gender quotas miraculously achieved a groundswell of public support, they would be nearly impossible to implement. The individualistic and candidate-centered nature of U.S. elections is established by the Constitution. A move away from winner-take-all, single member districts would require a series of amendments or a Constitutional Convention to rewrite parts of the founding document. From 1791, when the Bill of Rights was adopted, through 2014, approximately 11,600 constitutional amendments have been proposed. Only 17 have passed.[17] Given that people feel far more strongly about an Equal Rights Amendment, Balanced Budget Amendment, and Flag Burning Amendment—and all of those measures have failed—the likelihood of a gender quota amendment happening is next to zero.[18]

Closing the gender gap in political ambition is similarly unlikely, at least in the foreseeable future (see Chapter 3). And there's little way around the two factors that exacerbate it. Consider the incumbency advantage. The popular "fix" is often thought to be term limits. If members of Congress were barred from serving more than three terms, only about 40 percent of the incumbents in recent decades could have stood for reelection. Even with a less stringent 12-year limit, 28 percent of incumbents would have had to give up their seats.[19] Yet term limits at the federal level are unlikely, as the Supreme Court has ruled that states cannot impose term limits on their own members. They can be achieved only through a national law or constitutional amendment.[20] (Some enthusiasm for such an amendment existed in the early 1990s, but the movement has since evaporated.) Even if federal term limits were enacted, though, they probably would not have the intended effect. At the state legislative level, term limits have increased the number of open seats in the 15 states where they are mandated.[21] But these states have experienced no changes in the

percentage of female legislators. The number of incumbent women forced to
vacate their seats because they are "term limited" out often exceeds the number of women elected to seats that open as a result of term limits.[22]

Finally, the United States is firmly grounded in a two-party political system, but only one of those parties is making any progress running and electing
women. Although the Republicans are increasingly becoming a party of men,
this was not always the case. The Republicans were the first party to support
the Equal Rights Amendment. They were the first major party from which a
woman (Margaret Chase Smith) sought the presidency. And in the mid-1980s,
Republican women actually outnumbered Democratic women in the U.S. Congress. But as long as female candidates' electoral fortunes are linked disproportionately to the Democrats, then steady increases in women's representation
are precarious. When Democrats have a good year—like 2006 or 2012—women
see gains in their numbers. When Democrats have a bad year—like 2010 and
2016—women's representation stagnates or, sometimes, takes a hit. The growing network of women's organizations that successfully encourage pro-choice
and progressive women to enter the electoral arena further propel Democratic
women's candidacies. The Republicans have no such network.

Even an optimist would be hard-pressed to conclude that major increases
in women's representation are on the horizon, or that the United States will
improve its global position anytime soon. In fact, as other nations continue to
develop and move forward, it's more likely than not that the United States will
fall even further behind.

QUESTIONS FOR REFLECTION AND DISCUSSION

1. In the United States, we see little public outcry about women's underrepresentation in politics. Why do you think the dearth of female candidates and elected officials isn't more of a concern for voters or political leaders? Why do so few people seem to care?

2. Amid the wars in Iraq and Afghanistan, then secretary of state Condoleezza Rice, representing the U.S. government, played a pivotal role in orchestrating the design of the new Afghani and Iraqi governments. In doing so, she strongly advocated for, and ultimately succeeded in, implementing 25 percent gender quotas in the new parliaments. Rice, in other words, pushed for starting these new governments with a higher ratio of women in the national legislature than has ever been achieved in the U.S. Congress. Can you envision any circumstances under which electoral gender quotas might be adopted in the United States? Why or why not?

3. Choose one of the nations that outranks the United States in electing women (see Table 2.1) but that does not have a gender quota. Why does the country you've selected have more women in the national legislature than the United States does? The Interparliamentary Union (www.ipu.org/wmn-e/world.htm) might be a helpful source for answering this question.

4. Other than term limits, can you think of any ways to ensure that new people—and women, in particular—have more opportunities to run for and serve in elective office?

5. Why do you think so many more women in politics are Democrats than Republicans? Is it about policies and issues? The image of the two parties? Or something else?

FOR FURTHER EXPLORATION

Clinton, Hillary Rodham. 2014. *Hard Choices*. New York: Simon & Schuster.

Henderson, Sarah, and Alana S. Jeydel. 2013. *Women and Politics in a Global World*, 3rd edition. New York: Oxford University Press.

Inter-Parliamentary Union website: www.ipu.org/english/home.htm

Krook, Mona Lena. 2010. *Quotas for Women in Politics: Gender and Candidate Selection Reform Worldwide*. New York: Oxford University Press.

Lawless, Jennifer L., and Richard L. Fox. 2010. *It Still Takes a Candidate: Why Women Don't Run for Office*. New York: Cambridge University Press.

Madam Secretary. 2014–2017. Created by Barbara Hall. New York, NY: CBS Television Studios.

McDonagh, Eileen. 2009. *The Motherless State*. Chicago: University of Chicago Press.

Morojele, Naleli Mpho Soledad. 2016. *Women Political Leaders in Rwanda and South Africa: Narratives of Triumph and Loss*. Leverkusen, Germany: Barbara Budrich Publishers.

Veep. 2012. Season 1. Directed by Armando Iannucci. Baltimore, MD: HBO.

President Obama speaks with students at Ivy Tech Community College in Indianapolis. Although women now outnumber men on college campuses throughout the country, they are less likely to take political science and government classes, join College Democrats or College Republicans, or think that they'll ever be qualified to run for office.

CHAPTER 3

GIRL POWER ISN'T POLITICAL POWER: THE GENDER GAP IN POLITICAL AMBITION

Key Question: Will the next generation of elected leaders continue to be dominated by men?

M en dominate the face of American politics. Just think back to the 2016 presidential election: Of the 22 major party candidates, only two were women. But we don't need to conjure up images of presidential campaigns to see a similar picture. The Speaker of the U.S. House of Representatives, the majority leader in the U.S. Senate, and the Chief Justice of the Supreme Court are men. Forty-four states—including the largest 20—have male governors. And men outnumber women roughly four to one in key elected positions at the local, state, and national levels (see Figure 3.1). In fact, of the more than 12,000 people who have ever served in the U.S. Congress, only 362 (that's only 3 percent) have been women. The dearth of female political leaders not only reduces the likelihood that politicians will address a diverse array of issues and concerns, but it also compromises the legitimacy of U.S. democracy.[1]

Although it is troubling that women, who comprise more than half the population, constitute just 20 percent of elected officials, there are many reasons to be optimistic. According to a recent World Bank/*Economist*

FIGURE 3.1 WOMEN'S REPRESENTATION IN U.S. POLITICS, 2017

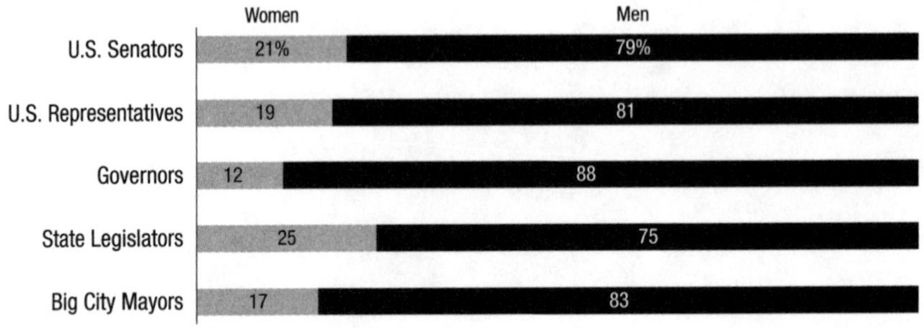

	Women	Men
U.S. Senators	21%	79%
U.S. Representatives	19	81
Governors	12	88
State Legislators	25	75
Big City Mayors	17	83

The bars reflect the percentage of women and men serving in each position as of June 2017. The "Big City Mayors" percentage reflects data through the end of December 2016.

report, the United States ranks 15th in the world (of more than 200 countries) in women's economic opportunities and legal protections.[2] Following the 2014 midterm elections, the total number of women serving in the U.S. Congress cracked 100 for the first time—quite the feat considering that it wasn't until 1993 that more than two women ever served in the U.S. Senate at the same time. The 2016 elections resulted in a record number of women of color serving in Congress (a total of 38).[3] Young women today have been exposed to more women in politics than any previous generation, growing up amid Hillary Clinton's 2008 and 2016 presidential bids, Sarah Palin's run for vice president in 2008, and Nancy Pelosi's ascension to Speaker of the U.S House (2007–11). Women are slowly catching up to men in entering the fields of law and business, the two professions that most often precede a career in politics. And contemporary culture is filled with messages of female empowerment. The pop music scene, for instance, is full of songs like Katy Perry's "Roar," Rachel Platten's "Fight Song," and Beyoncé's "Run the World (Girls)." The idea is simple: Women are a force to reckon with.

To many observers, gender parity seems to be on the horizon. As the "old boys' network" continues to crumble, young women will continue to embrace the opportunities available to them. This generational argument—that women's representation will improve markedly as younger women come of age, participate fully as citizens, and run for office themselves—certainly has intuitive appeal. But as we demonstrate in this chapter, it's unlikely. In the pages that follow, we establish and explicate this gender gap in political ambition. We base our analysis on the results of a 2012 survey we conducted of a national random sample of more than 2,100 college students (ages 18–25). No matter how we slice, dice, or even ginsu the data, the results are the same: When it comes to political ambition, young men tend to have it, and young women don't. Our findings suggest that the next generation of political leaders will continue to be dominated by men.

HE WILL RUN, SHE WILL NOT: GENDER DIFFERENCES IN BECOMING A CANDIDATE

Developing a prognosis for women's full inclusion in the U.S. political system requires determining whether young women are as likely as young men to aspire to seize the reins of political power. After all, a general interest in running for office early in life often sets the stage for a political candidacy decades later. Most 45-year-olds don't wake up one day, look in the mirror, and decide to run for public office. The idea has usually been in their heads and percolating for quite some time. Maybe they were not sure when they would run, or whether the right opportunity would ever arise. Perhaps they were not certain what office they would seek. They probably had not fully considered the nuts and bolts of what a campaign might entail. But the seed of a potential candidacy was likely planted years ago, often dating back to childhood or young adulthood. Bill Clinton serves as a perfect example. He writes in his memoir, "Sometime in my sixteenth year I decided I wanted to be in public life as an elected official. . . . I knew I could be great in public service."[4] U.S. Senators Ted Cruz and Marco Rubio, both of whom sought the 2016 Republican presidential nomination, credit their childhood hero, Ronald Reagan, with inspiring their careers in public service.

We realize that most people don't end up running for president, but political ambition still follows a similar track. Throughout the last 15 years, we have surveyed and interviewed thousands of lawyers, business leaders, and educators—people who have the backgrounds and credentials that most candidates possess. Nearly half told us that they had considered running for office. Of those, half said that they first thought about it by the time they were in college. A broad swath of research on career development finds the same thing—that young people's professional goals in high school and college are excellent predictors of the jobs they eventually get.[5]

So we asked a national sample of college students whether they ever thought that, someday, when they were older, they might want to run for political office. Forty-seven percent of college students told us that the idea of

FIGURE 3.2   HAVE YOU EVER THOUGHT THAT YOU MIGHT WANT
TO RUN FOR POLITICAL OFFICE?

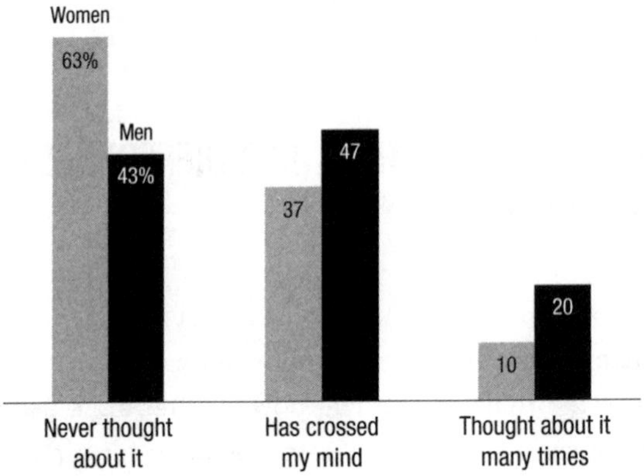

Data are based on responses from 1,020 male and 1,097 female college students (ages 18–25). Bars represent the percentage of men and women who fall into each category. The gender gap in each comparison is statistically significant.[6]

running for an elective position had at least "crossed their mind." But women and men were not equally politically ambitious. The data presented in Figure 3.2 reveal that men were almost twice as likely as women to have thought about running for office "many times."[7] Women, on the other hand, were roughly 20 percentage points more likely than men never to have considered it. Or think of it like this: Whereas just slightly more than one-third of women had thought about becoming a candidate, nearly six out of 10 men had. We also asked them to look to the future and consider whether running was something they might ever pursue. The gender differences were just as stark. Men in college were twice as likely as women to report that they "definitely" planned to run for office at some point down the road. Women were twice as likely to say they never would.

Importantly, the gender gap in political ambition persists across racial lines. The magnitude varies a bit, though. White men are two and a half times as likely as White women to report having thought about running for office regularly (21 percent of men, compared to 8 percent of women). Latinos are "only" twice as likely as Latinas to have thought about running for office many times (24 percent compared to 12 percent). And among Blacks, the gap dwindles even more (15 percent of men, compared to 10 percent of women, thought about running for office often). A similar pattern emerges when we consider the percentage of people who have never considered running (see Figure 3.3). Overall, though, the gender differences within each race are far

FIGURE 3.3   I'D NEVER RUN FOR OFFICE! (BY RACE AND SEX)

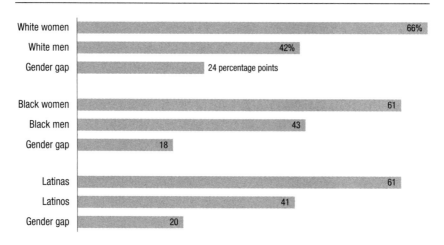

Data are based on responses from 1,205 White respondents, 260 Black respondents, and 387 Latino/a respondents. Bars indicate the percentage of college students who have never considered running for office. The gender gap is statistically significant in all comparisons.

more substantial than the differences across the races. After all, a majority of White, Black, and Latina women have never considered running for office, but a majority of men in each racial group report that the idea has at least crossed their minds.

Now, the idea of running for office is probably an abstract notion for most college students. To get a better sense of how young people feel about a career in politics, we also juxtaposed ambition for a political career with aspirations for other professional paths that might seem equally distant in the future. Again, we uncovered gender differences in political ambition.

In the first scenario, we presented college students with four potential career options—business owner, teacher, mayor of a city or town, and salesperson—and asked them which they would most like to be, assuming that each paid the same. Women and men ranked owning a business and being a teacher as more desirable than serving as a mayor. But men were almost twice as likely as women to select mayor as their preferred job (see the top of Figure 3.4). When we asked the students to indicate which of the four positions they liked least, 43 pecent of women, compared to 32 percent of men, selected mayor (it was the least desirable profession for women).

We then asked which of the following four higher echelon jobs was most appealing: business executive, lawyer, school principal, or member of Congress. Here too, women were significantly more likely than men to eschew the

FIGURE 3.4   IF THE FOLLOWING JOBS PAID THE SAME AMOUNT
OF MONEY, WHICH WOULD YOU MOST LIKE TO BE?

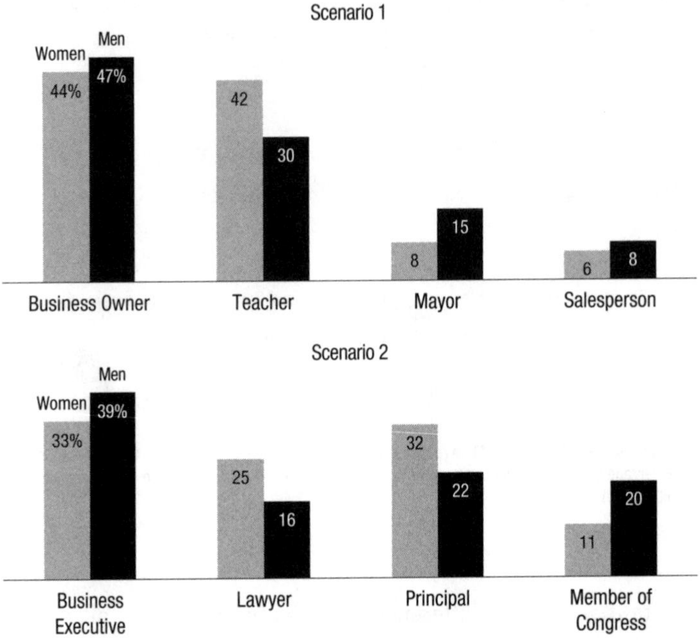

Scenario 1

Women 44% / Men 47% — Business Owner
42 / 30 — Teacher
8 / 15 — Mayor
6 / 8 — Salesperson

Scenario 2

Women 33% / Men 39% — Business Executive
25 / 16 — Lawyer
32 / 22 — Principal
11 / 20 — Member of Congress

Data are based on responses from 1,012 men and 1,088 women. Bars represent the percentage of men and women who ranked each position as their most desirable when presented with the list of four options. The gender gaps for mayor and member of Congress are statistically significant.

possibility of a political career. As we see in the bottom of Figure 3.4, men were 50 percent more likely than women to select member of Congress.

These scenarios suggest pretty convincingly that college women are far less likely than college men to be interested in running for office. But just to be sure, as a final way to measure political ambition, we provided our survey respondents with a list of 24 jobs and asked them to check off any in which they might ever be interested. Once again, we uncovered substantial gender gaps in receptivity toward the three political positions about which we asked. For the three public offices—president, member of Congress, and mayor—men were at least 50 percent more likely than women to be interested in the position. Men were also more likely than women to be attracted to a career in business and science, whereas women were more likely than men to express interest in being a teacher, nurse, or secretary. In fact, three times as many female college students were open to being a secretary as were open to serving in Congress.

These gender gaps in political ambition are striking not only because the young women and men were similar in race, household income, party affiliation, and academic background, but also because they were equally likely to have participated in political activities. From voting, to attending a protest or rally, to blogging or e-mailing about a cause, to posting about or following a politician on a social networking site, we uncovered generally comparable rates of activism (see Figure 3.5). When significant differences did emerge—voting in a student election and raising money for a candidate or cause—women were *more* likely than men to have engaged in the activity. Yet young women and men were not equally likely to consider running for office.

At first glance, the gender gap in political ambition we uncovered might not seem that significant. Is it really meaningful—given that so few young people plan to pursue a career in politics—that 20 percent of men, but only 10 percent of women, want to run for office someday? We'd say yes, the difference is very important. There are more than 500,000 elective offices in the United States. That means that for every 475 adults living in this country, one is an elected official. If only a small fraction of young people is seriously interested in seeking these positions, but young men are twice as likely as young women to fall into that category, then most elected officials will continue to be men, well into the future.

FIGURE 3.5   COLLEGE STUDENTS' POLITICAL ACTIVITY

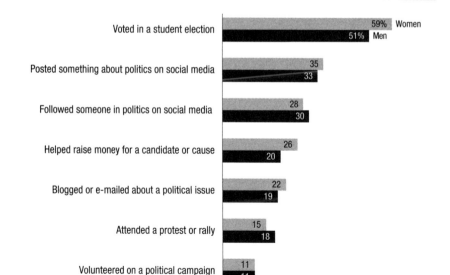

Data are based on responses from 1,020 men and 1,097 women. The gender gaps for voting and raising money are statistically significant.

TWO REASONS YOUNG WOMEN ARE LESS POLITICALLY AMBITIOUS THAN YOUNG MEN

What explains the striking gender gap in political ambition among college students? Certainly, the multifaceted lens through which individuals come to see the world politically—from interactions at home, at school, and through the media—affects interest in running for office. But two factors in particular contribute to the gender gap we uncovered: (1) support and encouragement that young people receive to run for office; and (2) the way young people feel about their suitability to participate in the political system. Together, these factors help explain why young women are less likely than young men to express interest in running for office.

You Don't Go Girl: The Gender Gap in Encouragement to Run for Office

We've long known that when people are encouraged to run for office, they're much more likely to think about it and to do it. And there's no reason to think this wouldn't be the case for young people. Campaigns for class representative in elementary, middle, and high school, to races for student government positions in college, can offer a first taste of what it might be like to campaign for an elective office as an adult. They can also provide young people with a first dose of encouragement or support to pursue a political position. The suggestion or support from friends, family members, teachers, or just about anyone can instill confidence and generate political ambition.

To assess whether young women and men are equally likely to receive encouragement to run for office, we began by asking about student government. In a nutshell, we found virtually no gender differences. When it came to receiving the suggestion to run for student body president or class representative, young women were just as likely as young men to report encouragement from their parents, family members, friends, and teachers (see the first two columns of Table 3.1). In academic settings, nothing suggests that adult mentors rate young women's leadership abilities or potential differently than they do young men's.

Not so when we turn to encouragement to run for public office later in life. Gender equity gives way to patterns that favor men. The comparisons presented in the right-hand columns of Table 3.1 reveal consistent gender gaps. Perhaps most notably, the gap was the largest when it came to encouragement from parents (we found the same thing when we asked separately about support from mothers and fathers). These results are especially noteworthy given that young women and men reported nearly identical rates of having

TABLE 3.1   GENDER DIFFERENCES IN WHETHER COLLEGE STUDENTS
            HAVE BEEN ENCOURAGED TO RUN FOR OFFICE

	Encouraged to Run for Student Government		Encouraged to Run for Political Office in the Future	
	MEN	WOMEN	MEN	WOMEN
Parent	24%	25%	40%	29%
Grandparent	9	7	14	9
Aunt / Uncle	9	6	10	7
Sibling	8	9	10	7
Teacher	19	18	19	12
Coach	5	3	7	4
Religious Leader	4	4	7	4
Friend	22	22	26	17
Received encouragement from three or more sources	**20**	**19**	**19**	**13**

Entries indicate the percentage of respondents who ever received encouragement or the suggestion to run for office
from each source. Data are based on responses from 1,020 men and 1,097 women. For political office, all of the gender
differences are statistically significant. For student government, only the gender difference on coach is significant.

political discussions with their parents, going to vote with them, or following
news together.

Gender differences in encouragement, however, came not just from
parents. In each of the other seven comparisons presented in Table 3.1, young
men were more likely than young women to receive the suggestion to run for
office later in life. When family members, mentors, and peers think beyond
the extracurricular activity of school government, gendered notions of what
political leaders look like seem to kick in.

The gender gap in encouragement to run for office is important because
it contributes directly to the gender gap in political ambition. Parents who
encourage their children to consider running for office exert a dramatic impact
on the likelihood that their children will. Fifty percent of college students whose
mothers regularly suggested that they run for office, and 46 percent whose
fathers made the suggestion, reported that they would definitely like to run in
the future. These people were 10 times more likely than those whose parents
never mentioned it to be interested in a candidacy down the road. College students who received encouragement to run from another source were roughly
three times more likely than those who did not to report interest in a future
candidacy.

Clearly, encouragement to run for office can motivate young women and men to think about a political career. That's why it is so concerning that college-age women are not as likely as college-age men to report receiving it. Attitudes about women as leaders have certainly changed over time, and public perceptions of women in politics have evolved. But the General Social Survey, which provides a benchmark of American public opinion, finds that roughly 25 percent of Americans still believe that men are better suited emotionally for politics than women are. A recent Gallup poll revealed that 14 percent of citizens still agree that "women aren't tough enough for politics." Sixteen percent of Americans still think that "women don't make as good leaders as men."[8] These numbers reflect dramatic improvement from only a few decades ago, but they also indicate that a substantial number of citizens do not view women and men as political equals. Even today's college students face vestiges of these cultural barriers.

I Could Never Do That: The Gender Gap in Self-Perceptions

Researchers have found that, from as early as elementary school, boys are taught to be confident, assertive, and self-promoting. Girls often receive the message—if even only subtly—that it is inappropriate or undesirable to possess these characteristics. As a result, from a young age, women are more likely than men to exhibit a tendency to diminish and undervalue their skills and achievements.[9] Male and female students in mathematics and language arts, for example, have vastly different perceptions of their own abilities; male students overestimate their skills and female students underestimate theirs relative to objective indicators of competence.[10] This carries over into college, where female students are perpetually more likely than men to doubt their academic abilities. A 2011 report on student leadership at Princeton University found that women regularly undersell themselves as strong leaders.[11] In 2013, a study at Boston College found that women's levels of confidence are lower when they graduate from college than when they entered, and that these self-doubts may limit their career aspirations.[12] Although college students may not have fully formed opinions about their qualifications to run for office, these studies suggest that men will be more likely than women to express the confidence that, someday, they will be qualified.

Indeed, that's exactly what we uncovered among the college students we surveyed. We asked them whether they thought that after they finish college and have been working for a while, they will know enough and be sufficiently prepared to run for office. The data presented in Figure 3.6 reveal that men

FIGURE 3.6   WHEN YOU'RE OLDER, DO YOU THINK YOU'LL BE QUALIFIED TO RUN FOR POLITICAL OFFICE?

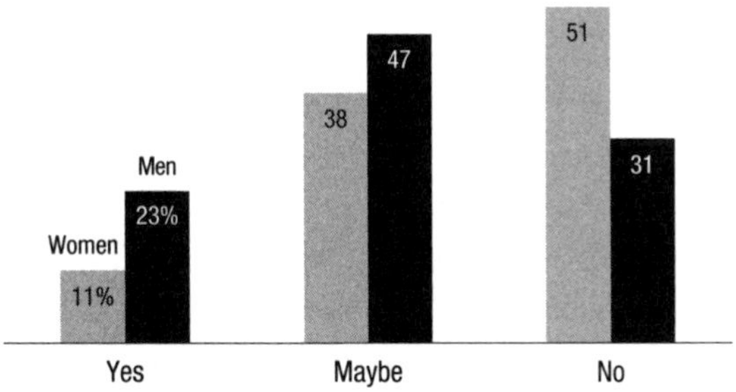

Data are based on responses from 1,020 male and 1,097 female college students. Bars represent the percentage of men and women who fall into each category when asked, "When you have finished school and have been working for a while, do you think you will know enough to run for political office?" The gender gap is statistically significant for all comparisons.

were more than twice as likely as women to answer the question affirmatively. Women were 50 percent more likely than men to doubt that they would be qualified candidates.

College women expressed more doubts about their qualifications than college men did, not only in this broad, abstract way. They also reported less confidence when we asked about specific skills needed to be a successful candidate. Men were about 20 percent more likely than women, for example, to contend that they were good at public speaking. They were also significantly more likely than women (22 percent of men, compared to 14 percent of women) to assert that they knew a lot about politics. It bears repeating here that the college men and women we surveyed had almost identical academic experiences and credentials. These gender gaps, therefore, are perceptual; they are not rooted in actual gender differences in young people's political knowledge or politically relevant skills.

Women's self-doubts are important for two reasons. First, college students who perceive themselves as qualified to run for office are more likely to consider running. Among those who thought they might be qualified to run for office someday, 53 percent of women and 66 percent of men considered politics a viable option for the future. Among those who did not think they were qualified, only 15 percent of women and 23 percent of men had considered a political career. Even though confidence makes young women and young men more likely to consider running for office, women are significantly less likely than men to exhibit that confidence and believe they will achieve the necessary qualifications.

Second, self-doubts inhibit female college students' interest in running for office more so than they do men's. After all, men who did not think they would be qualified to run for office were 50 percent more likely than women who felt the same way still to consider a candidacy. And men who thought they "might" be qualified were 25 percent more likely than their female counterparts to express interest in running. Women, therefore, are doubly disadvantaged on the qualifications criterion.

Women's lower self-assessments of their political skills are consistent with a political culture that has not traditionally impressed upon women the value of confidence, assertiveness, or competitiveness. The mostly male face of politics likely reinforces these doubts. And our candidate-centered electoral system exacerbates them. Running for office in the United States is a highly competitive endeavor that requires significant levels of entrepreneurship and self-promotion. Given the heavy weight young women and men place on their self-evaluations when considering a future run for office, closing the gender gap in political ambition looks unlikely, at least in the near future.

WHERE DO WE GO FROM HERE?

Our national survey of college students revealed a substantial gender gap in political ambition. In fact, the gap in political ambition we uncovered among 18- to 25-year-olds is very similar to the size of the gap we previously uncovered in studies of potential candidates already working in the feeder professions to politics (see Chapter 2). This suggests that the gender gap in ambition is already well in place by the time women and men enter their first careers, and that it doesn't get smaller over time. In addition, for adults and college students alike, the gender gap is driven by a lack of encouragement for women's candidacies and women's perceptions that they are not qualified to run. Ultimately, the generational argument that women's interest in running for office and their presence as elected officials will increase as women's educational and professional opportunities increase is quite precarious.[13]

It is critical to note, however, that young women's lower levels of interest in running for office do not stem from gender differences in a sense of civic duty or their broad aspirations for the future. When we asked college students about their priorities and life goals, we found few gender differences; young women and men were equally likely to want to get married, have children, earn a lot of money, and achieve career success. Male and female respondents were also equally likely to aspire to improve their communities. Yet despite their similar life goals, college women and men reported very different views when asked about the most effective way to bring about societal change. Thirty-five percent of young women, compared to 25 percent of young men, viewed working for a charity as the best way to bring about change. On the other hand, 26 percent of men, but only 17 percent of women, saw running for elective office as the best way to improve society. Women and men both aspire to change the world around them for the better, but women are less likely than men to see political leadership as a means to that end.

If we want to close this gap, then organizational efforts to engage young women politically during the college years seem like a practical and efficient way to proceed. Because female college students are less likely than men to take political science classes, discuss politics with their friends, and seek out political information through the media, there are substantial opportunities for women's organizations—on college campuses and nationally—to make a difference.

Consider IGNITE, which runs political and civic education and training programs in high schools in California, Colorado, and Texas. The organization identifies girls at participating high schools and offers an after-school training program for three hours each week throughout the school year. Annually, hundreds of participants learn about government (particularly at the local level), issues they consider personally relevant (such as immigration, reproductive rights, marriage equality, and education funding), and the importance of women in politics. A central component of the IGNITE model also involves introducing high school girls to female candidates and elected officials who can share their personal stories. At the college level, though, IGNITE's programming is far more limited. The organization offers a training session on participating campuses, but it's up to students to start IGNITE chapters and organize efforts to build women's political ambition.[14]

Another organization, Running Start, "introduces young women to role models, talks to young women about the importance of politics in their lives, and gives them the encouragement and skills to pursue a career in political leadership."[15] The bulk of their programming, however, focuses on high school students. Their flagship Young Women's Leadership Program is a six-day retreat for 60 high school girls from across the country. The weeklong foray into politics includes workshops on public speaking, networking, fundraising, media training, and issue advocacy. Young female candidates and elected officials are also integral to the program; they speak to participants about what it is like to run for office, why it matters, and how to get involved at the local level. Here too, though, programming beyond the high school level is far less developed. The organization offers an annual day-long Young Women's Political Summit (for women under the age of 35), which touches on many of the same topics.

Programs like these are vital for ensuring that high school girls are just as politically interested and engaged as high school boys. But given that the gender gap in political ambition is substantial on college campuses, initiatives directed at college women are at least as essential. High-profile, bipartisan women's advocacy groups, such as the National Organization for Women and the Women's Campaign Fund, would be well-served to launch national initiatives on college campuses. Partisan organizations, such as EMILY's List, Emerge America, or even the Democratic and Republican Parties themselves, would also benefit from developing a substantial collegiate presence that targets young women in particular. These organizations are well-positioned to provide college women with continued exposure to female candidates and elected officials. Their sustained efforts would show young women how running for office can bring about societal change. And the programs would help combat women's tendency to doubt their abilities to enter politics. The organizations would benefit, too. By casting a wider net, all of these groups would expand their own pools of potential female candidates down the road.

We know that once a young woman is encouraged to run for office, she is just as likely as a young man to be open to a future in politics. And we know that when young women feel confident about their political competence and knowledge, they are just as likely as young men to consider turning their political aptitude into a candidacy one day in the future. The challenge is to make sure that more young women receive the support and confidence boost. In the meantime, we must continue to deepen our understanding of how young women and men in contemporary society are still socialized about politics, the messages they receive about the acquisition of political power, and the characteristics that qualify individuals to seek it.

QUESTIONS FOR REFLECTION AND DISCUSSION

1. Would you ever want to run for office? Has anyone ever encouraged you to consider it? In thinking about your answer, reflect on how and when you arrived at your feelings about the idea of ever becoming a candidate.

2. In thinking about your friends and classmates, are there differences between men and women that might help explain the gender gap in political ambition? Do you see any behaviors inside or outside the classroom that are consistent with gender differences in interest in running for office?

3. Young women and men are equally likely to express interest in politics and to participate politically (see Figure 3.5). But these similarities don't translate into ambition to run for office. Why do you think that is the case? Are there unique aspects about running for office that pose particular challenges to women's inclusion?

4. If you were the head of an organization whose goal was to encourage more young women to run for office, what would your central message be? Once you decide what main idea you'd focus on, come up with three specific ways to communicate the message.

5. Hillary Clinton was the first woman to win a major party nomination and compete for president in a general election. Do you think her candidacy will serve to encourage more girls and young women to think they too can enter politics? Or might her candidacy (and defeat) have the opposite effect and depress interest among women? Regardless of the position you take, explain your thinking.

FOR FURTHER EXPLORATION

Campbell, David E., and Christina Wolbrecht. 2006. "See Jane Run: Women Politicians as Role Models for Adolescents." *Journal of Politics* 68(2): 233–47.

Election. 1999. Directed by Alexander Payne. Los Angeles, CA: Paramount Pictures.

Fox, Richard L., and Jennifer L. Lawless. 2014. "Uncovering the Origins of the Gender Gap in Political Ambition." *American Political Science Review* 108(3): 499–519.

The Good Wife. Season 6. 2014–2015. Created by Michelle King and Robert King. New York: CBS.

Lawless, Jennifer L., and Richard L. Fox. 2010. *It Still Takes a Candidate: Why Women Don't Run for Office.* New York: Cambridge University Press.

Lawless, Jennifer L., and Richard L. Fox. 2015. *Running from Office: Why Young Americans Are Turned Off to Politics.* New York: Oxford University Press.

McMinn, Lisa Graham. 2007. *Growing Strong Daughters: Encouraging Girls to Become All They're Meant to Be.* New York: Baker Books.

*Miss*Representation. 2011. Directed by Jennifer Siebel Newsom. San Francisco, CA: The Miss Representation Project.

Orenstein, Peggy. 1995. *Schoolgirls: Young Women, Self Esteem, and the Confidence Gap.* New York: Anchor Books.

Kamala Harris declares victory in her 2016 race for the U.S. Senate at a rally in Los Angeles. Even though women are just as likely as men to win elections, women occupy only 20 percent of the seats in the U.S. Congress.

CHAPTER 4

INTO THE FRYING PAN:
WOMEN'S EXPERIENCES
RUNNING FOR OFFICE

Key Question: Do women have a tougher time getting elected than men?

In March 2016, Democratic presidential candidate Hillary Clinton took to the stage in Detroit to deliver a speech about job creation and gender equality. Former Republican National Committee chair Michael Steele, however, took more interest in the tone of Clinton's voice than in the content of her remarks. "When you're going up every octave with every word, people are like, 'I have to get some popcorn and get away from this,'" said Steele, an MSNBC political analyst.[1] His was only the latest in what had become a sustained line of criticism directed at Clinton. Bob Woodward, a journalist at the *Washington Post*, warned Clinton that her constant "shouting" turned people off. He recommended that she "lower the temperature" and "get off this screaming stuff."[2] On *Fox News*, Geraldo Rivera described Clinton's voice as "unpleasant," "unrelaxed," and "bitter" and speculated that she might have a hearing problem.[3] Peggy Noonan, a *Wall Street Journal* columnist and former speechwriter in the Reagan White House, wrote that

Clinton reminds her of a "landlady yelling."[4] Even Clinton's Democratic opponent—Senator Bernie Sanders—demanded that she "stop shouting" about gun violence.[5]

Nearly as soon as the first voice-related critique was lobbed at Clinton, pundits and analysts condemned what they perceived to be a sexist electoral environment and raised concerns about holding female candidates to a different standard than men. "If Mrs. Clinton is shouting, what is Bernie Sanders doing?" asked Stephanie Schriock, the president of EMILY's List. Howard Dean, a former Democratic governor and 2004 presidential candidate, wondered if Clinton "were a male and she were making these kinds of speeches, would people be criticizing her?"[6] Clinton even found an unlikely ally in former Republican congresswoman and 2012 presidential candidate Michele Bachmann. In an interview with the *Huffington Post*, Bachmann empathized with Clinton's experiences, explaining that "the hill she has to climb . . . it's just a different hill than men have to climb."[7]

Criticisms about Clinton's voice, of course, may have had little to do with the fact that she was a woman. Many people just didn't like her and, as a result, were willing to criticize everything she said and how she said it. It's also important to remember that voice-related critiques weren't reserved for Clinton. Democratic candidate Bernie Sanders and Republican Donald Trump received plenty of press coverage regarding the tone of their voice and their speaking style.[8]

The high-profile discussion of Clinton's voice and the narrative about sexism in politics that followed, however, are what's important here. Indeed, they likely reinforced ordinary Americans' sense that female candidates face a more treacherous electoral environment than men do. According to a 2014 Pew Research poll—conducted well before Clinton announced her 2016 presidential bid—nearly two-thirds of the public said one reason there aren't more women in political office is that voters aren't ready to elect them. Six in 10 believed that women are held to higher standards than men. More than half said that women active in party politics are held back by men. Perceptions of bias in the electoral arena are even significantly higher than voters' doubts that women would be able to carve out sufficient time to run for office (see Figure 4.1). And that says a lot. After all, women—even those with the very successful careers and credentials typical of most candidates—are 10 times more likely than men to be responsible for the majority of the household tasks and child care.[9]

When asked more specifically about women's and men's experiences on the campaign trail, Americans also see a playing field that is far from level. Heading into the 2014 midterm elections, a national survey conducted by YouGov found that 60 percent of people thought that the media focus too much on how female candidates look. Nearly the same proportion said that women are subjected to sexist media coverage. Roughly half the country believed that women have to be more qualified than men to win office. It's no surprise then that nearly one-third said that women who run for office don't win as often as men do, and that they aren't as successful at raising money.[10] The same sentiments rang true among a national sample of "potential candidates"—women and men who work in the professions from which most candidates emerge.[11] The lack of women in top elective office only supports the view that politics is more difficult for women than men. Otherwise, there'd be more women in positions of political power.

Although it might seem intuitive to conclude that women have a tough time getting elected, or that the media, campaign donors, and voters are to blame, we show in this chapter that it's just not the case. Using the 2014 campaigns for the U.S. House of Representatives as an example, we demonstrate that the sex of a candidate matters little in general elections, regardless of where we look. When they run for office, male and female candidates receive almost identical news coverage, are evaluated by voters in similar ways, raise the same amounts of money, and win their races at equal rates. That's not to say that sexism and discrimination are altogether absent from electoral politics. And by no means are we suggesting that a female presidential candidate, such as Hillary Clinton, will not encounter gender bias on the campaign trail (see Chapter 1). But in the vast majority of campaigns, the twenty-first-century political landscape is far more equitable than most characterizations would lead us to believe.

FIGURE 4.1   PERCEPTIONS OF WHY MORE WOMEN DON'T HOLD POLITICAL OFFICE

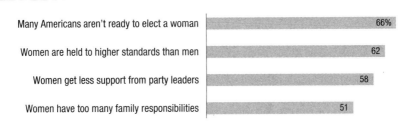

Many Americans aren't ready to elect a woman   66%
Women are held to higher standards than men   62
Women get less support from party leaders   58
Women have too many family responsibilities   51

Bars represent the percentage of 1,835 respondents who considered each factor a "major" or "minor" reason that more women don't hold high-level elective office in the United States. Source: Pew Research Center, November 12–21, 2014.

ALL THE NEWS THAT'S FIT TO PRINT: COVERAGE OF MALE AND FEMALE CANDIDATES

We begin our analysis with the news media. It is widely assumed that, compared to male candidates, female candidates are treated differently, and often worse, in the press. This conventional wisdom, of course, didn't come out of the blue. Some early research—mostly studies of gubernatorial and Senate candidates in the 1980s and 1990s—found that women received less coverage than men did, and that the content of the news attention they got differed.[12] More specifically, these studies showed that news tends to emphasize women's appearance and family roles, but focuses on men's credentials and political experience.[13] In addition, women are often associated with "feminine" traits—such as compassion and honesty—and advocacy for "women's" issues, like women's health, gender equity, and abortion rights. Men are more likely to be described with "masculine" attributes—such as leadership and competence—and strength in the areas of foreign policy, defense, and the economy.[14] These widespread gender differences in news coverage then work to undermine female candidates' credentials, temperament, and expertise.[15]

When we put this conventional wisdom to the test in contemporary elections, though, we found little supporting evidence. To draw this conclusion, we relied on a comprehensive study of newspaper coverage during the 2014 House races. Although it might seem old-fashioned in the digital age to focus on local newspapers, they remain the most important and influential source of information to voters during congressional campaigns.[16] In fact, local papers are often the only reliable, steady source of news in House elections. We have at our disposal every local news story during the 30 days leading up to the election that mentioned either the Democratic or Republican candidate. Overall, this amounts to more than 4,000 articles that appeared in the largest circulating newspaper in each congressional district across the country.[17]

First, we examined the claim that women receive less news coverage than men. If anything, we found the opposite to be true. The average number of stories in a race between two men was 11. Replace one of the men with a woman and the average number of stories went up to 13 per election. Races with two women competing against each other averaged almost 16 articles. Contests with two female candidates, in other words, saw roughly one more story per week in the month leading up to Election Day than contests featuring two men.

We also see no disadvantage for female candidates when we analyze the volume of coverage received by each candidate (as opposed to by the number of stories about the contest overall). The average female candidate appeared in approximately 14 news articles in the four weeks prior to the election. The average male candidate appeared in 11. These gender differences persist across racial lines. Black, White, and Latina female candidates saw two, three, and four more stories, respectively, than Black, White, and Latino male candidates. Women who run for Congress do not have a harder time than men attracting press attention.

It is important to note that both women and men of color garnered less media attention than White women and men. The overall story count for Latino/a candidates was, on average, about three fewer stories than for White candidates. And Black candidates had three fewer articles than that. This difference in volume, though, is a result of the fact that the Black and Latino/a candidates competed in less competitive races than those that featured White candidates. By less competitive, we don't mean that Black and Latino/a candidates ran as sacrificial lambs. Quite the contrary: They were actually more likely than White candidates to win, and to do so by large margins.[18] Because these contests weren't nail biters, they were somewhat "boring" by conventional press standards.

Next, we turned to four aspects of the substance of the news coverage the candidates received. Overall, we found very few gender differences—certainly none that disadvantaged women. Take first press attention to candidates' positions on policy issues. This kind of coverage was plentiful, with 88 percent of women and 83 percent of men receiving at least some of it. No significant differences emerged when we compared the average number of references to policy issues male and female candidates received. The top row of Figure 4.2 reveals that men (black bar) had an average of 23 mentions of policy issues in their news coverage; women (grey bar) had 26.

When we broke down the coverage and examined the specific policy issues associated with candidates, the results were again similar for women and men. Regardless of sex, among the top issues mentioned in relation to both Democratic and Republican candidates were the economy and health care. On most other policies that made their way into the news—defense and security, foreign affairs, taxes and spending—the amount of attention journalists gave to women was also indistinguishable from the amount they devoted to men. Women were slightly more likely than men to receive coverage about traditional "women's" issues—such as abortion, women's health, and gender equity—but it didn't come at the expense of attention to anything else. News media mentions of "women's" issues just represented the additional policy coverage female candidates received.

FIGURE 4.2   LOCAL MEDIA COVERAGE OF MALE AND FEMALE HOUSE
CANDIDATES

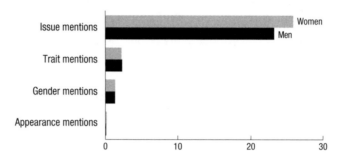

Bars represent the total number of mentions in each category a candidate received in his or her local newspaper in the 30 days leading up to the 2014 general election. None of the gender differences is statistically significant. Source: Hayes, Danny, and Jennifer L. Lawless. 2016. *Women on the Run: Gender, Media, and Political Campaigns in a Polarized Era.* New York: Cambridge University Press.

The second set of bars in Figure 4.2 indicates the total number of explicit references in news coverage to candidates' personal traits, both positive and negative (e.g., "capable" and "ineffective"). The overall amount of attention devoted to personal traits was much less than for issues—just about two references throughout the entire month. But men and women received it in equal amounts. We also turned up virtually no gender differences when we looked specifically at whether the trait referred to a candidate's competence and leadership ("male" traits), empathy and integrity ("female" traits), or when we considered positive versus negative adjectives.

Finally, the third and fourth sets of bars in Figure 4.2 make clear that journalists do not devote more attention to candidate sex, family roles, or appearance when they write about women than when they cover men. In the month leading up to the election, 60 percent of candidates saw no coverage of this type whatsoever. And those who did saw very little (on average, women and men alike received only one mention of their sex or gender). When we focus on the small number of references to a candidate's appearance—discussion of clothes, hairstyles, physical features—there's even less to analyze. Ninety-five percent of women and 96 percent of men received no coverage of their appearance. The handful of male and female candidates who did saw equal (and tiny) amounts of it.

All of this suggests that candidate sex, and all the stereotyping thought to go with it, is not routinely relevant in news coverage of U.S. House races. It's not just our analysis of 2014 coverage that finds this to be the case. The only other similarly exhaustive analysis of congressional candidates' news coverage focuses on 2010, and the findings are virtually identical. The sex of the candidate affected neither the volume nor the substance of the coverage he or she received.[19]

Why? One reason may be that journalistic norms encourage the media to reflect candidates' campaign messages, and women and men tend to communicate the same messages.[20] Another reason is that female candidates in most congressional districts are no longer a novelty. In just the last 20 years alone, women have run as general election candidates for the U.S. House in every state except Rhode Island. In most cases, when a woman runs for Congress, there's no history-making potential, no glass ceiling being cracked, no "first" associated with the candidacy. Her presence—unlike Hillary Clinton's on the national stage—does little to alter the way that journalists approach a campaign. Reporters regard electoral competitiveness, and especially the possibility of defeating an incumbent, as far more newsworthy than the presence of a female candidate.[21]

PARTY OVER SEX: VOTERS' ASSESSMENT OF MALE AND FEMALE CANDIDATES

When we turn to the voters, we see a pattern that mirrors media coverage. Lots of studies from the 1990s and early 2000s found that voters associated male and female candidates with different character traits and issue strengths. Citizens viewed female politicians as more compassionate and empathetic than men, but also as less competent and as weaker leaders. As a result, women were often stereotyped as adept at handling "compassion" issues, especially those relating to women, families, and children. Because male politicians were often seen as strong leaders, voters perceived them as better able to handle foreign policy, defense, and crime. But as was the case for journalists, voters nowadays don't rely on gender stereotypes when they evaluate candidates.[22]

Just look at the results of a national survey conducted in the days leading up to the 2014 midterms. First, voters were asked to rate both the Democratic and Republican House candidates in their districts on five traits: competence, leadership, empathy, trustworthiness, and whether the candidate was qualified. If traditional gender stereotypes affect the way citizens evaluate candidates, then women should outperform men on empathy and trustworthiness, but fare less well when it comes to competence and leadership (and probably perceived qualifications). They don't. Figure 4.3 presents the percentage of voters who reported that each trait described the

FIGURE 4.3   VOTERS' ASSESSMENTS OF MALE AND FEMALE HOUSE
CANDIDATES' PERSONAL TRAITS

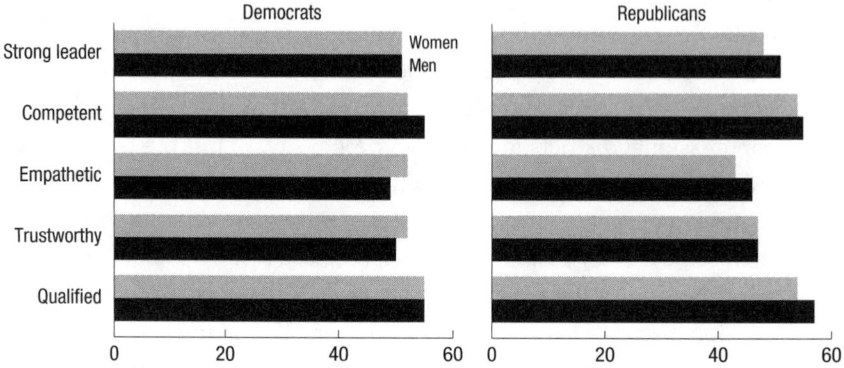

Bars represent the percentage of respondents who think these terms describe the Democrat and Republican U.S. House candidates in their districts "very well" or "quite well." None of the gender differences is statistically significant. Data come from the Women & Politics Institute's module of the 2014 Cooperative Congressional Election Study. Sample size ranges from 1,803 to 1,817.

Democrat (left panel) and Republican (right panel) House candidate "quite well" or "very well." Not one of the 10 comparisons between women and men reveals a significant difference.

Voters were also asked to rate, on a scale from 0 to 10, how capable they thought the candidates in their districts would be at dealing with a wide range of important public policy issues. Higher scores indicate more favorable evaluations. The left-hand panel of Figure 4.4 presents the average evaluation male and female Democratic candidates received; the right-hand panel presents scores for Republicans. Across all 10 comparisons—five issues for each party—women did just as well as men. These results aren't surprising, though. Assessments of candidates' personal qualities and character traits—where we found no gender differences—often serve as the foundation for evaluations of how well they'd handle a series of issues.

Why does gender matter only in the faintest of ways when it comes to voters' evaluations of candidates? One reason—as we've already shown—is that the news media don't encourage people to think about congressional elections in gendered terms. Another is the power of partisanship. Citizens tend to see the political world through a partisan lens, a view that is encouraged by campaign discourse and news coverage that focuses on differences and conflict between Republicans and Democrats. Many congressional campaigns are

FIGURE 4.4   VOTERS' ASSESSMENTS OF MALE AND FEMALE HOUSE
              CANDIDATES ON THE ISSUES

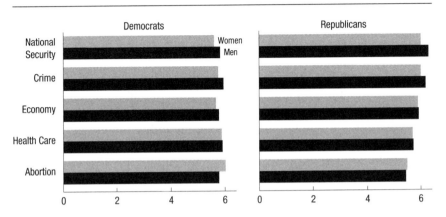

Bars represent the mean score that respondents gave the Democrat and Republican U.S. House candidates in their districts on how well they would handle each issue. A zero indicates "not well at all," and a 10 indicates "extremely well." None of the gender differences is statistically significant. Data come from the Women & Politics Institute's module of the 2014 Cooperative Congressional Election Study. Sample size ranges from 1,817 to 1,833.

"nationalized," with candidates within a party adopting a similar set of talking points.[23] Republicans in districts across the country in 2014 railed against President Obama, and Democrats accused Republicans of obstructionism and the failure to get anything done in Washington, DC. When partisanship dominates voters' evaluations of candidates and virtually dictates their vote choice, there's little room for sex to matter.[24]

MONEY AND VOTES: MALE AND FEMALE CANDIDATES' PERFORMANCE IN CONGRESSIONAL ELECTIONS

The earliest political science research about women's experiences when they ran for public office uncovered a political arena rife with discrimination.[25] Women were actively discouraged from throwing their hats into the ring, and when they did, they often faced a hostile environment.[26] For at least 30 years now, though, women and men have raised and spent similar amounts of money in House elections.[27] And women who run for Congress do just as well as men, in both primaries and general elections.[28] We focus once again on the 2014 midterms, but the results we present are consistent with previous election cycles dating back to the 1980s. The results also hold for 2016, where women constituted roughly 19 percent of the candidates in the general election and now occupy roughly 19 percent of the seats in the 115th Congress.[29]

Let's start with money. Overall, the 2014 midterm elections cost more than $3 billion. That is, if we add up the spending from candidates, parties, and outside groups, Republicans spent about $1.75 billion, Democrats $1.64 billion. The average winning House campaign cost $1.2 million.[30] Women on both sides of the aisle were just as likely as men to access the dollars needed to run a competitive race. On average, women spent $1,012,158; men spent virtually the same amount ($1,037,029). When we break the overall expenditures down by whether the candidate was an incumbent, challenger, or vying for an open seat, in no comparison is the gender difference statistically significant (see Table 4.1). Actually, where the dollar amounts differ substantively, they tend to advantage women. Female challengers in both parties, for instance, outspent men, as did women competing for open seats (often by sizeable amounts).

TABLE 4.1 U.S. HOUSE CANDIDATES' CAMPAIGN EXPENDITURES

	WOMEN	MEN
Democrats		
Incumbents	$1,353,622 (57)	$1,442,187 (126)
Challengers	519,449 (44)	301,059 (135)
Open Seats	1,594,035 (11)	1,069,646 (33)
Republicans		
Incumbents	1,293,730 (17)	1,519,129 (188)
Challengers	521,698 (27)	489,802 (120)
Open Seats	2,006,533 (6)	1,495,129 (41)

Column entries reflect the mean amount of campaign spending for the 2014 election. Numbers in parentheses indicate the number of candidates in each category. None of the gender differences is statistically significant. Data provided by Gary Jacobson.

Similar levels of financial success are important because the candidates who spend the most are more likely to win. In 94 percent of the House races in 2014, the candidate with the largest war chest came out on top. The numbers presented in Table 4.2 reveal that women and men were equally likely to fall into that category. This is the case regardless of whether we look at the percentage of the vote a candidate received (left side of the table) or simply whether the candidate won the election (right side of the table). Female incumbents were reelected with similar margins and at comparable (and incredibly high) rates as male incumbents. Notice that almost every single incumbent who sought reelection won reelection (see Chapter 2). Male challengers were just as likely as female challengers to lose their races (more than 95 percent did). And women seeking open seats had just as good a shot at winning, and by just as much, as did the men against whom they competed. As with fundraising, the few substantive gender differences we uncover—such as the percentage of Democratic candidates winning open seat races—benefit women. We don't want to make too much of these differences, though—even when they sometimes might seem substantial—because the number of female candidates in several categories is quite small. Only a total of 17 women (6 Republicans and 11 Democrats), for example, competed in open seat contests in 2014.

TABLE 4.2   U.S. HOUSE CANDIDATES' PERFORMANCE ON ELECTION DAY

| | Mean Vote Share | | Percent Winning | |
Democrats	WOMEN	MEN	WOMEN	MEN
Incumbents	66%	65%	98%	91%
Challengers	35	33	1	2
Open Seats	56	44	55	27

Republicans	WOMEN	MEN	WOMEN	MEN
Incumbents	65	66	100	99
Challengers	37	36	4	9
Open Seats	47	51	67	67

Entries are based on the 2014 House elections and include the same number of candidates in each category as presented in Table 4.1. The only difference is that the 32 races in which a candidate received 100% of the vote (five featuring female candidates) are omitted from this analysis. None of the gender differences is statistically significant.

It's also important to note that female candidates of color performed at least as well as White women. Whereas 46 percent of White Democratic women won their races, 55 percent of Latina and 75 percent of Black Democratic women claimed victory. We can't offer similar statistical comparisons on the Republican side of the aisle because the GOP fielded only 11 women of color (six Black and five Latina). The Democrats ran more than three times as many.

The data presented in Tables 4.1 and 4.2 certainly confirm the absence of widespread gender bias on the part of campaign donors and voters. But keep in mind that just because we observe no gender disparities in fundraising and election outcomes does not mean we should conclude unequivocally that the electoral process is "gender neutral." If the women who run for office are more qualified than the men against whom they compete, or if political gatekeepers encourage only the most qualified women to run, then the apparent absence of bias against female candidates might reflect their higher average quality, as compared to men (see Chapter 3). Even though gender remains relevant in the candidate emergence process, among people who make it to Election Day, men don't outperform women on any indicator of electoral success.

WHERE DO WE GO FROM HERE?

This chapter highlights a critical puzzle for people who care about women and elections. On one hand, the public opinion data we presented early in the chapter show how deeply citizens subscribe to the conventional wisdom that gender bias permeates the electoral arena. On the other hand, our analysis of the key indicators of electoral success in U.S. House races—media coverage, voters' assessments of candidates, campaign contributions, and election results—reveals no systematic bias against women.

Why is there such a disconnect between perception and reality? Several reasons. For some people, it's hard to believe that women don't face unrelenting gender bias because men hold most positions of political power. Except for bias, why else would the electoral system be so male dominated? For others, sexism and gender bias regularly emerge in their personal and professional lives. How could these factors not also influence the outcomes of campaigns and elections? And for still others, exposure to high-profile examples of overt sexism in the political arena conveys the impression that these circumstances are typical of what female candidates more generally endure. After all, national news coverage regularly frames female candidates as facing sexism, if not outright discrimination. If you happened to be a *Washington*

Post reader in September 2015, for example, you were informed that "all female politicians" receive "enormous scrutiny" of the way they look.[31] Talking heads and political pundits also often state as simple fact that the political environment is biased against women.[32]

The 2016 presidential race did nothing to dispel the myth. Instead, it perpetuated the idea that women in politics face widespread discrimination and hostile treatment when they run for office. Donald Trump's barrage of sexist attacks against his female opponents received extensive coverage and became a major feature of the 2016 campaign. It began when Trump, still a couple of months prior to announcing his candidacy, retweeted a supporter's doubts about Clinton's appeal: "If Hillary Clinton can't satisfy her husband, what makes her think she can satisfy America?"[33] (The tweet referenced the long history of marital infidelities that dogged President Bill Clinton throughout his political career.) Trump quickly deleted the tweet and a staffer took responsibility for it. Nevertheless, it certainly foreshadowed what was to come.

After entering the crowded 17-person Republican presidential field later that year, Trump, in an interview with *Rolling Stone* magazine, singled out his one female primary opponent, Carly Fiorina, and said, "Look at that face! Would anyone vote for that? Can you imagine that, the face of our next president?!"[34] When asked during a televised presidential debate to elaborate on the comment and respond to the criticism that ensued, Trump did not apologize. Rather, he said that Fiorina "has a beautiful face and is a beautiful woman."[35]

And by the time Trump secured the Republican nomination in spring 2016, he had ramped up the sexist attacks considerably. In a series of interviews, Trump tore into Clinton: "If Hillary Clinton were a man," Trump speculated, "I don't think she would get 5% of the vote. . . . The way she is, she would get virtually no votes."[36] The justification for Trump's assertion? Well, according to Trump, "Without the woman's card, Hillary would not even be a viable person who could even run for a city council position."[37] By questioning Clinton's qualifications this way, Trump invoked the age-old stereotype that women are less qualified than men to be political leaders. It mattered none to him that Clinton had a lengthy legal career, or that she had served as First Lady, U.S. senator, and secretary of state.

Every time Trump uttered a comment like this, he faced a media uproar, with many pundits calling him blatantly sexist. Claire Cohen, an editor for *The Telegraph*, wrote, "Donald Trump is sexist and he doesn't care."[38] Ben Cohen, of *The Daily Banter*, referred to Trump as a "sexist monster."[39] Even *Fox News* accused Trump of "sexist verbal assaults" directed at their own Megyn Kelly.[40] These comments just scratch the surface, though. Simply google "Donald Trump" and "sexism," and you'll turn up more than 2.2 million hits, including a long list of sexist quotes and articles written by people condemning him. Typical is this headline from *Vox*: "Read every horrible thing Donald Trump has said about women and tell me he's not a sexist."[41] Anyone following the 2016 presidential election, even peripherally, would have been aware of Trump's sexist statements and mistreatment of women. Indeed, 70 percent of voters on Election Day indicated that they were bothered by it. Many were not so bothered that it kept them from voting for him, but they were bothered nonetheless (see Chapter 1).

The greater point here is that Trump's sexist attacks, and the media's response to them, conveyed to the public that sexism and gender bias in politics are alive, well, and serve as obstacles that women still must regularly confront in the electoral arena. There's no question that they were obstacles Trump's female opponents had to navigate. But what was lost in the discussion is the fact that the circumstances of the 2016 presidential election were highly unusual. Yet for many people, the 2016 presidential election will reinforce the perception that gender bias is pervasive and consequential for all levels of office, in all realms of politics, including at the polls.

The perception that gender bias is prevalent in most campaigns, when the reality is that it's not, matters because it ties into one of the main reasons women don't run for office. Many women doubt they have the qualifications and the thick skin needed to endure a political campaign in which women have to be twice as good to get half as far. They think that they have to be twice as good because they assume they will confront a political landscape rife with sexism. Upending the conventional wisdom about what happens to most female candidates on the campaign trail, therefore, could go a long way in closing the gender gap in political ambition and increasing women's representation. The challenge now is to make sure that potential candidates, and the activists who recruit them, realize that rarely will women face the highly discriminatory electoral environment they perceive to be a major impediment. Unfortunately, the spectacle of the Trump-Clinton race might go a long way in setting back these efforts.

QUESTIONS FOR REFLECTION AND DISCUSSION

1. Are you skeptical of the central claims of this chapter—that most women do not face discrimination when they run for office? Why or why not?

2. In this chapter, which focuses on women who run for Congress, we find no evidence of systematic bias. Would gender bias be more likely in elections for other offices, such as president, governor, or even mayor? What about in primaries?

3. Local newspapers cover male and female candidates similarly. But what about social media or late-night television? Would gender differences be more likely to appear in political satire programs, blogs, or on Twitter and Facebook? Why? Find a few examples from these types of media to support your answer.

4. What do you think is the best explanation for the disconnect between the data we presented in this chapter and the perceptions of politicians, pundits, and voters, most of whom assume that things are tougher for female candidates?

5. If you had to create an advertising campaign to encourage more women to run for office, what messages or slogans would you use based on the evidence presented in this chapter? Come up with at least three points you would want to emphasize to prospective female candidates.

FOR FURTHER EXPLORATION

Brooks, Deborah Jordan. 2013. *He Runs, She Runs: Why Gender Stereotypes Do Not Harm Women Candidates*. Princeton: Princeton University Press.

Burrell, Barbara. 2014. *Gender in Campaigns for the U.S. House of Representatives*. Ann Arbor: University of Michigan Press.

Cohen, Nancy L. 2016. *Breakthrough: The Making of America's First Woman President*. Berkeley, CA: Counterpoint.

The Contender. 2000. Directed by Rod Lurie. Washington, DC: Cinerenta.

Dolan, Kathleen. 2014. *When Does Gender Matter? Women Candidates and Gender Stereotypes in American Elections*. New York: Oxford University Press.

Gillibrand, Kirsten. 2015. *Off the Sidelines: Speak Up, Be Fearless, and Change Your World*. New York: Ballantine Books.

Graber, Doris A., and Johanna Dunaway. 2014. *Mass Media and American Politics*, 9th edition. Washington, DC: Congressional Quarterly Press.

Hayes, Danny, and Jennifer L. Lawless. 2016. *Women on the Run: Gender, Media, and Political Campaigns in a Polarized Era*. New York: Cambridge University Press.

Woods, Harriet. 2000. *Stepping Up to Power: The Political Journey of American Women*. Boulder: Westview Press.

Mega-donor Sheldon Adelson with 2012 Republican presidential nominee Mitt Romney at the Republican Jewish Coalition's Winter Leadership Meeting in 2011. The Supreme Court's decision in *Citizens United* paved the way for billionaires—the overwhelming majority of whom are men—to donate unlimited amounts of money to support their preferred candidates in federal elections.

CHAPTER 5

SHOW ME THE MONEY:
THE MALE-DOMINATED WORLD
OF CAMPAIGN FINANCE

Key Question: Are women and men equally likely to use money to grease the wheels of the political system?

Amid grumbling from Republicans, Colleen Bradley Bell assumed the position of ambassador to Hungary in January 2015. President Obama selected Bell, according to White House spokesperson Josh Earnest, because of her success in "the business world" and her ability to maintain relationships "with the government and people of Hungary."[1] Bell's critics, however, weren't impressed with her credentials. Many senators (including some of the 42 who voted against her confirmation) concluded that the appointment had little to do with her primary professional achievement: producing the long-running soap opera *The Bold and the Beautiful.*[2] Instead, they assumed Bell received the position as a reward for the $2.1 million she raised for Obama's 2012 campaign.

Obama's decision to nominate Noah Bryson Mamet as ambassador to Argentina similarly raised eyebrows. Unlike Bell, Mamet was fully immersed in the political process. He'd been a political operative for years, working in the 1990s for Bill Clinton and Congressman Dick Gephardt, and then starting a consulting firm in California.[3] But with the exception of a short stint as an election monitor in Sierra Leone in 2007, Mamet had little foreign policy experience.[4] More to the point, he had never even been to Argentina. Mamet did, however, raise more than $3.2 million for Obama in 2012.[5] Despite Republican opposition, the Senate ultimately confirmed Mamet by a narrow margin (50 to 43).

Barack Obama wasn't the only president to reward major campaign donors with plum positions and political favors. In 1988, presidential candidate George H. W. Bush offered members of "Bush Team 100"—supporters who agreed to raise at least $100,000—an invitation to a black-tie dinner at the White House and a job in his administration. By the time his son, George W. Bush, ran for reelection in 2004, $100,000 only got you a sleepover at either the White House or Camp David.[6] Bill Clinton, on the last day of his second term in 2001, pardoned billionaire financier Marc Rich, who fled the United States decades earlier when charged with tax evasion, fraud, and racketeering.[7] During Clinton's presidency, Rich's wife, Denise, donated $450,000 to the Clinton Library and more than $1 million to Democratic candidates Clinton supported.[8] Most recently, Donald Trump appointed many large donors from his 2016 presidential campaign to key cabinet posts, including secretary of Commerce, secretary of Education, and secretary of the Treasury.[9]

Selling access and influence has even landed politicians in jail. In 2011, an Illinois jury found Democratic Governor Rod Blagojevich guilty of 18 counts of conspiracy and corruption, many of which were related to trying to sell to the highest bidder an appointment to the U.S. Senate seat vacated by Barack Obama.[10] Blagojevich received a 14-year prison sentence. Republican Congressman Randy "Duke" Cunningham completed a seven-year prison term in 2013. He had accepted $2.4 million in bribes from defense contractors while serving on the House Defense Committee. From that post, Cunningham steered $90 million in government defense contracts to his contributors.[11] The list could go on and on.

High-profile political favors, coupled with egregious political corruption cases, likely give rise to the perception that politicians in general are "bought and paid for." That was certainly a central message—on both sides of the political aisle—in the 2016 presidential election. Republican Donald Trump and Democrat Bernie Sanders both argued that the political system is beholden to moneyed special interests. Books such as Darrell West's *Billionaires*[12] and Jane Meyer's *Dark Money*[13] document the ways that extremely wealthy individuals influence elections, governance, and public policy. These dynamics have also taken a toll on the public's perceptions. A 2015 *New York Times* poll found that 84 percent of people believed that money plays too big a role in campaigns. Eighty-five percent thought that politicians regularly prioritize their donors' interests.[14]

In reality, the link between campaign contributions and political influence over politicians is quite complicated. Many political science studies, especially those that focus on politics at the federal level, don't find a direct relationship between campaign contributions and elected officials' legislative voting records. This could be because people donate to the candidates they already agree with and know they can count on.[15] If we move beyond voting records, though, some research does uncover a link between campaign money and political influence. A recent experiment found that members of Congress and their senior staffers were more likely to agree to a meeting with "local donors" than with "local constituents."[16]

Even if the relationship between campaign contributions and political influence is more complex than it appears, the critical role that money plays in the electoral process in the United States is pretty straightforward. First, a candidate's ability to raise money at the beginning of an election signals to the news media, potential opponents, and future donors that a campaign is serious.[17] This is actually a central premise of many political organizations, including EMILY's List. Founded in 1985 with a mission to elect pro-choice Democratic women, the organization believes that female candidates' viability depends on raising a lot of money early in the campaign. So they endorse candidates, connect them to donors, and provide financial contributions early in the process. In fact, there is no Emily at EMILY's List. The name is an acronym for "Early Money Is Like Yeast"—it makes a candidate rise.

Second, competitive elections are expensive. California Assembly Speaker Jesse Unruh's famous 1966 quote—"Money is the mother's milk of politics"—is more true today than ever before.[18] Campaigns hire staff, hold events, produce and run ads, execute field operations, and conduct polls. And these imperatives have become increasingly costly over time. The data presented in Figure 5.1 show that the amount of money spent on federal elections—both presidential and congressional—more than doubled from 1998 to 2016. For the typical House incumbent in 2016, running for reelection cost, on average, close to $1.7 million. The average incumbent U.S. Senator spent more than $9 million that year. And these totals don't even include the millions of dollars that are often spent by independent groups trying to influence the outcomes in House and Senate races. The total cost of the 2016 federal elections came in just below the $7 billion mark.

FIGURE 5.1   PRESIDENTIAL AND CONGRESSIONAL ELECTION
EXPENDITURES (IN BILLIONS OF DOLLARS)

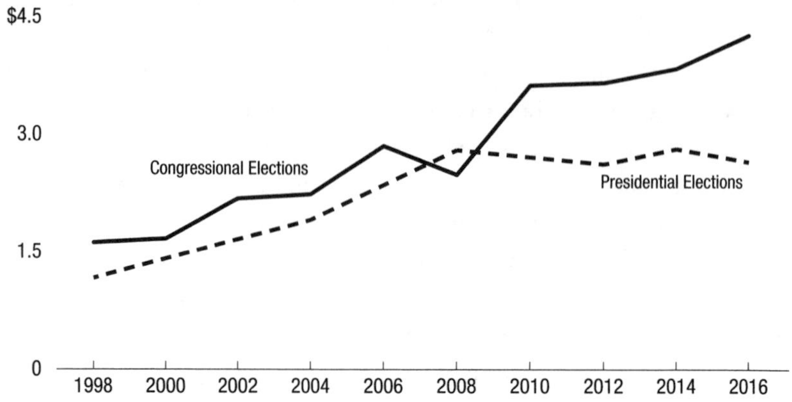

Dollar amounts include money spent directly by presidential, Senate, and House candidates, as well as by political parties and independent interest groups on behalf of federal candidates. Source: "Total Cost of Election," OpenSecrets.org.

Third, candidates vie to maximize the number of people who contribute to their campaigns—especially in small amounts—because donors have become a proxy for the broad, grassroots support that can give a campaign momentum.[19] In 2016, Bernie Sanders proudly asserted that his average contribution was "27 bucks."[20] Donald Trump, in an unprecedented move for a Republican presidential candidate, raised more than $100 million from people giving less than $200 each. In 2012, Barack Obama counted among his donors 3.6 million people who contributed less than $200. In all three cases, strong populist support—often from people who had never before given to a political candidate—helped propel these candidates' campaigns.

Money clearly makes the political system run. And as we show in this chapter, men are far more likely than women to use dollars to grease political wheels. Because men have historically had greater access than women to money and wealth, they've become accustomed to funding the political system and its candidates. Beyond demonstrating gender differences in whether and how much people donate to campaigns, we also show that men have even greater influence after the Supreme Court's *Citizens United* decision. These gender differences are important not only because campaign finance remains an exceedingly male-dominated domain, but also because when they do give, women and men support different parties, candidates, and causes.

HE GIVES, SHE GIVES LESS: POLITICAL CONTRIBUTIONS TO CANDIDATES, PACs, AND PARTIES

In 1974, Congress passed the Federal Election Campaign Act, which serves as the basis of current federal campaign finance law. In a nutshell, the law places limits on contributions to federal candidates, political organizations, and political parties. It also mandates a system for disclosing donor information.

Under the law, citizens may contribute to federal election campaigns in several ways. First, they can give directly to a candidate. These donations were initially limited to $1,000 per candidate for the primary and another $1,000 per candidate for the general election. In 2002, Congress modified the law to increase the limit and link it to inflation. By 2016, individuals could contribute a maximum of $5,400 to a candidate ($2,700 in each the primary and the general election). Second, people can contribute to Political Action Committees (PACs), organizations that exist for the sole purpose of giving money to candidates. The maximum allowable contribution a citizen can make to any given PAC is $5,000 per year. Third, contributors can give larger amounts by donating to political parties, which may then use the funds however they choose. In 2016, individuals were limited to a total of $10,000 per year to state and local parties, and $133,600 to national parties.[21] Under the current rules, candidates, PACs, and parties must itemize all contributions that exceed $200 and disclose the name and employment information of the donor.

It's important to keep in mind, of course, that only a small segment of the population donates to federal candidates, parties, and PACs. In recent election cycles, only about 13 percent of U.S. adults reported making a contribution to a presidential candidate.[22] And in 2016—as well as in every other federal election dating back to 1990—less than half of 1 percent of citizens made a political donation that exceeded $200, so it's only those contributions we can thoroughly analyze. But regardless of the type of contribution, gender differences in political giving abound. As the top two bars in Figure 5.2 show, men were almost twice as likely as women to contribute more than $200, accounting for 70 percent of the $2.1 billion in itemized contributions to federal candidates in the 2016 cycle. The next four bars in the figure reveal that as the contribution amount increases, so does the percentage of donations made by men. Whereas men accounted for a little more than 60 percent of political contributions in the amount of $200–$2,699, they made nearly three-quarters of the contributions that exceeded $100,000. Moreover, in recent election cycles, men have

FIGURE 5.2   GENDER DIFFERENCES IN POLITICAL CONTRIBUTIONS

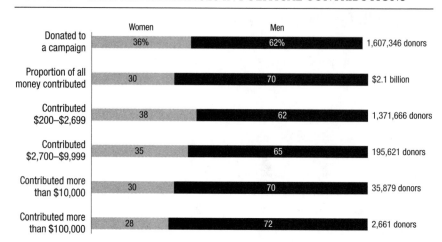

Donors include all people who gave more than $200 to a federal candidate, PAC, or party during the 2016 election cycle.
Source: "Donor Demographics," OpenSecrets.org, based on Federal Election Commission data as of December 9, 2016.

also accounted for more than two-thirds of the individuals who "maxed out"—that is, who gave the maximum allowable contribution in both the primary and the general election.

Women are not only less likely than men to donate to political campaigns—at all levels of giving—but the average size of the contributions they make is significantly less than men's, too. In the 2016 federal election cycle, the women who donated more than $200 gave, on average, $1,082. The average donation from men who contributed more than $200 was 40 percent more than that ($1,522). Donations to PACs tell a similar story. Men's average PAC donations in 2012 were almost four times the amount of women's ($244 compared to $65).

THE POST–*CITIZENS UNITED* WORLD: CHASING THE MALE BILLIONAIRE

Women's lower likelihood of making political donations, and their smaller contribution amounts, always limited the extent to which candidates and parties depend on them for support. But in 2010, when the U.S. Supreme Court dramatically shook up the campaign finance world by handing down its decision in *Citizens United v. Federal Election Commission*, women's influence became even more muted. The Court, in a 5–4 ruling, declared unconstitutional a section of the campaign finance law that banned corporations, labor unions, nonprofit organizations, and other associations from donating—in unlimited amounts—to groups that advocate for or against political candidates. Although these organizations are still not permitted to contribute directly to candidates for federal office, the ruling opened the floodgates for "super PACs" to play a major role in elections. These PACs can now seek out contributions in any amount, from almost any source, to support or oppose any candidate. Their only restriction is that they can't coordinate their activities with a candidate's campaign.[23]

The restriction on coordination doesn't mean that candidates—especially those running for president—don't engage in the unseemly process of wooing billionaire donors to fund super PACs on their behalf.[24] In one of the most blatant examples of seeking support from mega-wealthy contributors, the field of Republican presidential candidates in 2016 made it a top priority to meet with Sheldon Adelson, the casino magnate who spent $98 million supporting Republican candidates trying to defeat Barack Obama in 2012. In what became known as the "Adelson Primary," every top Republican contender paid Adelson and his wife a visit in the early stages of the 2016 presidential race, hoping to secure a large financial commitment to a super PAC.[25] In the end, the Adelsons did not back a candidate in the primary, and they endorsed Donald Trump only after he secured the nomination.

We now live in a world where super-wealthy donors, all by themselves, can launch and sustain candidates. And since the *Citizens United* ruling, every single billionaire donor who has publicly supported a presidential candidate has been either a man or a husband and wife team. This is hardly surprising. The *Forbes* magazine list of the 400 wealthiest Americans includes only 51 women. Moreover, only seven women on the list are "self-made"—the others inherited their wealth or share it with their husbands.[26]

It's not just among billionaire donors that men outnumber women. We identified the 20 largest contributors to candidates and parties, as well as to super PACs and other outside groups, in the 2012 and 2014 elections. In both cycles, and for both types of donations, men dominated the world of big political money. Consider Table 5.1. The top 20 contributors to candidates and parties gave a minimum of $195,000 in the 2012 election cycle. Eighty percent of these donors were men. When it came to the top-20 super PAC contributors in 2012, 15 men, four couples, and one woman made the list. The story wasn't much different in 2014, although women's presence was slightly diminished. Women comprised 15 percent of the largest donors to candidates and parties, and this time, no woman broke into the top-20 Super PAC donors in her own right (but 13 men did).

TABLE 5.1a   TOP-20 CONTRIBUTORS TO FEDERAL ELECTIONS, 2012

CONTRIBUTIONS TO CANDIDATES AND PARTIES		CONTRIBUTIONS TO SUPER PACs/OUTSIDE GROUPS	
Guy Bowers	$333,551	Sheldon and Miriam Adelson	$92,796,625
Jeffrey Hurt	245,100	Harold and Annette Simmons	26,865,000
Marie-Therese Tibbs*	241,296	Robert Perry	23,950,000
Ray Oden	232,376	Fred Eychaner	23,950,000
Richard Uihlein	226,500	Michael Bloomberg	13,672,973
David Wallace	224,500	John Ricketts	13,050,000
Diane Wilsey*	221,650	James and Marilyn Simons	9,575,000
Donald Simms	219,700	Fred Eshelman	6,558,150
Paul Isaac	219,200	Robert Mercer	5,409,354
Richard Spencer	213,400	Steve Mostyn, Amber Anderson	4,753,850
F. W. Corrigan	211,950	Peter Thiel	4,735,000
Susan Groff*	210,000	John Childs	4,225,000
Parker Williams	206,440	Jerrold Perenchio	4,100,000
Philip Geier	206,400	Robert Rowling	3,635,000
Prem Reddy	206,100	Amy Goldman*	3,600,000
Susan Simms*	204,600	Robert McNair	3,175,000
David Herro	201,640	John Ramsey	3,155,933
Sean Fieler	197,700	Jeffrey Katzenberg	3,150,000
David Fischer	196,100	Lawrence Ellison	3,000,000
Robert Reynolds	195,045	Paul Singer	2,815,316

Entries are restricted to individuals whose contributions were disclosed by the recipient. Some categories of outside spenders, such as 501(c)(4) groups, are not required to disclose the identities of their contributors. Sole-female donors (not part of a couple) are indicated with an *. Source: OpenSecrets.org.

The 2016 election followed suit. Women accounted for five of the 20 largest donors, and only one of the top-20 super PAC contributors.[27] If we expand that list a little bit, the gender gap in political giving becomes even more apparent. The top 100 individual donors gave $401 million to political campaigns and super PACs in 2016. Only 14 percent of that money came from women. Or think about this statistic: The top 10 male donors contributed roughly $155 million in the 2016 election cycle. The top *100* female donors contributed a combined $97 million. It took 10 times as many women to reach just 62 percent of the total contributions made by men.[28]

TABLE 5.1b TOP-20 CONTRIBUTORS TO FEDERAL ELECTIONS, 2014

CONTRIBUTIONS TO CANDIDATES AND PARTIES		CONTRIBUTIONS TO SUPER PACs/OUTSIDE GROUPS	
Paul Singer	$569,150	Thomas Steyer	$73,725,000
Ronnie Cameron	480,300	Michael Bloomberg	28,379,929
Charles Schwab	459,900	Paul Singer	10,622,824
Marsha Laufer*	444,450	Robert Mercer	9,220,000
John Childs	437,343	John Ricketts	8,845,000
Susan Groff*	435,000	Fred Eychaner	8,400,000
William Clark	425,798	James and Marilyn Simons	7,300,000
Paul Isaac	405,622	Sheldon and Miriam Adelson	5,524,236
Marcus Hiles	398,700	Charles and Elizabeth Koch	5,000,000
S. Donald Sussman	389,241	Richard Uihlein	4,676,000
James Stanard	372,400	Robert McNair	4,050,000
Stephen Bechtel	350,601	George Soros	3,560,000
Edmund Schweitzer	338,666	Robert Perry	3,100,000
Ronald Abramson	321,342	Kenneth Griffin and Anne Dias	3,075,000
Linda McMahon*	318,800	Jerrold Perenchio	3,000,000
Charles Joyce	318,500	Seth and Beth Klarman	2,950,000
Stephen Wynn	316,000	Kenneth Davis	2,892,495
Imaad Zuberi	314,600	George Marcus	2,750,000
Jeffrey Gural	313,200	Vincent and Linda McMahon	2,740,000
Howard Groff	312,800	Warren and Harriet Stephens	2,685,000

Entries are restricted to individuals whose contributions were disclosed by the recipient. Some categories of outside spenders, such as 501(c)(4) groups, are not required to disclose the identities of their contributors. Sole-female donors (not part of a couple) are indicated with an *. Source: OpenSecrets.org.

WHERE DOES THE MONEY GO? GENDER DIFFERENCES IN PARTISAN AND IDEOLOGICAL CONTRIBUTIONS

Women give less money to politics than men do. But that's not the only gender difference in the campaign finance landscape. Among donors, women and men direct their contributions to different parties and causes. Consider donations to candidates. Figure 5.3 tracks the percentage of contributions made by women to presidential and congressional candidates dating back to the 1990s.

The solid lines represent the percentage of Democratic candidates' donors who are women; the dotted lines do the same for Republicans.

Notice that for both types of candidates, across election cycles, women comprised a larger portion of donors to Democratic than to Republican candidates. In fact, Democratic presidential candidates have steadily come to rely more heavily on female donors over time. Whereas women made up 36 percent of donors to Democratic candidates including Bill Clinton in 1996 and Al Gore in 2000, they played a more substantial role in the 2004, 2008, and 2012 presidential campaigns (accounting for more than 40 percent of the donors to Democratic candidates John Kerry and Barack Obama).

FIGURE 5.3   WOMEN'S CONTRIBUTIONS TO CONGRESSIONAL AND PRESIDENTIAL CANDIDATES, BY PARTY

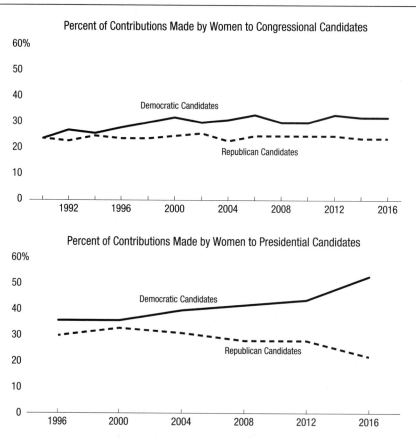

Source: OpenSecrets.org (based on data collected through June 9, 2016).

In 2016, for the first time in history, women accounted for the majority of a presidential candidate's donors. Indeed, one of the big campaign fundraising stories of 2016 was that, by the time the Democratic primaries wrapped up, Hillary Clinton became the first major-party candidate to raise a majority of her direct contributions—53 percent—from women.[29] Meanwhile, GOP presidential candidates have come to rely increasingly heavily on men. More than 70 percent of John McCain's contributions in 2008 and Mitt Romney's in 2012 came from men, as did close to 80 percent of Donald Trump's in 2016.

Women are also more likely to direct their campaign contributions to Democratic congressional candidates than they are to Republicans. Starting in the late 1990s, a gap opened, with women accounting for, on average, a little more than 30 percent of Democratic congressional candidates' donors, but only about 20 percent of Republicans'. This giving pattern has remained relatively stable over time.

A likely cause of the bump in the mid-1990s—as well as Hillary Clinton's experience in 2016—is that EMILY's List had become a major force in fundraising. The organization effectively solicits and directs political contributions from women to female, pro-choice Democratic candidates.[30] The 2012 U.S. Senate elections serve as a case in point. That year, female Democratic candidates relied on a 49 percent female donor base. Compare that to Democratic men, whose donors were 41 percent female. Female Republican Senate candidates in 2012 also relied more heavily on women than male candidates did. Twenty-nine percent of Republican women's donations came from women, compared to 23 percent of men's.[31] Because women are so much less likely to contribute to Republicans than to Democrats, we are a long way off from female GOP candidates being able to rely on women as a key source in funding their campaigns.[32] In the meantime, though, despite differences in their donor bases, similarly situated male and female candidates—Democrats and Republicans alike—raise comparable amounts of money when they run for office (see Chapter 4).[33]

Women give more to Democrats than to Republicans because they are more likely to affiliate with the Democratic Party and because they are more likely to support many of the progressive causes that Democrats champion. Men, on the other hand, are more likely to identify as Republicans and to support conservative causes (see Chapter 6). This becomes evident when we examine the donor base of four ideological PACs: NARAL Pro-Choice America and EMILY's List, both of which advocate for progressive positions on reproductive freedom; and the Chamber of Commerce and the National Rifle Association, which back candidates with conservative positions on business and gun rights, respectively.

Figure 5.4, which presents the gender breakdown of each PAC's donors, reveals dramatic differences in where women and men direct their contributions. When it comes to donating to pro-choice PACs, women comprise more than three-quarters of the donor base. And they're not only more likely than men to give; they also give more than the men who donate. Whereas female donors gave, on average, $567 to NARAL and $109 to EMILY's List, male donors gave less than 80 percent of that (roughly $450 to NARAL and $80 to EMILY's List). Women also constituted the majority of donors to MoveOn.org and the National Education Association, both of which are PACs that advocate progressive positions on issues beyond reproductive rights. The pattern reverses itself when it comes funneling political dollars to PACs that support pro-business and pro-gun candidates. The Chamber of Commerce's donor base includes more than five times as many men as women, and the NRA's is even more lopsided: Only 423 of the more than 17,000 donations it received in 2012 came from women.

Female donors are distinct from men. They are more likely to give to Democrats. They are more likely to give to women. And they are more likely to give to progressive causes. To the extent that campaign contributions affect candidate success and, ultimately, the legislative agenda that elected officials and interest groups pursue, women's underrepresentation as political donors carries important consequences.

FIGURE 5.4 GENDER DIFFERENCES IN POLITICAL CONTRIBUTIONS TO ISSUE-BASED POLITICAL ACTION COMMITTEES

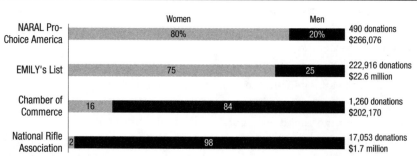

Source: Adam Bonica's 2013 Database on Ideology, Money in Politics, and Elections (for the 2012 election cycle).[34]

WHERE DO WE GO FROM HERE?

Based on the data presented in this chapter, it's clear that substantial gender differences characterize the campaign finance landscape in the United States. *Citizens United*, by loosening contribution limits and expanding potential funding streams, has increased the role of mega-donors and billionaires. As a result, campaign financiers today are even more male-dominated—and more instrumental—than the donors on whom candidates had traditionally depended. In the 1990s, small donors were responsible for about half of all contributions in an election cycle. By 2004, these donors accounted for only about 40 percent of contributions. By the middle of 2016? Only one-third.[35]

Of course, the world of campaign finance is more than simply male-dominated; it's older, Whiter, and more geographically concentrated than the general population, too. Here's how a recent *New York Times* article described the 158 families who contributed approximately half of the seed money to Democratic and Republican presidential candidates in 2016:

> They are overwhelmingly White, rich, older and male, in a nation that is being remade by the young, by women, and by Black and Brown voters. Across a sprawling country, they reside in an archipelago of wealth, exclusive neighborhoods dotting a handful of cities and towns. And in an economy that has minted billionaires in a dizzying array of industries, most made their fortunes in just two: finance and energy.[36]

And for two fundamental reasons, it's likely that older, White men will continue to dominate the world of political contributors.

First, wealthier individuals are more likely to make political donations, and White men are the demographic group most likely to reach those ranks. Women contribute less to political campaigns, in other words, because they have less money to give (see Chapter 8). Just consider the top 1 percent of income earners in the United States. Women comprise just 17 percent of those top earners. Women constitute only 10.5 percent of citizens in the top 0.1 percent.[37] Within the other 99 percent of the population, women are also in a weaker economic position than men. Among full-time workers in 2015, women earned roughly 80 cents to every dollar earned by men.[38] Pay disparities are even more striking among women of color. African American women and Latinas earn even less (64 and 55 cents on the dollar, respectively).[39]

Second, there seems to be a socialized or cultural component to how women and men think about using their money. Men are comfortable using money to shape politics and to determine who wields power, whereas women prefer to use dollars to help nonprofit and charitable organizations leverage change in the community, country, and world. At almost all income levels, women are more likely than men to direct dollars to philanthropic causes. Baby-boomer and older women actually give almost 90 percent more to charity than men their age. Women in the top 25 percent income bracket give approximately 150 percent more to charitable causes than men do.[40] Women are also twice as likely as men to report that giving to charity is the most satisfying aspect of having wealth.[41] Some research attributes women's greater likelihood of charitable giving to a deeper sense of empathy and concern for fellow citizens.[42] Others find that women are more likely than men to consider philanthropic work more rewarding and effective than political involvement.[43]

The good news is that women do not have an aversion to making contributions to causes they support. Their relatively limited financial resources don't inhibit them. The bad news is that the reasons for gender differences in giving patterns are deeply embedded. Thus, it's probably premature to conclude that women's political contributions will even out with men's even as women continue to make economic progress and gain access to more financial resources.[44] Until they do, men will continue to dominate—pretty overwhelmingly—the world of campaign finance.

QUESTIONS FOR REFLECTION AND DISCUSSION

1. Some analysts and pundits argue that men are comfortable using money to gain influence and women are not. Do you think this is true? Or are the gender differences we uncover really about women's lesser financial standing? Explain your answer.

2. Thirteen states provide some form of public financing for campaigns at the state level. The specifics vary, but in general, if a candidate chooses to run, then he or she accepts public money for the campaign in exchange for a promise to limit how much he or she will raise and spend on the election. Do you think that female candidates would be especially likely to benefit from a system like this? Why or why not?

3. Some analysts argue that the *Citizens United* ruling empowers rich men. Do you believe people should be allowed to contribute as much money as they want to support a candidate? Or do you think the *Citizens United* ruling should be overturned? Explain your answer.

4. Beyond the groups discussed in the chapter, list three interest groups or political causes you think men would be more likely to contribute to and three that women would be more likely to support. Visit opensecrets.org or other sources to see if you can find evidence to support your hypotheses.

5. Candidates, parties, and PACs do not have to list the names of people who donate $200 or less in an election cycle. If we had full information on small contributors, do you think we would uncover the same gender gap? Explain your answer.

FOR FURTHER EXPLORATION

Bulworth. 1998. Directed by Warren Beatty. Los Angeles, CA: 20th Century Fox.

Citizens United v. Federal Election Commission, 130 S. Ct. 876–Supreme Court 2010.

Magleby, David. 2014. *Financing the 2012 Election*. Washington, DC: Brookings Institution.

Mann, Thomas E., and Anthony Corrado. 2014. "Party Polarization and Campaign Finance." *Center for Effective Public Management*. Washington, DC: Brookings Institution.

Mayer, Jane. 2016. *Dark Money: The Hidden History of the Billionaires behind the Rise of the Radical Right*. New York: Doubleday.

Mr. Smith Goes to Washington. 1939. Directed by Frank Capra. Hollywood, CA: Columbia Pictures.

Opensecrets.org.

Powell, Lynda. 2012. *The Influence of Campaign Contributions in State Legislatures: The Effects of Institutions and Politics*. Ann Arbor: University of Michigan Press.

West, Darrell M. 2014. *Billionaires: Reflections on the Upper Crust*. Washington, DC: Brookings Institution Press.

A male Trump supporter and a female Clinton supporter argue outside a Trump rally in Pensacola, Florida. The "gender gap" is a regular feature of American politics. And given its deep-seated roots, it's likely here to stay.

CHAPTER 6

HIS AND HER POLITICS:
EXAMINING THE GENDER GAP

Key Question: Do women and men
have different political views?

In the wake of the 2012 elections, journalists and political commentators readily concluded that the Republican Party had a "woman problem." Not only did Democratic President Barack Obama outperform Republican Mitt Romney by 11 percentage points among female voters, but women also favored Democrats in every competitive Senate election that year.[1] The "gender gap"—a term used to describe differences in women's and men's political views and the candidates they support—was close to an all-time high. And post-election headlines all blared the same message. From the *New York Times* ("Women's Issues Were a Problem for the GOP"[2]), to *CNN.com* ("How Women Ruled the 2012 Election and Where the GOP Went Wrong"[3]), to the *Daily Beast* ("Respect Women, or Keep Losing"[4]), reporters attributed much of the GOP's defeat to its inability to resonate with female voters.

The headlines were hardly a surprise given some controversial statements conservative pundits and Republican candidates made in the months leading up to Election Day. Rush Limbaugh, the nation's highest-rated conservative talk radio host, took to the airwaves in February 2012 to call Sandra Fluke "a slut . . . a prostitute."[5] Fluke, a Georgetown University law student, caught Limbaugh's attention when she testified before Congress that health plans, including those offered by Catholic universities like Georgetown, should cover contraceptives. Later that year, Todd Akin, who sought a U.S. Senate seat in Missouri, suggested that abortion does not need to be legal in cases of rape and incest because "if it's a legitimate rape, the female body has ways to try to shut that whole thing down."[6] In Indiana, U.S. Senate candidate Richard Mourdock argued that abortion should not be legal in cases of rape because "that is something God intended to happen."[7] Although Republicans have long opposed abortion rights, to many voters, these comments seemed unusually extreme. The statements also added substantial fuel to the Democrats' fire. They'd already been campaigning against what they termed the Republican Party's "war on women."[8]

The GOP's solution to their "woman problem"? A series of meetings and tutorials to teach Republican men how to speak to female voters. As then–Speaker of the House John Boehner acknowledged, some members of his party just weren't "as sensitive as they ought to be" when it came to communicating with women.[9] The training sessions, for male candidates and staffers alike, urged attendees to avoid talking about social issues and, whenever possible, to refer to their wives and daughters as an important source of how they came to understand "women's" issues.[10] A senior Republican staffer familiar with the trainings told CNN, "First and foremost what we tell them to do [is] talk about yourself as a husband and a father," and issue a "blanket statement [that] rape is horrible."[11] It was essential, as far as Republican Party leaders were concerned, to avoid any Mourdock- or Akin-style pronouncements.[12]

Liberal columnists and activists howled at the notion of these trainings. Dahlia Lithwick, for example, mocked the idea in *Slate* by writing a counter article for female constituents titled, "How to Talk to Republican Congressmen: A Guide for Women."[13] Since these men were being trained to connect to women as wives and daughters, Lithwick suggested that female constituents begin any discussion of policy issues by referring to their Republican congressman as "Daddy" or "Honey." Columns on *Jezebel.com*, a self-defined "blog for women," applauded Republicans for recognizing the problem but doubted that "a workshop on not calling colleagues 'broads' [would] do much to undo an entire lifetime of sexist socialization."[14] Even conservative-leaning *Washington Post* columnist Kathleen Parker wrote that teaching men how to speak to women might be "well-intended and much-needed," but the idea that men need training on how to do it "is sort of 1950s prep school-ish."[15]

As out-of-touch as many perceived the trainings to be, the Republicans' focus on rhetoric and style appeared to help. The 2014 midterms saw no signature moments in which GOP candidates or commentators offended female voters en masse. Yet there was also no sign of a narrowing gender gap. When asked the party of the candidate they voted for in the election for the U.S. House of Representatives, 51 percent of women, but only 41 percent of men, favored the Democrat.[16] And in 2016, when voters were greeted with a relentless torrent of news stories about Republican presidential nominee Donald Trump's offensive behavior toward women? The gender gap was only slightly larger; 54 percent of women, compared to 41 percent of men, voted for Democrat Hillary Clinton. Is the gender gap so durable that, regardless of what happens in the campaign, Republicans will always struggle with women and Democrats with men?

In this chapter, we dissect the gender gap in U.S. politics, moving past media accounts that often provide only a superficial assessment, or a campaign-specific analysis of candidates jockeying for female voters' support. First, we present the foundation of the gap, demonstrating widespread gender differences on contemporary public policy issues. We then link these policy differences to the persistent gender gap in party affiliation and highlight the key electoral consequence: Women and men regularly vote for different candidates. Given the deep-seated reasons for the gap—which we discuss in the chapter's final section—it will likely continue to influence electoral politics for the foreseeable future.

THE BATTLE OF THE SEXES IN U.S. POLITICS

When John Gray's *Men Are from Mars, Women Are from Venus* hit the bookshelves in 1992, it immediately became a smash hit. And why wouldn't it? Mass media and popular culture relish focusing on the differences between women and men, and Gray's pop-psychology book did just that. By chronicling all the ways that women and men want different things in relationships, speak different languages, and hold contrasting life views, the book sold more than 50 million copies worldwide. It's in good company, too. Bookstores, both real and virtual, are filled with pages devoted to the different dating, marital, and work habits of women and men. An endless parade of romantic comedies and television sitcoms also highlights major differences in women's and men's values, philosophies, and goals as they make their way through the world.

Of course, it's not just pop culture that sends the message that women and men are different. Harvard psychologist Carol Gilligan's famous book, *In a Different Voice*, argues that women and men experience social reality in fundamentally different ways. Women tend to see their roles and relationships as being connected to one another, whereas men make decisions and arrive at judgments in a far less interdependent way. Gilligan's account spawned work across the social sciences. In the decades since she published it (in the early 1980s), economists, sociologists, and political scientists have also come to examine gender differences in their own disciplines.[17]

Accounts of differences between women and men resonate with people because they seem to emerge in so many facets of daily life. Ask men and women a series of simple questions—If you could have only one child, would you prefer a boy or a girl? How religious are you? What motivated you to pursue your career?—and there's a good chance you'll get different answers. Men are 60 percent more likely than women to prefer a boy to a girl,[18] are less religious,[19] and are more motivated in their careers to achieve financial independence.[20] When it comes to sexual values, the gender divide is just as striking. A 2012 city of Los Angeles exit poll uncovered a 26-point gender gap on a city ordinance to require male porn stars to wear condoms on the job.[21] Not surprisingly, women favored the ordinance, and men did not.

All of this paints a picture of marked differences in women's and men's values and preferences—differences that often transcend into the political world. They shape people's political views, party affiliation, and, ultimately, the candidates they prefer.

She's More Liberal, He's More Conservative: The Gender Gap in Policy Preferences

We begin our examination of the gender gap with an array of policies that are important in contemporary American politics. Table 6.1 presents the results of public opinion polls on 14 major political issues and attitudes. Each falls into one of three broad areas: the role of government, domestic and social policy, or foreign policy. The first two columns indicate the percentage of women and men who agree with each statement. The table's final column reports the gender gap for each (women's support for the policy minus men's support for it). All of the policies are worded such that higher percentages (and positive gender gaps) correspond with the more liberal position.

Clear gender gaps (of at least 7 percentage points) emerge on 11 of the 14 issues. And on these 11, women are more likely to support the liberal position, whereas men are more likely to favor the conservative view. More specifically,

TABLE 6.1   THE GENDER GAP ON POLICY ISSUES

	WOMEN	MEN	GAP
Role of Government			
Unfairness in the economic system is a bigger problem than the government's over-regulation of the free market	54%	42%	12 points
Government does not do enough to help poor people	61	52	9
Government should be bigger and provide more services	45	36	9
Government should do whatever it takes to protect the environment	75	67	8
Government should do more to solve national problems	44	37	7
Domestic and Social Policy			
Support major restrictions on gun ownership	62	34	28
Oppose nuclear energy as a way to provide more electricity	51	27	24
Oppose the death penalty	45	30	15
Believe that same-sex couples should be allowed to marry legally	46	42	4
Approve of health care reform known as Obamacare	47	46	1
Believe that abortion should be legal in all or most cases	50	52	-2
Foreign Policy			
Concerned about whether drones endanger civilians	60	46	14
Worried that military action in Iraq to combat ISIS will go too far	46	37	9
Believe that the best way to ensure peace is through diplomacy	62	53	9

Percentages indicate levels of support or agreement with each policy statement.[22]

women are more likely than men to favor a larger role for government, especially when it comes to providing services and helping the poor. On domestic policies, they are more likely than men to support gun control and environmental protection, and to oppose the death penalty. And in the realm of foreign policy, women express more concern than men do about drone strikes and the use of military force abroad.

That's not to say men and women are diametrically opposed to each other on every issue. When it comes to increasing the size of government, for example, a majority of women and men oppose expanding the government's reach. In a similar vein, majorities of men and women think the government should do more to help the poor. And on three of the highest profile issues in contemporary U.S. politics—abortion, same-sex marriage, and health care—men's and women's views are virtually indistinguishable from each other. For the most part, though, we see a gender divide—and often a sizeable one—that speaks to women's and men's disparate philosophies about the role of government, the policies it should adopt, and the principles it should follow.

She's a Democrat, He's a Republican: The Gender Gap in Party Affiliation

Gender gaps in public opinion are relevant not only because they reflect fundamental differences between women's and men's policy views, but also because they work their way into electoral politics. After all, the contemporary two-party system embodies these differences to a tee.

The most recent official party platforms make this clear. The preamble to the 2016 national Republican Party platform explains that the federal government must be smaller and control must be returned "to the people and the states." The body of the platform includes passages advocating the need to reduce the "regulatory juggernaut, particularly from the Environmental Protection Agency," recognize the right to use and store firearms and ammunition "without federal licensing or registration requirements," and "abandon arms controls treaties that benefit our adversaries."[23] The Democratic Party's platform espouses a different set of values and positions. The document devotes attention to rebuilding the middle class, protecting the environment, expanding and supporting background checks for gun ownership, and favoring diplomatic outcomes as an initial approach to confronting global threats.[24] In general, women's and men's policy views—as presented in Table 6.1—map pretty well onto the priorities and positions of the two major parties.

It makes sense, then, that women are more likely than men to affiliate with the Democratic Party, whereas men are more likely to identify as Republicans. In 2016, for example, women were 14 percentage points more likely than men to consider themselves Democrats.[25] Of course, about 40 percent of Americans identify as "independents." A lot of research, however, has shown that most independents reliably "lean" toward one of the two major parties.[26] When we group together partisan identifiers with "independent leaners," the gender gap remains. Women are approximately 13 percentage points more likely than men to consider themselves Democrats. Men, by the same 13-point margin, are more likely to be Republicans. The size of the gender gap in party identification has varied slightly over time, but it has been a defining feature of the electorate for decades (see Figure 6.1).

FIGURE 6.1   THE GENDER GAP IN PARTY AFFILIATION

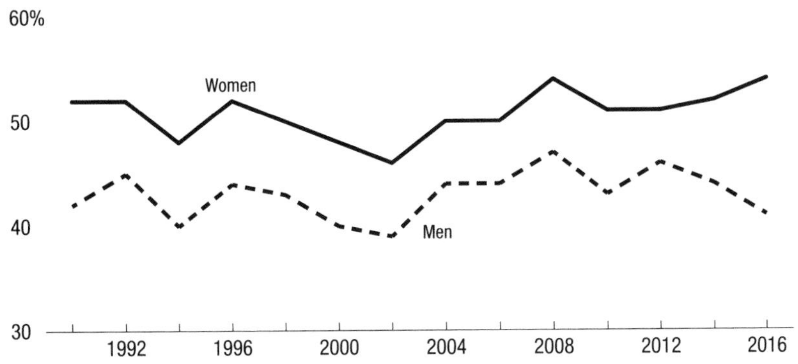

Lines represent the percentage of people who identify as Democrats, or as independents who "lean Democratic."[27]

She Votes Democratic, He Votes Republican: The Gender Gap in Candidate Selection

Citizens tend to see the political world through a partisan lens, a view that is encouraged by campaign messages and news coverage. So whether someone is a Democrat or a Republican exerts substantial influence over how he or she evaluates candidates and casts a ballot.[28] Just look at the data presented in Table 6.2. The left side of the table reports the percentage of Democrats and Republicans who voted for the Democratic presidential candidate dating back to the 1980 election between Ronald Reagan and Jimmy Carter. The right side of the table displays the same information for the Republican candidate in each race. On average—across these 10 contests—86 percent of Democrats voted for the Democrat, and 90 percent of Republicans voted for the Republican. Even in 1984, when Walter Mondale won just one state (his home state of Minnesota), eight out of every 10 Democrats still chose him over Reagan. In 1992, when George H. W. Bush faced two competitors in the general election—Democrat Bill Clinton and independent Ross Perot (who received 19 percent of the popular vote)—he still received the support of almost eight out of 10 Republicans. And in the most recent election, when both Hillary Clinton and Donald Trump were rated the two most unfavorable presidential candidates in modern history, they could still count on the votes of almost 90 percent of their respective party base. The extent to which people select candidates based on whether they share a party affiliation is striking, especially considering how much time and money candidates spend appealing to voters.

TABLE 6.2   PRESIDENTIAL VOTE CHOICE

	Voted for the Democratic Presidential Candidate		Voted for the Republican Presidential Candidate	
	DEMOCRATS	REPUBLICANS	DEMOCRATS	REPUBLICANS
1980	69%	8%	26%	86%
1984	79	4	21	96
1988	85	7	15	93
1992	82	7	8	77
1996	90	10	6	85
2000	89	7	10	92
2004	93	5	7	95
2008	93	7	7	93
2012	95	3	5	97
2016	89	8	8	88

Support for each candidate does not always sum to 100% because third-party candidates received a portion of the vote in 1980, 1992, 1996, and 2000. From 1980 to 2012, we rely on Gallup estimates. The 2016 data come from CNN's exit polls.[29]

Because the D or R in front of a candidate's name often tells us almost everything we need to know about how a person will vote, the fact that women are, and have consistently been, more likely than men to identify as Democrats matters in elections. Indeed, in all presidential contests since 1980, women have been more likely than men to support the Democratic candidate, on average by about 9 percentage points (see Figure 6.2). Men have been more likely than women—by about 10 percentage points—to favor the Republican. The same has been true in all congressional election cycles since 1986.

To be clear, the gender gap doesn't mean that a majority of women always vote for Democrats. Presidential candidates Walter Mondale in 1984 and Michael Dukakis in 1988 couldn't gain a majority of support among women. Nor does it mean that a majority of men always cast ballots for Republicans. Exit polls showed that more men voted for Obama in 2008 than they did Republican John McCain. But in most presidential elections, male and female voters prefer different candidates. Sometimes by a lot (the gender gap reached double digits in 1996, 2000, 2004, 2012, and 2016). Sometimes by just a little (in 1992, for example, there was only a 4 percentage point difference in the percentage of women and men supporting Democrat Bill Clinton). If women had their druthers in 2000, 2004, and 2016,

FIGURE 6.2   THE GENDER GAP IN PRESIDENTIAL ELECTIONS

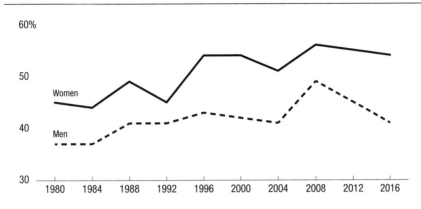

Lines represent the percentage of people who reported voting for the Democratic presidential candidate. Percentages are based on exit polls conducted by CNN, CBS News/*New York Times*, the Voter News Service, and Edison Media Research and Mitofsky International.

though, George W. Bush and Donald Trump would never have occupied the Oval Office. And if men had their way, Barack Obama would have been a one-term president.

Women Are Not All the Same: A Sub-Group Examination of the Gender Gap

Throughout this chapter, we've discussed the gender gap in public opinion, party affiliation, and voting by comparing all women to all men. This is a common way to analyze gender differences, but it also assumes that all women are the same and that all men are the same. So we want to spend a little time looking beyond the overall numbers to determine whether the gender gap plays out differently among subgroups of women and men. To this end, Figure 6.3 presents the percentage of women and men who voted for Hillary Clinton in 2016, broken down by three subgroups—race, marital status, and party affiliation.

Let's start with race. Despite some variation, the gender gap is sizable across the three largest racial groups in U.S. society. Among White voters, there was a 12-point gender gap, with women more likely than men to favor Clinton over Trump. Among Blacks, the gender gap was exactly the same size. Among Latinos, it was smaller (6 points). Regardless of race, women were more likely than men to support Clinton, the Democratic candidate.[30] The more telling story to emerge from the exit poll data, however, has to do with similarities within the races, as opposed to across them. Black and Latino voters were significantly more likely than Whites to cast a ballot for Clinton in 2016.

FIGURE 6.3 SUPPORT FOR HILLARY CLINTON IN THE 2016 PRESIDENTIAL ELECTION

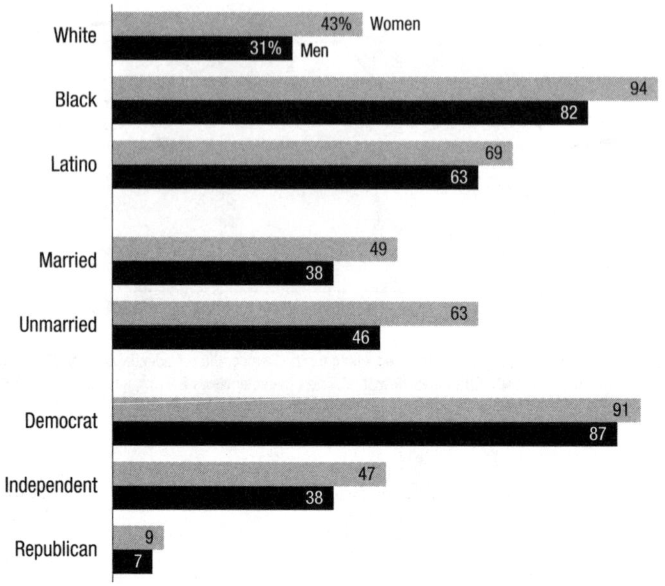

Bars indicate the percentage of women and men in each subgroup who voted for Hillary Clinton in 2016, according to CNN exit polls.

The gap between White and Black voters' support for Clinton was 52 points. The gap between Whites and Latinos was 29 points. As a result, Clinton won a majority of Black and Latino voters—men and women alike—but Trump defeated her among both White women and White men.

Turning to marital status, the gender gap among unmarried voters was 17 points, more than 50 percent larger than the size of the gap among married people (11 points). This is a substantial difference. But here, too, it's marital status that really affects vote choice. Whereas Clinton beat Trump among unmarried women and men, Trump won married men handily and lost married women to Clinton by only 2 points.

And when it comes to party affiliation, the magnitude of the gender gap is even smaller—just 4 points among Democrats and 2 points among Republicans. It's much larger among independents, with independent women favoring Clinton by 5 points and independent men giving Trump a 12-point edge. Again, though, the differences across the parties are far larger than the gender gaps within them.

Despite some sub-group differences when we focus on race, marital status, and party identification, the general patterns and gender gaps we presented earlier in the chapter persist. And although we use vote choice in the 2016 presidential election for this analysis, the story looks very similar when we examine different election cycles, as well as party affiliation.[31]

WHERE DO WE GO FROM HERE?

We've spent this chapter documenting the gender gap in public opinion, party affiliation, and voting. And we've demonstrated that it's quite durable. Its magnitude doesn't change much from election to election, and gender differences in political views and candidate choice persist across several important demographic categories. This suggests pretty compellingly that the gender gap is a phenomenon that is deeply embedded in U.S. politics. So where does it come from? Why do women and men have different political beliefs, affiliate with different parties, and cast ballots for different candidates? Answers to these questions have received sustained scholarly attention since the 1980s. And although scholars have not reached a consensus on the most important contributing factor, three primary explanations shed quite a bit of light on the reasons for the gender gap.

The first explanation is about economics. Women in the United States have substantially less wealth and lower incomes than men (see Chapter 8). They are also more likely to be the heads of single-parent households. In addition, because women live longer than men, they are more likely to be financially dependent on the government in the later years of their lives.[32] Their economic circumstances tend to mean that women are more likely than men to support the policies that bolster the social safety net—policies that the Democratic Party and Democratic candidates also tend to support.[33] Conversely, men—in large part because they're wealthier—are much more likely to favor Republican policy positions, such as lower taxes and less spending to allay poverty. In essence, the gender gap is a result of individuals pursuing their economic self-interest.

Explanation number two is about compassion. Drawn primarily from research in social psychology, the argument is that women display more compassion for their fellow citizens than men do. Whether women's greater sense of compassion is something they're born with or something they're raised to develop is a long-standing debate. But regardless of where this compassion comes from, it's politically relevant. It means that women are more supportive of rights for women, racial minorities, and gay people, and more likely than men to favor increased spending for child care, health care, and assistance to the poor and elderly.[34] Because they see a larger role for government to protect these rights and provide this assistance, women are more likely than men to support policies consistent with those of the Democratic Party. Alternatively, because men favor a smaller government and less spending, they are more likely to line up behind the GOP.

The third prominent explanation for the gender gap focuses on the rise of women's autonomy in the 1970s and 1980s and what many perceive to be the feminist agenda of the Democratic Party (see Chapter 1). This generates a gender gap in two ways. First, it drives women who identify as feminists to support Democrats because the Democratic Party is more favorably disposed toward women's economic, political, and reproductive rights.[35] Second, it fosters a sense of male backlash, which results in men moving away from the Democratic Party and favoring the GOP.[36] Men, in other words, feel threatened by the economic and political progress for women that the Democratic Party favors, so they band together in opposition to it.[37]

If there's any doubt as to the utility of each of these explanations, a quick look at the contest between Democrat Hillary Clinton and Republican Donald Trump in the 2016 presidential race should quell it. As we've shown, Clinton beat Trump by 13 points among women, and Trump carried men by a similar (11 point) margin.[38] The exit poll data suggest that it's because of economics, differences on "compassion issues," and antiwoman sentiment. Consider these facts:

- Americans earning less than $50,000 a year—a group made up mostly of women—preferred Clinton to Trump by 12 points.

- Voters who supported "Obamacare" and were concerned that the criminal justice system doesn't treat everyone fairly—the majority of whom are women—favored Clinton over Trump by double-digit margins. Voters who cared most about curbing illegal immigration, even if it meant separating families or deporting them, preferred Trump by 30 points.

- As Donald Trump made an increasing number of sexist statements, his unfavorable rating among women grew. In March 2016, roughly 50 percent of women had a "very unfavorable" opinion of Trump. By May, the percentage of women with a very negative view was up to 60 percent.[39] On Election Day, 70 percent of voters said that they were "somewhat" or "very bothered" by Trump's treatment of women. Throughout the campaign, polls showed that women were more likely than men to be dismayed by Trump's behavior.

As this chapter and the results of the 2016 election make clear, the gender gap is here to stay. Candidates like Donald Trump—who make expressly sexist comments during a campaign—or Hillary Clinton—who mobilize women because of their potential to make history—might move the gender gap a couple of points one way or the other. That's what we saw in 2016 with a 13 percentage point gap, as opposed to the average gap of 9 points. But with men's and women's political attitudes and beliefs firmly planted much deeper than in the particular circumstances of any one election, the gender gap will persist as one of the most stable forces in U.S. politics.

QUESTIONS FOR REFLECTION AND DISCUSSION

1. When you think about your peers and friends, does the "Men Are from Mars, Women Are from Venus" storyline apply? Do you see examples of gender differences in how you interact with each other or in your opinions and attitudes? List at least three gender differences you experience in your daily life.

2. Lots of attention is devoted to how Republicans can better appeal to female voters. But the gender gap cuts the other way, too. If you were a Democratic campaign consultant, what kind of campaign message would you develop to appeal to men? What character traits would the ideal candidate have, and what policy issues would he or she emphasize?

3. We've noted here, and in Chapter 1, that Donald Trump made several sexist statements throughout his campaign. Do you think his rhetoric affected the size of the gender gap in 2016? Or did the presence of the first female candidate account for the fact that it was a little larger than usual? Why wasn't the gender gap bigger in this historic matchup? In crafting your response, consult exit poll data from 2016 and 2012 to provide evidence for your argument.

4. In the conclusion of the chapter, we briefly identified three leading explanations for the gender gap. Which of these do you think is the most compelling? Why? Can you think of any other explanations that might account for gender differences in political attitudes?

5. Do you think there will always be a gender gap in political attitudes and voting? Or do you think as society continues to move toward greater gender equality in politics, as well as in professional and family life, the gap will go away? Explain your answer.

FOR FURTHER EXPLORATION

Behrendt, Greg, and Liz Tuccillo. 2004. *He's Just Not That into You: The No-Excuses Truth to Understanding Guys*. New York: Simon and Schuster.

Caughell, Leslie. 2016. *The Political Battle of the Sexes: Exploring the Sources of Gender Gaps in Policy Preferences*. Lanham, MD: Lexington Books.

Gilligan, Carol. 1982. *In a Different Voice: Psychological Theory and Women's Development*. Cambridge: Harvard University Press.

Gray, John. 1992. *Men Are from Mars, Women Are from Venus: The Classic Guide to Understanding the Opposite Sex*. New York: HarperCollins.

He Said, She Said. 1991. Directed by Ken Kwapis and Marisa Silver. Los Angeles: Paramount Pictures.

Kathlene, Lyn. 1995. "Alternative Views of Crime: Legislative Policymaking in Gendered Terms." *Journal of Politics* 57(3): 696–723.

Seabright, Paul. 2012. *The War of the Sexes: How Conflict and Cooperation Have Shaped Men and Women from Prehistory to the Present*. Princeton: Princeton University Press.

Tannen, Deborah. 1990. *You Just Don't Understand: Women and Men in Conversation*. New York: HarperCollins.

Whitaker, Lois Duke. 2008. *Voting the Gender Gap*. Urbana: University of Illinois Press.

Members of the bipartisan congressional women's softball team celebrate their 10–5 victory over women in the press corps at Watkins Recreation Center on Capitol Hill in June 2014. Activities with colleagues outside of Congress have been a big part of building the social fabric inside the institution. But in the era of partisan politics, these friendships are often insufficient for promoting cooperation and collaboration on the House and Senate floors.

CHAPTER 7

HE'S A PARTISAN, SHE'S A PARTISAN: GENDER IN THE U.S. CONGRESS

Key Question: Do male and female members of Congress do their jobs differently?

In politics if you want anything said, ask a man. If you want anything done, ask a woman.

Margaret Thatcher
Prime Minister of Great Britain, 1979–1990[1]

Women have the ability to reach across the aisle. In addition, I think women bring a unique perspective ... and I think it's important to represent that perspective in Congress.

Republican Elise Stefanik
Youngest woman ever elected to Congress (in 2014)[2]

Women are actually more inclined toward ... collaborative problem-solving, enabling, consult[ing], not just trying to assert a kind of hierarchical power.

Mary Robinson
Former High Commissioner of The United Nations[3]

A cross the globe, people tend to believe that women and men differ when it comes to how they approach positions of leadership and authority. They're thought to have different styles, different priorities, and different preferences. This doesn't mean that women and men can't be equally effective. In fact, most people—75 percent, according to a 2015 national survey of voters in the United States—think they are. But citizens also recognize clear differences in male and female leaders' strengths and characteristics. Voters view female leaders as more compassionate and organized than men, and men as more ambitious and decisive than women. People also think that women have a greater propensity than men to strive for compromise and to be honest and ethical.[4]

These stereotypes and conventional notions are particularly salient when we think about political leaders. The perception that women in politics place a higher premium than men do on cooperating to get the job done isn't based simply on abstract stereotypes or old clichés. From time to time, women do exhibit this behavior, and when they do, it's often newsworthy. Just consider the federal government shutdown in the fall of 2013. Republicans in the House and Senate deadlocked with their Democratic colleagues and President Obama over the federal budget. Republicans refused to pass any budget that included funding for the Affordable Care Act (Obamacare). Democrats vowed to filibuster any measure that cut Obamacare funding or tried to delay its implementation. At a clear impasse, and with no budget in place, the federal government shut down on October 1. In the days that followed, political posturing and blame games dominated the discussion on Capitol Hill. Meanwhile, furloughed federal workers, disgruntled tourists trying to enter closed national parks, and would-be travelers who couldn't get their passport applications processed wondered with frustration why members of Congress couldn't do their jobs.

A week into the shutdown, and with no compromise in sight, Republican Senator Susan Collins spoke to her colleagues from the Senate floor and urged them "to come together . . . [and] legislate responsibly and in good faith."[5] Democrat Barbara Mikulski and Republican Lisa Murkowski joined her, encouraging cooperation to reopen the government. Ultimately, a bipartisan group of senators, working from a proposal drafted by Collins, reached an agreement that ended the shutdown 16 days after it started. Republican John McCain praised the outcome, asserting that the leadership shown in ending the crisis "was provided primarily from women."[6] Democrat Heidi Heitkamp also credited women for ending the stalemate, explaining to a reporter, "One of the things we do a little better is listen. It is about getting people in a room with different life experiences who will see things differently."[7] It wasn't only senators patting women on the back. From the *Huffington Post* ("Men Got Us into the Shutdown, Women Got Us Out"[8]) to *Time* magazine ("Women Are the Only Adults Left in Washington"[9]) to the *New York Times* ("Senate Women Lead in Effort to Find Accord"[10]), headlines lauded the female senators' efforts.

Stories like these can give the impression that women regularly work together this way to find common ground. But from George W. Bush's presidency through the Trump White House, members of Congress—women and men alike—have had plenty of opportunities to set partisanship aside and collaborate to solve the nation's problems. And they usually haven't taken them. Cooperation tends to take a backseat to heated debates over raising the debt ceiling, repeated battles over the budget, and sustained partisan warfare over immigration and health care reform. In fact, during the 2016 budget dispute—in which Republicans and Democrats led the country once again to the precipice of a shutdown—a key sticking point was a critical "women's" issue: funding for Planned Parenthood. Yet no part of the debate's news coverage, deliberations, or eventual resolution suggested that women in Congress were any more civil, collaborative, or bipartisan than men.

So what's the real story? Do male and female political leaders do their jobs in fundamentally different ways? Are women any more likely than men to put collaboration ahead of partisanship to find legislative solutions? In this chapter, we move beyond well-known anecdotes and broad assertions and tackle these questions systematically by focusing on the U.S. Congress. Despite the sense—from the media, the voters, and even the politicians themselves—that congresswomen are more collegial, collaborative, and bipartisan than congressmen, we just don't uncover much evidence for these claims. That doesn't mean that women's presence in Congress is not critically important. They foster a more representative and open governing process, which is key for democratic legitimacy in any government.

FRIENDS DON'T LET FRIENDS CROSS THE AISLE: SEX VERSUS PARTISANSHIP IN THE U.S. CONGRESS

As we begin to assess whether women and men differ in how they approach and conduct their responsibilities as members of Congress, it's important to step back and consider how to measure political leadership and identify its key components. This is tricky because there are so many aspects of leadership: team building, problem-solving, agenda setting, effecting change. The list goes on and on. No one analysis can address every facet of how members of Congress do their jobs. But we've identified four central aspects of the job to test whether women and men legislate differently. We consider (1) members' collegiality and social interactions with each other, (2) the bills they sponsor and cosponsor, (3) the way they vote on procedural matters, and (4) the votes they cast on substantive bills. Taken together, our results paint a picture of a political institution that's far more influenced by partisanship than by the sex of its members.

Gender and Social Engagement among Members of Congress

The first way we examine whether women and men approach their congressional roles differently is by considering how much they value building the social fabric of the institution. Studies show that socializing and developing friendships with your colleagues can promote general trust and cooperation within the workplace.[11] Tracking social engagement, though, is easier said than done. No one records who sends whom a holiday card, who attends whose children's weddings, who works out together at the congressional gym, or which members regularly meet for coffee or cocktails. Three regularly scheduled activities, however, do provide men and women, Democrats and Republicans, an opportunity to spend time with their colleagues in a social setting if they choose to participate:

1. *Democratic Senator Al Franken's Secret Santa Gift Exchange.* Franken describes the annual holiday gift exchange, which he started in 2011, as a way to "create comity and good cheer in an institution badly in need of both."[12] Senators who participate are held to a $15 limit and are encouraged to select a gift with special meaning for the giver or the recipient.

2. *Seersucker Thursday, started by then senator Trent Lott in 1996.* On one Thursday each spring, senators are encouraged to join the "fashion parade" and don a seersucker suit. According to the official webpage of the U.S. Senate, "Senators voluntarily make this annual fashion statement in a spirit of good-humored harmony."[13]

3. *The annual congressional baseball and softball games.* Both events allow members of Congress to "settle scores and solidify friendships off the floor and on the field."[14] These games, in the words of Democratic Congressman Ed Perlmutter, "are a great time to meet other members of Congress, it's just fun, we're out doing something different than legislating."[15]

FIGURE 7.1   SOCIAL ENGAGEMENT ACTIVITY AMONG WOMEN
AND MEN IN THE U.S. CONGRESS

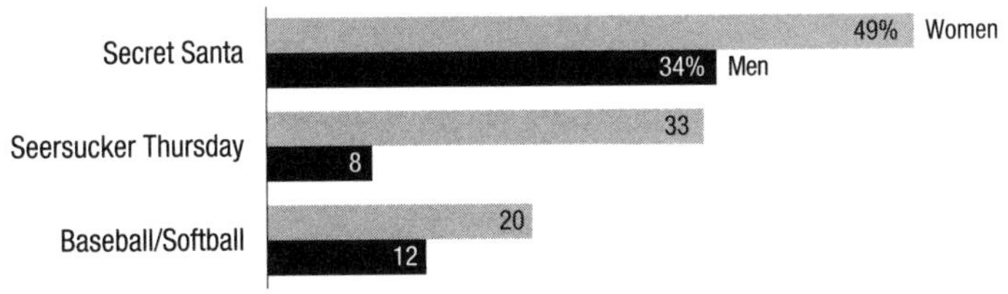

Bars represent the percentage of members of Congress who participated in each activity. Secret Santa participation includes the 2011–2015 gift exchanges in the Senate. Seersucker Thursday data are from 2004–2016 in the Senate. Baseball/softball participation rates include members of the House and Senate from 2009–2016. All three gender comparisons are statistically significant, with women more likely than men to participate in the activity.

These three lighthearted activities allow us to gauge whether women are more likely than men to participate in the kinds of social interactions that can build collegiality within Congress. Put simply, they are. Across time, women have been more likely than men to participate in all three activities.[16] Consider the Secret Santa gift exchange. Although participation rates vary from one congress to the next, approximately 40 percent of senators partake each year. But from 2011 to 2015, 49 percent of women, compared to 34 percent of men, joined the festivities (see Figure 7.1). With the exception of the inaugural year—when women and men participated at equal rates—female senators on both sides of the aisle have always been more likely than their male colleagues to participate. The same is true of Seersucker Thursday and congressional baseball and softball. The overall rates of participation are lower than they are for the holiday gift exchange, but gender differences are evident over time and across party lines. Women are four times as likely as men to participate in the fashion parade. And they're almost twice as likely as men to wear a uniform and swing a bat.[17]

These results support a substantial body of research that finds that women are more likely than men to prioritize the personal relationships that are a key ingredient for cooperation in the workplace.[18] Whether women's collegiality translates into legislative behavior is another question.

Gender and Bill Sponsorship and Cosponsorship

Sponsoring and cosponsoring bills is a second aspect of the legislative process that presents an opportunity for women and men to behave differently. When a member puts his or her name on a bill, it's a prominent way to stake out and publicize a position on a policy.[19] It's also a way to demonstrate how much support a bill has before it comes to a vote. In particular, securing a cosponsor from the other party can be especially valuable. All it takes is one Republican to sign onto a Democrat's bill, or one Democrat to support a Republican's, and the bill has "bipartisan" support. For our purposes, analyzing cosponsorship activity can shed light on whether women leverage the personal relationships they build outside of Congress as a basis for collaborating on legislation with colleagues across the aisle.

To examine cosponsorship activity, we rely on the Lugar Center's "Bipartisan Index."[20] This measure accounts for how often a senator cosponsors bills introduced by members of the opposite party, as well as how often a senator's bills attract cosponsors from the other party. The measure excludes ceremonial bills, such as commemorative coin bills and post office namings, which receive near unanimous support. The index varies from -1 to +1, with higher scores indicating greater levels of bipartisan activity.

Figure 7.2 presents women's and men's scores from the 103rd through the 113th congresses (1993 to 2014). We display the results for Democrats, but the image would look very similar for Republicans. Basically, women on both sides of the aisle behave the same way as their male copartisans. In no congress did Democratic women's scores differ from Democratic men's.

FIGURE 7.2   DEMOCRATIC SENATORS' COSPONSORSHIP SCORES

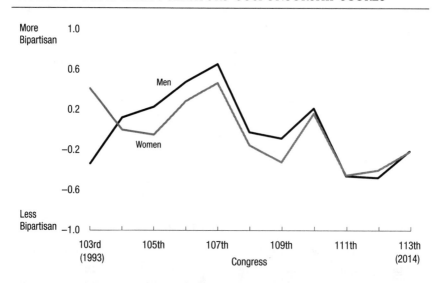

Data provided by the Lugar Center. Scores closer to +1.0 indicate greater bipartisan activity. None of the gender differences is statistically significant.

In only one of the 11 congresses we analyze (the 112th Congress) were Republican women's scores statistically more bipartisan than Republican men's.[21]

Women came together to end the government shutdown in the fall of 2013, but in general, they are no more likely than men to lend bipartisan support to their colleagues' bills or attract bipartisan support for their own. This wasn't always the case. In the 1980s and early to mid 1990s—at least when it came to "women's" issues, such as gender equity, child care, abortion, and poverty—Democratic and moderate Republican women in Congress were more likely than men to cosponsor each other's bills.[22] But as the parties have polarized, party loyalty has come to trump the gendered behavior that previously characterized cosponsorship patterns even on this small subset of issues.

Gender and Procedural Votes

The third area where gender differences could emerge in how members of Congress legislate has to do with procedural votes. These include things like resolutions setting up the rules for debate, motions to adjourn, and cloture motions to restrict filibusters. Most procedural votes create the voting agendas and rules that structure how to get to the final passage vote for a bill. A member who values cooperation and moving the legislative process along should cast more bipartisan procedural votes pertaining to how bills are debated and handled. Importantly, procedural votes do not lock members into a final passage vote. So, if women are more likely than men to have a penchant for moving the process along, they can cast bipartisan procedural votes and still vote along party lines when it comes to final passage.[23]

To analyze procedural votes, we rely on data collected by Jennifer Lawless and Sean Theriault. Their data set includes all procedural votes dating back to the 100th Congress in 1987. This amounts to 5,261 votes in the House and 4,107 in the Senate. For each member in each congress, they generated a "score" from -1 to +1. In each chamber of Congress, the two members who disagreed with each other the most on procedural votes are at the endpoints. In every case, one of the endpoints turns out to be a Democrat (-1) and the other a Republican (+1). Everyone else is lined up along the continuum according to how often they voted with each of the endpoints. Numbers closer to zero indicate a procedural vote profile that is more bipartisan than at either endpoint.

Figure 7.3 presents the mean procedural vote score for House Democrats and Republicans from the 100th through the 113th Congress (1987–2014). Given the way the scores are calculated, Democrats' scores typically fall between

FIGURE 7.3   PROCEDURAL VOTE "SCORES" IN THE U.S. HOUSE

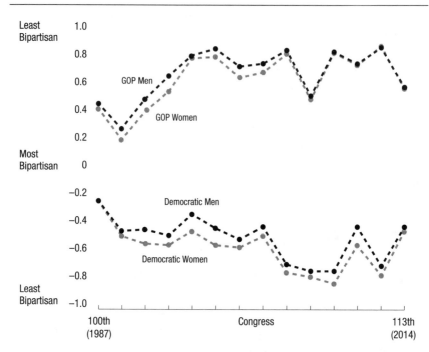

Voting profiles closer to zero are more bipartisan than those at either endpoint. For Democrats, none of the gender differences is significant. For Republicans, in the 103rd (1993–1994) and 105th through 107th (1997–2002) Congresses, the gender difference is statistically significant, with women more likely than men to cast bipartisan procedural votes.

-1 and 0, and Republicans' scores range from 0 to +1. This means that the closer to zero a Democrat's score, the more frequently the member voted with Republicans. On the flipside, the closer to zero a Republican's score, the more frequently the member voted with Democrats. The black circles indicate the mean score for men in each congress; the gray circles represent the mean score for women.[24]

Notice that in every congress, the mean score for female Democrats is *more negative* (in other words, less bipartisan) than the mean score for male Democrats. In 11 of the 14 cases, the gender difference is even statistically significant. For the most part, the results are the same for House Republicans. Although GOP women were somewhat more bipartisan than men in the mid to late 1990s, that trend has been absent from the six more recent congresses. If they ever did, GOP women no longer hold a premium on procedural bipartisanship. Instead, the mean procedural vote scores—for women and men of both parties—never cross the zero-line. Party differences are far more dramatic than the limited gender differences that emerge.[25]

Gender and Final Passage Votes

The final aspect of the legislative process we examine is votes on substantive bills. These are the bills we hear most about since they lead to enactment or defeat of the laws that affect us all. Repealing the Affordable Care Act, rejecting a series of gun control measures, or sending to the president a bill that allows families of 9/11 victims to sue the Saudi Arabian government all fall in this category. Analyzing these bills allows us to compare women and men on two dimensions: the extent to which they are bipartisan, and how liberal or conservative they are.

For this analysis, we identified all substantive votes dating back to 1987 (roughly 12,000 votes in the House and 5,000 in the Senate) and generated an ideology score for each member in each congress. These scores are just like the procedural vote scores, only here, the votes used to array members along the continuum are substantive votes, so the scores are more explicitly ideological in nature. The two endpoints, once again, represent the two members whose vote profiles are the most different from each other, and everyone else is lined up in between them. The scores range from -1 (the most liberal) to +1 (the most conservative). Scores closer to zero represent more bipartisan, and thus more moderate, profiles.

Figure 7.4 presents the results for the House of Representatives, broken down by sex and political party. Notice the same trends we uncovered when examining procedural votes. Most notably, party differences are far more telling than gender differences. Male and female Democrats, in every congress, are more liberal than male and female Republicans. Never does the mean score for either sex in either party approach, let alone cross, the zero-line. Importantly, in the few congresses where we do find statistically significant gender differences, they're all in the same direction. Democratic women are slightly more liberal than Democratic men, and Republican women are slightly less conservative than Republican men. But the magnitude of these differences is quite small, and they've disappeared altogether in the most recent congresses. The results for the Senate are similar to the House.

For years, scholars uncovered gender differences in members' priorities and preferences, especially among Republican women who crossed party lines to cast more liberal votes on policies pertaining to women, families, and children.[26] But as the parties have polarized, which has resulted in fewer moderates in both the House and Senate, these patterns have dissipated.[27] Today, the small gender differences that do emerge are all within the political parties, not across them.

FIGURE 7.4   IDEOLOGY "SCORES" IN THE U.S. HOUSE

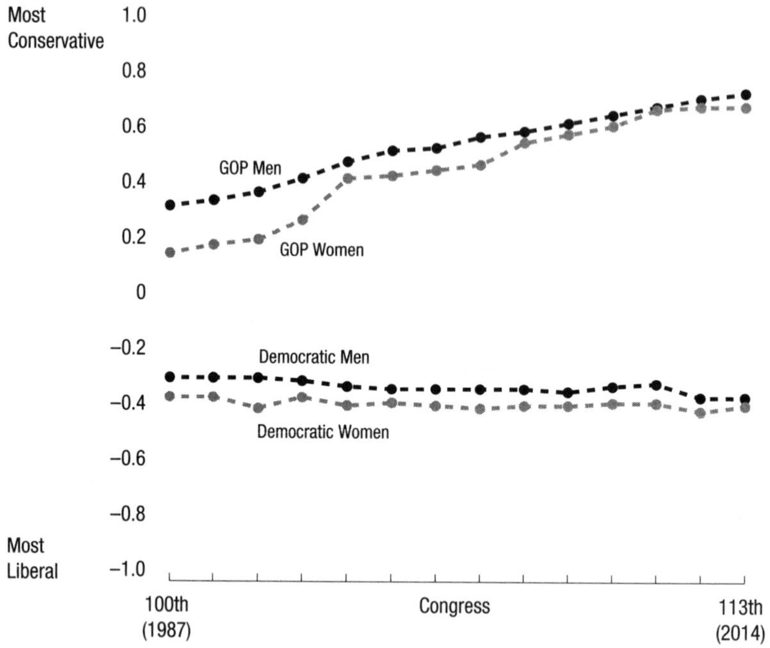

Voting profiles closer to zero are more bipartisan (and moderate) than those at either endpoint. For Democrats, in the 102nd (1991–1992), 104th (1995–1996), and 106th–112th (1999–2012) Congresses, women were more liberal than men. For Republicans, in the 100th–103rd Congresses (1987–1994), and the 105th (1997–1998) and 107th (2001–2002) Congresses, women were less conservative than men.

WHERE DO WE GO FROM HERE?

Despite the widespread perception that women have a unique leadership style—a perception fueled by incidents like the 2013 government shutdown, where female legislators led the way to arrive at a bipartisan solution—this chapter demonstrates that women and men are more similar than different when it comes to doing their jobs as members of Congress. Women are no more bipartisan than men when it comes to cosponsoring legislation or voting on the procedures that govern the legislative process. Nor are they any more moderate when voting on the substantive pieces of legislation that will result. As far as legislative outcomes are concerned, the sex of the member of Congress makes little difference. These findings leave us with two big questions. First, are the patterns we've identified likely to persist? And second, if they do, does it even matter if we elect women to the House and Senate? These answers are yes and yes.

Turning to the first question, two aspects of the contemporary U.S. Congress fundamentally constrain the way members behave: congressional rules and the power of partisanship. And there's nothing to suggest that these constraints are going anywhere anytime soon. Take first how rule-driven and rigid both the House and Senate are. In the House, the Speaker, Majority Leader, and committee chairs control virtually the entire policy agenda and structure the terms of debate for all legislation. In the Senate, individual senators have more power, but along with that power comes the filibuster, which makes it easy to stymie any initiative or proposal that doesn't have supermajority support. Both chambers also operate under strict rules of parliamentary procedure. Studies reveal that "feminine" leadership styles—those that are more collaborative and based on consensus-building—are more likely to emerge in open, flexible environments. Rule-based, hierarchical contexts are more likely to see "masculine" leadership styles, which are based less on cooperation than on top-down decision-making.[28] The House and the Senate epitomize the conditions conducive to masculine leadership.

Then there's a second factor that affects how members of Congress behave: the extreme partisanship that now dominates the chamber. In the 1960s and 1970s, party unity scores—the percentage of time a senator or representative voted with a majority of his or her party—averaged roughly 70 percent.[29] By the time the 113th Congress (2013–2015) convened, party unity scores were close to 95 percent.[30] This is hardly surprising. In contemporary elections, congressional candidates run campaigns as partisans; whether they're Democrats or Republicans features far more heavily into their campaign messaging and media coverage than whether they're women or men (see Chapter 4).[31] The partisan battle continues after they win their elections and enter the House or Senate. Members of Congress face sustained pressure to vote with their party and to oppose the other party. When they do so, they're rewarded. Party loyalty, in other words, is a way to ensure support in the next election and to curry favor with the party leadership.[32]

In this era of unprecedented levels of party polarization—levels that continue to intensify from one congress to the next—it may be unrealistic for women to be any less likely than men to play partisan politics. After all, women and men face the same electoral constraints and incentives. The fact that our results don't change during 2007–2011, the years when women held two of the most important leadership positions in the House (Nancy Pelosi was Speaker and Louise Slaughter chaired the Rules Committee), demonstrates the power of institutional rules and partisanship. It's not a coincidence that social engagement is the one place where we uncovered clear gender differences. This is one of the few aspects of the legislative process far less influenced by congressional rules and party labels. After all, building social relationships tends to take place outside the House or Senate and off the campaign trail, so women might have more flexibility to behave in a way that's consistent with expectations that they value collegiality more than men do.

Even if congresswomen and congressmen aren't markedly different on most of the aspects of how they legislate, women's presence in U.S. political institutions still matters in several meaningful ways. First, some evidence suggests that women work harder for their constituents, delivering more federal spending to their districts and sponsoring more legislation than their male colleagues.[33] Women also have greater success than men in keeping their sponsored bills alive, especially when they are in the minority party.[34] And when given an opportunity to speak about issues of their choosing during one-minute speeches on the floor, congresswomen in both parties are more likely than men to speak, and to speak about women.[35] Where rules and partisanship aren't front and center, gender differences in the legislative process do emerge.

Moreover, we shouldn't minimize the fact that women are more likely than men to value and contribute to a collegial work environment. In times of gridlock, obstructionism, and inefficiency, collegiality and comity are especially welcome. Even if it doesn't affect legislative outcomes or the procedural steps through which a bill becomes a law, it might make Capitol Hill a more civil and pleasant place to work. It could reduce the ad hominem attacks and hostility that have depressed citizens' approval of and trust in the federal government. And it could even be a reason that Congress manages to get anything done. Maybe it's because women invest more in building the social fabric of Congress that it functions even as well as it does.

Beyond these benefits, electing more women matters for symbolic reasons. Many scholars link the presence of female candidates and elected officials to female citizens' political attitudes and participation. When women live in districts with female House candidates, they are more likely to report that they're interested in politics, and they're more likely to have political discussions.[36] Female voters are more likely to be familiar with their senators' records when those senators are women.[37] And highly visible female politicians can even spur adolescent girls' political engagement.[38] There is also growing commentary and discussion about how women in high-profile political positions normalize women's presence in politics for boys and girls and young women and men.[39] As is the case with most research, the findings are not entirely uniform.

But there's a general consensus that women's presence in politics likely conveys a sense of democratic fairness and inclusivity that are important in their own right.

Heading into the 2016 elections, *Cosmopolitan* magazine profiled 19 "path-breaking" women who would make history if elected to Congress.[41] These women would be the first Indian or Thai American woman in Congress. The first woman ever elected to the Senate from Arizona, Pennsylvania, or Nevada. The first transgender member. The first Latina to serve from a particular state. The article doesn't say it explicitly, but the piece clearly implies that these women, if elected, would bring change and a new style of leadership to Washington. Not all of them won their races, but three Democratic women of color—Tammy Duckworth (IL), Kamala Harris (CA), and Catherine Cortez Masto (NV)—were elected to the U.S. Senate. And three Democratic women of color were newly elected to the House: Lisa Blunt Rochester (DE), Stephanie Murphy (FL), and Pramila Jayapal (WA). These new faces will certainly contribute to diversity in Congress. But the reality is that any new faces on Capitol Hill—female or male, White, Black, Latino, or Asian—will have little flexibility to lead differently. The rule-based, partisan environment subsumes everything else.

QUESTIONS FOR REFLECTION AND DISCUSSION

1. In this chapter, we presented several ways that men and women in Congress are similar (cosponsorship activity, procedural votes, political ideology). Can you think of other aspects of the legislative process where they might differ?

2. This chapter focuses on members of Congress. Do you think that in other types of political positions—such as mayor, state legislator, governor, or judge—it might be more likely for gender differences to emerge? Why or why not?

3. At the end of the chapter, we mentioned that the six new women of color elected to the 115th Congress are all Democrats. How typical is this party breakdown? Visit the official website of the U.S. Congress and draw at least three conclusions about the women of color who have served throughout history: http://history. house.gov/Exhibitions-and-Publications/WIC/Historical-Data/Women-of-Color-in-Congress

4. Some scholars argue that there are still too few women in positions of political power for them to exert their own "brand" of leadership. Do you think that when women occupy one-third, or even half, of the political positions, they'll be less likely to toe the party line and more likely to work together? Why or why not?

5. Since women and men appear to perform their jobs as members of Congress quite similarly, is it important to elect more women? Beyond legislative performance, what kinds of societal benefits might more women in Congress provide? We mention a few possibilities in the conclusion to this chapter. You should feel free to elaborate on these or add others. If you believe that electing more women to Congress isn't important, explain your position.

FOR FURTHER EXPLORATION

Advise and Consent. 1962. Directed by Otto Preminger. USA: Otto Preminger Films.

The American President. 1995. Directed by Rob Reiner. Los Angeles, CA: Universal Pictures.

Brownstein, Ronald. 2008. *The Second Civil War: How Extreme Partisanship Has Paralyzed Washington and Polarized America*. New York: Penguin Books.

Harbridge, Laurel. 2015. *Is Bipartisanship Dead? Policy Agreement and Agenda-Setting in the House of Representatives*. New York: Cambridge University Press.

House of Cards. 2014. Season 2. Created by Beau Willimon. Baltimore, MD: Netflix.

Newton-Small, Jay. 2016. *Broad Influence: How Women Are Changing the Way America Works*. New York: Time, Inc.

Rhode, Deborah. 2016. *Women and Leadership*. New York: Oxford University Press.

Sinclair, Barbara. 2006. *Party Wars: Polarization and the Politics of National Policy Making*. Norman: University of Oklahoma Press.

Swers, Michele L. 2013. *Women in the Club: Gender and Policy Making in the Senate*. Chicago: University of Chicago Press.

Lilly Ledbetter (center) and members of Congress watch Barack Obama sign into law the Lilly Ledbetter Fair Pay Act in January 2009. Although the law represents a step toward pay equity for women and men, the wage gap remains a prominent feature in today's labor force.

CHAPTER 8

HE EARNS, SHE EARNS (LESS):
THE WAGE GAP AND PAY EQUITY
IN THE UNITED STATES

**Key Question: Do women really make only
80 cents for every dollar earned by men?**

In 1979, Lilly Ledbetter took a job at the Goodyear Tire Company. Although most of the women employed by Goodyear at that time worked as secretaries or receptionists, Ledbetter was hired as an area manager and supervisor—one of the first women to hold such a position. Shortly before her retirement in 1998, Ledbetter received an unsigned letter that compared her pay to her male colleagues'.[1] She learned that the most highly compensated male manager earned $5,236 per month, significantly more than Ledbetter's monthly paycheck of $3,727. In fact, even the lowest paid male manager earned more than she did ($4,286 per month).[2] According to Ledbetter, the information validated her intuition: "Toward the end of my 19 years at Goodyear, I began to suspect that I wasn't getting paid as much as men doing the same job. An anonymous note in my mailbox confirmed that I was right."[3]

With evidence of these pay inequities in hand, Ledbetter filed a gender discrimination lawsuit against Goodyear. The Equal Pay Act of 1963, after all, bars employers from paying women and men different wages for performing the same job. Goodyear fought the lawsuit intensely, on both substantive and procedural grounds. On the merits of the claim, Ledbetter's employers maintained that poor performance evaluations, not gender discrimination, accounted for the absence of merit-based raises and her lower pay.[4] Beyond that, Goodyear argued that even if they had discriminated against Ledbetter, she missed the opportunity to make that claim. Title VII of the 1964 Civil Rights Act requires that wage discrimination claims be brought within 180 days of the initial act of discrimination.[5] Ledbetter's claim fell outside that window.

By 2007, the case had made its way to the U.S. Supreme Court. A district court had awarded Ledbetter more than $3.5 million, but an appeals court overturned the ruling on the procedural grounds of the 180-day rule. In a 5–4 decision, the Supreme Court affirmed that claims of wage discrimination must be filed within 180 days of the initial discriminatory paycheck.

The decision outraged Democrats and women's rights advocates. In her dissent, Justice Ruth Bader Ginsburg accused the Court of not comprehending the "insidious way in which women can be victims of pay discrimination." She explained that "pay disparities often occur, as they did in Ledbetter's case, in small increments; only over time is there strong cause to suspect that discrimination is at work."[6] Marcia Greenberger, co-president of the National Women's Law Center, characterized the ruling as a "setback for women and a setback for civil rights."[7] Many Democrats were so incensed by the decision that they campaigned in 2008 on the promise to overturn it.

And that's what they did. In 2009, Congressional Democrats (along with a handful of Republicans) passed the Lilly Ledbetter Fair Pay Act, which became the first piece of legislation that newly elected president Barack Obama signed into law. The act mandates that the 180-day limit reset every time a paycheck reflects unequal treatment. It doesn't matter when the initial discriminatory act occurred.

Since then, the Ledbetter case and questions of pay equity have come to represent a constant point of contention between Democrats and Republicans. Whereas Democrats rally around the call for women to receive "equal pay for equal work," Republicans consider fair pay legislation little more than an unnecessary, cumbersome government regulation. We need to look no further than the 2016 presidential election to see these dynamics at play. Democratic candidates repeatedly pressed for legislation to ensure pay equity. U.S. Senator Bernie Sanders included "equal pay for equal work" in his overall Economic Agenda for America.[8] Former secretary of state Hillary Clinton's general election stump speeches prioritized equal pay, too: "The last time I checked, there's no discount for being a woman. Groceries don't cost us less, rent doesn't cost us less, so why should we be paid less?"[9]

GOP candidates seeking the presidential nomination sang another tune. According to U.S. Senator Rand Paul, "The minute you set up a fairness czar to determine what wages are, you give away freedom." Texas Senator Ted Cruz dismissed calls for fair pay legislation because equal pay had already "been the law for decades." Florida Senator Marco Rubio argued that any effort to legislate fair pay is nothing more than "a welfare plan for trial lawyers."[10] And Donald Trump, who said that if women "do the same job, they should get the same pay," was quick to add a significant caveat: "It's very hard to say what is the same job. It's a very, very tricky question."[11]

So what's the real story when it comes to women's and men's wages? Is Lilly Ledbetter an anomaly, or is the pay gap far more prevalent than Republicans tend to admit? What explains the gap? And what can be done to close it? This chapter presents systematic evidence that women who work full-time do indeed earn less money than full-time working men. The disparity is particularly pronounced for women of color. When we turn to the primary causes of the pay gap, though, it's clear that the situation is more complex than either Democrats or Republicans would have us believe. Laws on the books prohibit employers from paying women less for doing the same job as men, so the gap doesn't result primarily from overt discrimination. But deep-seated patterns of occupational gender segregation, women's greater child care responsibilities, and gender differences in salary negotiation result in lower wages for women than men. And existing laws do nothing to generate fairness or equity on these fronts. Ultimately, we argue that legislation is the only way to remedy the root causes of the pay gap. But ideological divisions and partisan politics make it unlikely that the federal government will combat pay inequity any time soon.

THE WAGE GAP: ALIVE AND WELL, NO MATTER HOW WE MEASURE IT

Every year, the American Association of University Women (AAUW) "celebrates" Pay Equity Day. That day in April marks the moment when women's annual earnings catch up to men's from the previous year.[12] The celebration is a clever way to call attention to the fact that it takes women roughly an extra 100 days to earn what men do in a typical calendar year. AAUW isn't the only organization to recognize this economic disparity. The National

Organization for Women places pay equity right up there with reproductive rights when listing the key policy issues in the fight for gender equality. And the National Women's Law Center characterizes the pay gap as a "harsh reality," one that costs the average woman in the workforce more than $10,000 per year.[13] Of course, not everyone agrees with these claims. Conservative media sources, such as *Breitbart.com* and *The Weekly Standard*, periodically feature editorials asserting that there is no pay gap.[14] They allege that it's simply "taken as an article of faith on the left," even though there's actually no merit to the claim.[15] The best place to begin our analysis, therefore, is with an assessment of whether women's earnings trail men's and, if they do, by how much.

Several government agencies and research organizations release annual pay gap statistics. The U.S. Census Bureau and the Bureau of Labor Statistics report the yearly earnings of male and female full-time wage and salary workers. The Pew Research Center documents the annual pay awarded to men and women by comparing workers' hourly wages, including people who work part-time. Before we consider the magnitude of the pay gap, it's important to be explicit about what the data collected by these agencies represent and what they don't. Pay gap statistics do not compare women's and men's pay for doing the same job. It is illegal to compensate women differently from men for the

FIGURE 8.1 THE PAY GAP IN THE UNITED STATES

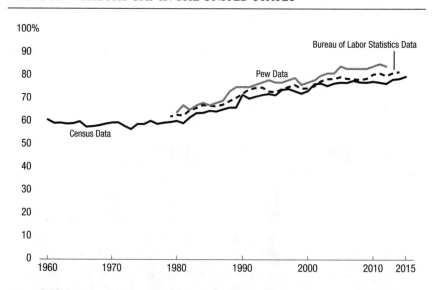

U.S. Census Bureau and Bureau of Labor Statistics data reflect women's earnings as a percentage of men's among full-time wage and salary workers. Pew data reflect women's earnings as a percentage of men's among hourly wage workers, including part-time workers.

same work. Instead, the pay gap reflects the difference in what the average female and average male worker earn overall, even though they're often doing different jobs. We want to be very clear about this because it's a distinction often lost in political arguments. As a result, misinformation is widespread. A 2013 Pew survey of millennials, for example, found that 60 percent of women and 48 percent of men believe that women get paid less than men for doing the same job.[16] That's not a conclusion that can be drawn from the general statistics gathered by the Census Bureau, the Bureau of Labor Statistics, or Pew.

Figure 8.1 presents the data from all three agencies and organizations; the lines represent women's wages as a percentage of men's. Although the size of the pay gap varies slightly depending on the data source, all of the statistics point to women making somewhere around 80 cents for every dollar earned by men. The trend lines also indicate that while women's pay made steady gains starting in about 1980, the progress stalled in the early 2000s.

The marked income disparities presented in Figure 8.1 represent averages for all women and men. But women of color face a double disadvantage.[17] Consider the comparisons illustrated in Figure 8.2. Here, we set the base level

**FIGURE 8.2   PENNIES ON THE DOLLAR: MEDIAN HOURLY EARNINGS
BY RACE AND SEX**

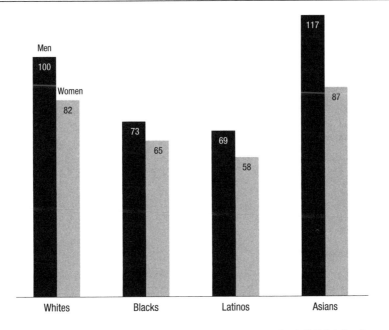

Entries reflect each group's hourly earnings as pennies on the dollar of White men's earnings in 2015. Data from the Pew Research Center.

of pay as the average hourly earnings of a White man. That's represented by the 100 percent in the figure's leftmost bar. The other bars indicate everyone else's pay as pennies on the dollar of what White men earn. White women, for example, make 82 cents for every dollar earned by a White man. Black women and Latinas earn significantly less. Within each racial group, women also fare worse than men. Black women's hourly wages are just 89 percent of Black men's. Latinas earn only 84 percent of what Latinos do. And although Asian women and men earn the most, the gender gap in pay among them is still roughly 30 cents on the dollar.[18]

The real consequences of these pay gap ratios hit home when we consider average weekly wages and annual earnings. Whereas the typical man earns $895 per week, the average woman earns just $726. When it comes to median annual earnings for full-time work, men make a little more than $50,000. Women? A little less than $40,000. The gap is even bigger when we compare single-parent households. There, men's median earnings are $48,634 per year; women's come in at just $34,002. That means that the average single mother relies on an annual income that's only about 70 percent of what a single father can depend on. In large part because of the pay gap, women are in a more precarious financial position than men. They are more likely to live in poverty and less likely to save for retirement. When women do manage to save, they save less (see Table 8.1).

TABLE 8.1   THE FEMINIZATION OF POVERTY IN THE UNITED STATES

	WOMEN	MEN
Poverty Rates		
Living in poverty (overall)	15%	12%
Ages 18 to 64	14	11
Ages 65 and older	10	7
Ages 70 to 79	17	11
Single-parent families living in poverty	30	16
Retirement Savings		
Saved for retirement	53%	67%
Average retirement savings (of those who have saved)	$34,900	$76,800

Data compiled from the U.S. Census Bureau, Catalyst Inc., and a BlackRock survey of investors.

For decades, scholars have written about the feminization of poverty—the notion that poverty is increasingly dominated by women. And researchers offer many reasons for it: substantial increases in the number of households led by single women, regional factors, the changing nature of family dynamics, and variation in measures of poverty and wealth.[19] There's no doubt, however, that gender disparities in full-time pay play a substantial role, too.

STUCK AT 80 CENTS: EXPLAINING THE ROOT CAUSES OF WOMEN'S LOWER PAY

As the pay gap persisted and progress grew stagnant by the early 2000s, policy analysts, sociologists, and labor market economists began to pinpoint its foundation. A general consensus emerged: Gender discrimination in salaries and wages accounts for only a small portion of the pay gap. Rather, the different jobs and careers women and men pursue, coupled with women's greater likelihood of taking time off from work to care for children, serve as the two primary explanations for women's lower pay. Gender differences in salary negotiations throughout a career then exacerbate the pay gap that already exists. We elaborate on each of these explanations, treating them in order of the magnitude of their impact as women and men navigate the labor market.

Men and Women at Work: Gender and Occupational Segregation

Prior to the 1950s, the notion of a woman's "independent career" was just not a thing. To the extent that women worked at all, it was often either doing menial labor or supporting a family business. *Goesart v. Cleary*, a case decided by the U.S. Supreme Court in 1948, illustrates the prevailing ethos of the time. The justices ruled that a Michigan law that prohibited women from working as bartenders was constitutional. The Court agreed with the state's argument that allowing women to work in bars could "give rise to moral and social problems."[20] The Court also agreed with the one exception specified by the law: A woman could serve as a bartender if she was the wife or daughter of the bar owner. Even as women began to enter the workforce in greater numbers by the '50s and '60s, they found themselves largely relegated to low-status jobs. Among the most prestigious was airline stewardess. As United Airlines advertised at the time, the job offered the possibility of traveling the world. It also required women to be between 5'2" and 5'7" and "never" weigh more than 135 pounds.[21]

Obviously, a lot has changed since the 1960s. Women have access to educational and professional paths that had once been open only to men. Formal barriers that previously limited women's career opportunities have diminished. And women have legal recourse when confronted with unequal treatment or hostility in the workplace. But these changes have gone only so far in chipping away at the occupational gender segregation that has always characterized the workforce. Many categories of jobs continue to be dominated by either women or men. And it's not difficult to guess which ones. Jobs that focus on caring for or supporting other people—such as nurse or clerical assistant—even today still fall largely to women. Jobs that involve protecting people and building or repairing things—such as police officer or mechanic—remain dominated by men.

These occupational divisions serve as a central explanation for the pay gap. Table 8.2 lists the 20 jobs that, based on Department of Labor statistics, are the most gender segregated. The top half of the table rank orders the 10 jobs with the most male-dominated workforce. In each of these positions, men constitute at least 98.5 percent of the workers. The bottom half of Table 8.2 presents the most female-dominated jobs. In each of these, women represent at least four out of every five employees. Next to each job, we specify the annual average salary. Notice that the highest paying male-dominated job on the list (firefighter supervisor) pays about 11 percent more than the highest paying female-dominated job (registered nurse). The gap is even more pronounced for the lowest paying positions. Auto technicians or mechanics—98 percent of whom are men—earn nearly 90 percent more than child-care workers do, 94 percent of whom are women. Overall, the male-dominated jobs pay, on average, about 50 percent more than the female-dominated positions.

These patterns also persist across professions that require advanced degrees or credentials. Roughly 80 percent of architects, for example, are men, and they earn on average about $66,000 a year. Eighty-two percent of social workers, on the other hand, are women. Social workers, like architects, hold college degrees and a professional license or certification, work full-time, and generally log the same number of hours. Yet social workers typically bring home only about 67 percent of architects' pay. Comparisons like this are nearly endless.

Women aren't paid less because they work less or because they don't perform as well as men. They're paid less because jobs typically held by men, at all skill levels, yield higher average salaries than jobs dominated by women. That's why the wage gap narrowed through the 1980s and 1990s, decades when women were breaking into traditionally male occupations. And that's why, as women's integration into the full range of male professions began to stall in the 2000s, so did their pay relative to men's.[22]

TABLE 8.2   AVERAGE SALARIES FOR JOBS WITH THE HIGHEST RATES
OF GENDER SEGREGATION

	PERCENTAGE WOMEN	AVERAGE SALARY
10 Most Male-Dominated Jobs		
Brick, Block, and Stonemason	0.1%	$39,640
Drywall and Tile Installer	0.3	40,470
Mining Machine Operator	0.3	49,270
Bus and Truck Mechanic	0.5	46,110
Home Electronic Installer/Repairer	0.5	55,160
Fire Fighter Supervisor	0.5	74,970
Tool and Die Maker	0.8	42,110
Heavy Vehicle Servicer	1.0	47,120
Auto Technician or Mechanic	1.2	37,850
Construction Equipment Operator	1.3	49,110
Mean Salary for 10 Most Male-Dominated Jobs		**$48,173**
10 Most Female-Dominated Jobs		
Secretary/Administrative Assistant	95.3%	$36,500
Child Care Worker	94.1	20,320
Receptionist	91.5	28,430
Teacher's Assistant	91.1	26,550
Registered Nurse	90.6	67,490
Bookkeeping/Accounting Clerk	89.1	38,990
Maid/Housekeeper	88.1	22,990
Home Health Aide	87.9	21,920
Personal Care Aide	84.7	20,980
Office Clerk	83.4	31,890
Mean Salary for 10 Most Female-Dominated Jobs		**$31,606**

Data compiled from the Department of Labor and the Bureau of Labor Statistics' 2015 report.

Should She Stay or Should She Go? Gender, Child Care, and Leaving the Workforce

The cost of child care, coupled with gender differences in child care responsibilities, also contribute substantially to the pay gap. When women and men both work full-time, families often need to find full-time child care. And it's not cheap. On average, one young child's full-time enrollment in a private child care center in the United States costs $9,711 per year. That number, in and of itself, is high. But when considered as a percentage of an individual's annual income, it is often prohibitive. Figure 8.3 displays child care costs by state; the more darkly shaded the state, the greater the expense.

Child care is most affordable in South Dakota, where it eats up "only" 11 percent of a full-time wage earner's pay. At the other end of the continuum, Washington, DC, is most expensive; child care costs comprise 31 percent of a typical annual income. The national average is 16.4 percent. These figures

FIGURE 8.3 CHILD CARE EXPENSES AS A PERCENTAGE OF MEAN ANNUAL INCOME, BY STATE

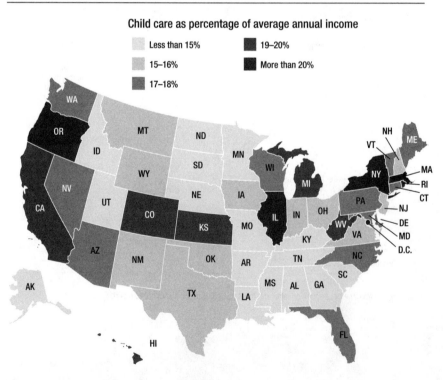

Data provided and compiled by the Census Bureau and *The Boston Globe*.

are based on one child. Multiply them by two or three for larger families, and costs become untenable. Because women earn, on average, only 80 percent of what men do, it's often women who leave the workforce, even temporarily, to provide child care they otherwise can't afford.

Financial realities are not the only reason that women are more likely than men to take time off from work when they have children. Striking a balance between work and family also weighs more heavily on women than men. There's no question that we've reached a point in time when both mothers and fathers articulate a desire to gain a better handle on managing work and family life. When asked whether they would be willing to relocate, give up a promotion, or even change their career or job if doing so would help them reconcile competing career and family responsibilities, roughly 50 percent of people say they would be. Perhaps somewhat surprisingly, men are even more likely than women to say they're willing to make these sacrifices (see the top of Figure 8.4).

But when the rubber hits the road, women are more likely than men to make these changes. The bottom half of Figure 8.4 reports the percentages of women and men who have taken specific actions to prioritize their families over their jobs or careers. Women are 30 percent more likely than men to have

FIGURE 8.4 STRIKING A WORK/FAMILY LIFE BALANCE: WOMEN'S AND MEN'S ATTITUDES VERSUS ACTIONS

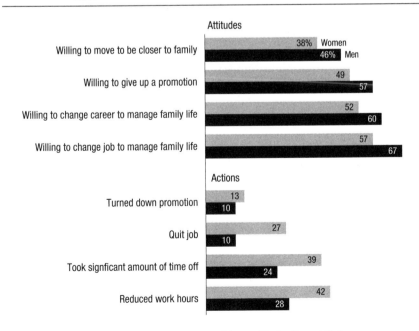

Data compiled from a Harris poll conducted on behalf of Ernst and Young and the Pew Research Center.

turned down a promotion, nearly three times as likely to have quit their job, and 50 percent more likely to have taken significant time off from work or to have reduced their work hours.

Regardless of whether these decisions are driven by a family's economic situation or women's greater sense of responsibility when it comes to putting family ahead of work, these circumstances bear directly on the pay gap. When roughly 40 percent of women either take significant time off or reduce their hours to care for their children, they stymie their potential for career advancement and the higher incomes that come with it. Indeed, the wage gap is smallest among women and men under the age of 35, many of whom have not yet been confronted with the dilemma over how to balance their family with their professional roles and responsibilities.[23]

She Doesn't Ask for Much: The Gender Gap in Salary Negotiations

Even when women and men work in the same career field, and even when women don't leave the workforce for child care–related reasons, they still often earn less than men do. Although it's against the law for employers to pay women less for doing the same job, most jobs have salary ranges. In many cases, part of arriving at a salary involves negotiations between employer and employee; here, significant gender differences emerge.

Studies of salary negotiations reveal that when there's no explicit statement that a salary or wage is negotiable, women are more likely than men to accept the salary they're offered. Men, even without being told that it's appropriate or possible to ask for higher pay, tend to do so.[24] A study of MBA students found, for example, that 50 percent of men, but only 13 percent of women, negotiated their starting salaries out of business school.[25] As a result, even after accounting for previous work experience, female MBAs accepted salary offers that were 5.5 percent lower than those accepted by their male counterparts.[26] It's not only among MBAs where we see this pattern. Across a wide range of professions and disciplines, women are less likely than men to ask for more pay.[27] In fact, surveys find that when asked to select metaphors to describe the idea of negotiating a salary, men choose "winning a ball game." Women equate the experience with "going to the dentist."[28]

These gender differences in behavior and perceptions contribute to the pay gap because their effects accumulate over time. Compare, for instance, the lifetime earnings of two lawyers—one male and one female. For the sake of argument, let's assume that both graduated from law school and began working in the same division of the same firm at the same time. And let's assume that both received initial salary offers of $85,000 (which is the average starting salary for lawyers across the country).[29] The female lawyer accepted the offer. The male lawyer bargained for a better package. He successfully negotiated a starting salary of $91,000, an 8.3 percent increase over his female colleague. (By the way, this is a conservative estimate. Researchers find that, on average, men ask for roughly 30 percent more than women do.[30]) The top two bars in Figure 8.5 represent these starting salaries.

Now let's assume that both employees perform equally well, take no significant time off, and receive annual merit raises of 5 percent. By the time they've been working at the firm for five years, the gap in their wages will have grown by 50 percent (what started out as a $6,000 salary differential is now a $9,000 difference). The remaining bars in Figure 8.5 carry this simulation out over a 30-year career. Based on annual merit raises of 5 percent and two negotiated raises—one when the lawyer makes partner and one to keep the employee from leaving the firm—at the end of a 30-year legal career, the woman earns 81 percent of what the man earns. In terms of lifetime earnings,

FIGURE 8.5   A CAREER'S WORTH OF GENDERED SALARY NEGOTIATIONS

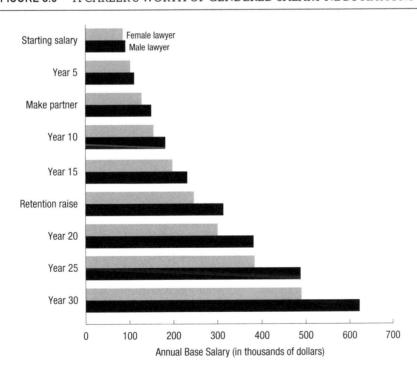

Figures based on annual merit raises of 5 percent, and two negotiated raises with an 8.3 percent differential rate (consistent with the starting salary negotiation gap). At the end of a 30-year legal career, the woman earns 81 percent of what the man earns.

the woman makes $7.4 million, compared to the man's $9.2 million. Differences in the propensity to negotiate at three moments across a career lead to a situation in which the female employee's lifetime earnings trail the man's by nearly $2 million.

WHERE DO WE GO FROM HERE?

The evidence of a substantial and enduring pay gap between women and men is clear, and the reasons for it are relatively straightforward. Developing, passing, and implementing policy solutions to close the gap, however, are far more complex than simplistic political debates suggest. And given the political environment, they're also not likely to gain much traction.

Let's take as a starting point occupational segregation and the way it contributes to the pay gap. Republicans contend that the wage gap is not a problem in need of a solution because it is already illegal for employers to pay women less for the same work. For the GOP, "equal pay for equal work" means the exact same job, and we already have it. For Democrats, "equal work" means something different. They are concerned that women work just as much as men, but earn significantly less. It doesn't matter that women and men perform different jobs; what matters is that women are compensated less than men for the work they do. A "comparable worth" policy that attempts to recalibrate wage scales to match professional qualifications and skills across jobs could potentially address the problem. But we'll likely never have a serious debate about such a proposal because enacting comparable worth legislation is a political nonstarter. After all, Republicans in Congress don't even support the Paycheck Fairness Act. This bill, which has consistently been introduced by Democrats since 1997, would (1) punish employers for retaliating against workers who share wage information, (2) place the burden on employers to justify why someone is paid less than someone else, and (3) allow workers to sue for punitive damages in cases of wage discrimination. Given that this relatively modest proposal is continually blocked, a bill that aims to address and remedy the root causes of occupational segregation would be dead on arrival.

The same political dynamics prevent the kind of comprehensive child care policy that could provide incentives for women to remain in the workforce. During the 2016 presidential campaign, Donald Trump promised a plan that would allow families to deduct the costs of child care from their income taxes. Even if such a law passes, it would likely disproportionately benefit high-income parents, since the credit is designed as a tax deduction for those who can already afford the initial costs of child care. Low-income wage earners, who are dispro-portionately women, wouldn't have an opportunity to take advantage of the deduction.[31] They often can't afford child care in the first place, so they are more likely to reduce their hours or leave the workforce to provide it themselves. Thus, there's no cost to deduct. Proposals to expand the plan to include poor women, or to provide child care subsidies for low-income working women so that they can remain fully employed, have little chance of making it through Congress.

Of course, it's not only the costs of child care that can pose a financial hardship. Taking time off from work to have a child can be difficult as well. And here, too, the potential for passing some sort of federal legislation to allay the pain is unlikely. Currently, the Family and Medical Leave Act (FMLA), which was signed into law by President Bill Clinton in 1993, guarantees new parents job protection if they take up to 12 weeks of *unpaid* leave in a one-year period.[32] During this time, although they receive no pay, workers maintain their health care and other benefits under the same terms and conditions as if they had not taken leave.[33] Because women represent 56 percent of the workers who take advantage of FMLA, the law ostensibly creates incentives for women to remain in the workforce when they have children.[34]

But many argue that the job security provided by the FMLA is not enough. Rather, they believe that paid leave is a necessary step toward devel-oping a series of policies that make it possible for parents to balance their families and their careers. Several states and cities have passed measures to supplement the FMLA, whereby employees receive at least partial pay for part of the leave. Some private sector companies have stepped up, too. At Facebook, for example, all new parents receive four months of paid leave plus a $4,000 cash stipend for each child. Netflix goes even further. People who work in its streaming services division receive up to one year of leave at full salary.[35]

Congressional Democrats pushing for paid leave contend that the federal government should follow suit and, at a minimum, guarantee that women and men, regardless of where they work or where they live, benefit from 12 weeks of paid leave. After all, the United States (along with Oman and Papua New Guinea) is one of only three countries in the world without some sort of paid-maternity-leave law.[36] Yet passing a policy like this is nowhere on the horizon. Granted, during the 2016 presidential campaign, Donald Trump broke from the typical Republican position and proposed a paid leave policy. The plan fell far short of what paid leave advocates champion, as it called for only six weeks of paid leave, and only for women.[37] But even this limited plan goes far beyond what the GOP-controlled Congress seems willing to support.

The final aspect of the pay gap that legislation could potentially address pertains to salary negotiations. This is difficult because negotiating pay is part of a broader set of gender dynamics that transpire in the workplace. Beyond their reluctance to negotiate their pay, women are also more likely than men to diminish and undervalue their professional skills and achievements. In general, men are more likely than women to express confidence in skills they do not possess and overconfidence in skills they do possess.[38] Men tend to be more "self-congratulatory," whereas women tend to be more modest about their achievements.[39] And whereas men tend to overestimate their intelligence, women tend to underestimate theirs.[40] These differences in self-assessments are deeply engrained and, accordingly, difficult to undo. The proposed Paycheck Fairness Act includes a provision that makes grants to organizations and entities that provide negotiation skills training programs for girls and women.[41] This might be a good start in addressing this problem, but the provision remains linked to a bill with dim prospects.

Regardless of the political feasibility of these potential responses to the pay gap, millions of American women face wage disparities every day. And without major legislative efforts to close the gap, it will persist. A 2014 study estimated that even in states with the most hospitable political and economic environments—states in which women's integration into male-dominated career fields outpaces the national average—women will still have to wait decades for their pay to catch up to men's.[42] In a handful of other states—Wyoming, Louisiana, Utah, North Dakota, and West Virginia—economic and political conditions continue to reinforce the pay gap. As a result, pay equity won't happen until the next century. Because money and wealth equate with power and status in U.S. society, women's full equality hinges on achieving gender parity in wages. Given the political climate, though, it's unlikely that we'll reach that milestone anytime soon.

QUESTIONS FOR REFLECTION AND DISCUSSION

1. If a friend asked you whether women are paid less than men, what would you say? Is the answer obvious, or is it more complicated than you thought before reading this chapter?

2. Go online and search for the average salary of three historically male-dominated jobs and three historically female-dominated jobs that you consider equally important in U.S. society. Payscale.com and salary.com are two good sources to locate this information. What did you find? Are the results of your search similar to the data we presented in this chapter?

3. Most explanations for the pay gap downplay the role of overt gender discrimination in the workplace. Yet surveys continue to reveal that women regularly report facing gender bias at work. Beyond pay, what other forms of gender bias might occur in the workplace? Identify at least three other types of workplace discrimination.

4. Can you identify any political implications of the pay gap? How might it affect women's and men's party identification, the candidates they support, or their political participation and engagement?

5. A 2016 study by the Pew Research Center found that among 41 developed countries, only the United States did not have a law mandating that when a woman or man has a child, he or she may take time off from work at full pay. Why do you think the United States lags behind other wealthy countries on this front?

FOR FURTHER EXPLORATION

Babcock, Linda, and Sarah Laschever. 2003. *Women Don't Ask: Negotiation and the Gender Divide*. Princeton, NJ: Princeton University Press.

Ehrenreich, Barbara. 2011. *Nickel and Dimed: On (Not) Getting By in America*, 10th year anniversary edition. New York: Picador.

Erin Brokovich. 2000. Directed by Steven Soderbergh. Ventura, CA: Universal Pictures.

Fast Food Women. 1992. Directed by Ann Lewis Johnson. PBS and Appalshop.

Ledbetter, Lilly. 2012. *Grace and Grit: My Fight for Equal Pay and Fairness at Goodyear and Beyond*. New York: Crown Publishing Group.

Meet the Parents. 2000. Directed by Jay Roach. Brooklyn, NY: Universal Pictures and Dreamworks LLC.

Nine to Five. 1980. Directed by Colin Higgins. Glendale, CA: IPC Films and Twentieth Century Fox.

Sokoloff, Natalie. 1993. *Black Women and White Women in the Professions: Occupational Segregation by Race and Gender, 1960–1980*. New York: Routledge.

Verba, Sidney, Key Lehman Schlozman, and Henry E. Brady. 1995. *Voice and Equality: Civic Voluntarism in American Politics*. Cambridge: Harvard University Press.

Activists on both sides of the abortion issue demonstrate on the steps of the U.S. Supreme Court in June 2016. The Supreme Court is the final arbiter in determining whether the right to an abortion remains protected, but state legislators, members of Congress, and presidential candidates regularly try to shape the landscape of reproductive rights as well.

CHAPTER 9

THE PAST, PRESENT, AND FUTURE OF REPRODUCTIVE RIGHTS IN THE UNITED STATES

Key Question: How secure is a woman's right to an abortion?

In late November 2015, Robert L. Dear Jr. arrived at a Planned Parenthood clinic in Colorado Springs and opened fire with an assault-style rifle. He killed three people and wounded nine others during a standoff that lasted five hours. When interviewed by the police about the reason for the shootings, Dear muttered, "No more baby parts."[1] This was a reference to widely reported allegations that, after performing abortions, Planned Parenthood sells fetal tissue for a profit.[2]

Public reaction to the attack amounted to a sorrowful shrug, as events like the ones in Colorado have become commonplace. Since 1977, there have been 11 murders, 26 attempted murders, 42 bombings, 185 instances of arson, and more than 7,000 incidents of other criminal activities—such as vandalism, trespassing, and stalking—directed at abortion providers. If we include hate mail, harassing phone calls, and bomb threats, then that number climbs into the hundreds of thousands.[3] The debate over abortion is vitriolic, unrelenting, and sometimes violent.[4]

The beginning of the contemporary fight over abortion can be traced back to January 22, 1973, the day the U.S. Supreme Court handed down its decision in *Roe v. Wade*.[5] In a majority opinion written by Justice Harry Blackmun, the Court struck down a Texas state law that prohibited abortion, as well as similar laws in 37 other states. The ruling established that abortion was part of the constitutionally guaranteed right to privacy.[6] But it also made clear that it's not unconditional. During the first three months of a pregnancy, a woman's right to an abortion is protected. In the second and third trimesters, states can regulate and even restrict abortion as long as they are acting to protect the mother's health or the "potentiality of human life."[7] Put simply, the decision made legal abortion the law of the land, but not without limits.

Shortly after the Court handed down the decision, activists on both sides of the issue came to see themselves in a life and death struggle. For pro-choice organizations, keeping abortion safe and legal became synonymous with protecting women's rights more broadly. In the words of the National Women's Law Center, "Abortion is a key part of women's liberty, equality, and economic security."[8] On the other side of the debate, groups opposing abortion rights considered the Court's decision, as well as the decision to terminate a pregnancy, a "profound tragedy" that not only harms the mother but also "deprives society of the gifts of the unborn."[9] As such, organizations such as Operation Rescue endeavor to "take direct action to restore legal personhood to the pre-born."[10] Incidents of violence are not the norm, but a profound and intense battle roars on between these competing camps outside of abortion clinics, in state legislatures, at congressional hearings, during the Supreme Court confirmation process, and on the airwaves amid hotly contested political campaigns.[11]

Who is winning the fight? What is the status of women's reproductive freedom today? What can we expect in the future? The answers to these questions depend on where you look. In this chapter, we assess the contemporary state of abortion politics from four vantage points: public opinion, the Supreme Court, state legislatures, and the U.S. Congress. Our analysis reveals two clear—and competing—realities about reproductive rights. On one hand, when it comes to what Americans think about abortion, the public is divided, and this division has been relatively stable over time. On the other hand, state legislators and members of Congress have moved sharply in recent years to ramp up abortion restrictions and curtail access. Ultimately, we conclude that, as has been the case for the last 45 years, it will be the Supreme Court that determines whether abortion remains a right for generations to come.

A DIVIDED BUT STABLE NATION: ABORTION AND PUBLIC OPINION

In the wake of *Roe v. Wade*, pollsters started measuring Americans' support for reproductive rights. Sometimes they ask people whether they think *Roe* should be overturned. Sometimes they ask citizens whether they consider themselves "pro-choice" or "pro-life." Sometimes they pose questions to gauge support for particular laws that would limit abortion access. Relying on responses to these questions is tricky when it comes to tracking support for abortion rights over time. The same questions aren't always asked, and even when the substance of the question stays the same, the wording often changes. One question, however, has been asked consistently since 1975: "Do you think abortion should be legal under any circumstances, legal only under certain circumstances, or illegal in all circumstances?" The question wording is vague—the "circumstances" are never defined—but the responses nevertheless provide a general idea of where the public comes down on the issue and whether support for abortion rights has changed over time.

In a nutshell, a little less than half the country takes an absolute position—favoring abortion rights either in all cases or in none at all. Figure 9.1 illustrates that the "always legal" position is more popular than the "never legal" view. If we take an average of poll results dating back to 1975, 26 percent of people believe that abortion should always be legal, compared to 18 percent who think it should always be illegal. The rest of the country takes a more

FIGURE 9.1   CITIZENS' ATTITUDES TOWARD ABORTION

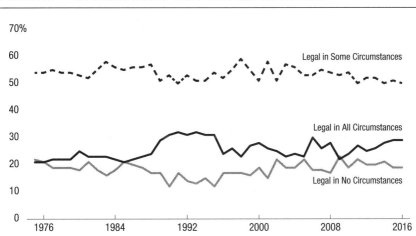

Data compiled from Gallup polls conducted between 1975 and 2016.

qualified position, supporting the legality of abortion in some situations but opposing it in others. And this has been the case since 1975.

Moving beyond these broad classifications, there's general consensus on the part of the American people as to many of the circumstances that justify legal abortion and those that don't. When a woman's physical health or life could be endangered by carrying a pregnancy to term, more than eight out of 10 people support her right to end the pregnancy. Three-quarters of Americans feel the same way when the pregnancy results from rape or incest. There's also quite a bit of agreement at the other end of the spectrum. A majority of the public opposes abortion in cases where a woman simply doesn't want a child or when a family can't afford to raise a child. Americans are more divided when the abortion is sought because the pregnancy would result in a baby who would be physically or mentally impaired (see Figure 9.2).

Young people, those with a college degree, and those with no religious affiliation are the most supportive of reproductive rights. White Evangelical Protestants, those with only a high school diploma, and citizens over the age

FIGURE 9.2   WHEN SHOULD ABORTION BE LEGAL?

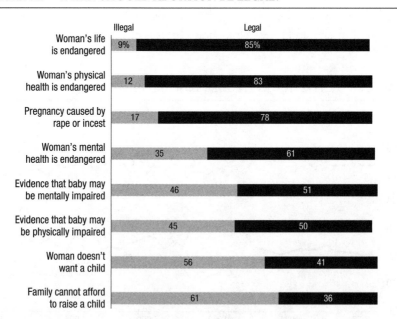

Data come from the most recent Quinnipiac, CNN, and Gallup polls that asked about support for these restrictions. The polls were conducted between 2011 and 2015.

of 65 are less likely to support legal abortion.[12] Importantly—and perhaps surprisingly—public opinion on abortion doesn't differ between women and men. Although the news media typically present abortion as a "women's" issue, and the highest profile spokespeople from pro-choice organizations such as Planned Parenthood and the National Abortion Rights Action League (NARAL) are women, there's no gender divide in support for or opposition to abortion rights (57 percent of men and 55 percent of women believe that abortion should be legal in all or most circumstances).

Black and White citizens also report similar views (57 percent favor abortion rights). This might initially seem somewhat surprising because Black and White women's history with reproductive freedom differs dramatically. During slavery, birth control and abortion were regularly practiced to prevent the production of additional slaves for abusive masters. When the movement to liberalize and expand family planning began to take hold in the 1950s and 1960s, many Black activists rejected legal abortion because they saw it as an attempt by Whites to control Blacks and reduce the Black population.[13] Of course, party affiliation is among the most significant factors correlating with attitudes toward reproductive rights. Whereas 70 percent of Democrats and 60 percent of independents think abortion should be legal, only 38 percent of Republicans feel the same way.[14] And Black women and men today are overwhelmingly Democratic.

Public opinion polls are helpful for understanding people's attitudes toward abortion rights, but a more definitive indicator of where the public stands on the issue is what they do at the ballot box. Since 2006, citizens in 11 states have voted on ballot initiatives pertaining to abortion.[15] The types of measures have varied widely. In South Dakota, for example, citizens in 2006 voted in a state referendum to "prohibit any person, at any time, from providing any substance to a pregnant woman or using any instrument or procedure on a pregnant woman for the purpose of terminating her pregnancy, except to prevent the death of the pregnant woman." Four years later, Alaska voters weighed in on a parental notification initiative to "forbid a minor from getting an abortion without having a doctor inform at least one parent before moving forward with the procedure." In 2014, North Dakotans considered the "Life Begins at Conception Amendment," which would confer all rights held by a citizen to any unborn fetus. The outcomes of these attempts to restrict abortion are in sync with public opinion polls. Parental notification laws tend to pass muster with the voters (as was the case in Alaska). Full-fledged efforts to ban abortion, or to restrict it even in cases of rape and incest, typically fail (which happened in North and South Dakota).

THE "LAW OF FIVE": ABORTION AND THE SUPREME COURT

Citizens weigh in directly on abortion when confronted with state ballot initiatives. But it's the U.S. Supreme Court that determines whether the restrictions voters support or oppose comply with the Constitution. Understanding the Court's logic on this contentious issue is anything but straightforward. The nine-member Court is the most archaic and secretive of the branches of government. It keeps no official records of deliberation and no videos of its proceedings.[16] Rather, the justices hear a case, collect written legal arguments from both sides, go behind closed doors, and issue a ruling several months later. Majority rules on the Court, so five justices are all it takes to declare a new law of the land. As iconic justice William Brennan famously quipped, with five justices voting your way, "You can do anything around here."[17] Nowhere is that more apparent than in cases having to do with abortion.

Following the 1973 decision in *Roe v. Wade*, more than 30 cases that address some aspect of abortion law have made their way to the Supreme Court. Most involve a challenge to a state law that restricts or regulates first trimester abortion access. These restrictions take many forms: mandatory waiting periods after a woman seeks an abortion, parental consent requirements for minors, mandatory counseling about alternatives, to name just a few. Table 9.1 summarizes the four most significant cases that have allowed restrictions on abortion rights since *Roe*. Notice that all four were decided with a 5-4 margin.

The Court also periodically debates whether to reconsider the central holding in *Roe v. Wade*, which underscores its centrality in the abortion debate. This was especially clear in the late 1980s and early 1990s. In *Webster v. Reproductive Health Services*, Chief Justice William Rehnquist and his conservative colleagues determined that fetal viability tests, mandatory counseling, and an abortion ban in public facilities were all legal and permissible under *Roe*.[18] But Rehnquist sought to go a step further. He urged his colleagues not only to uphold these major restrictions but also to take the dramatic step of overturning *Roe v. Wade*. The Court didn't go for it.

Three years later, Rehnquist's position gained traction. In *Planned Parenthood v. Casey*, the Court considered whether a series of abortion restrictions in Pennsylvania—including a 24-hour waiting period, parental consent, and spousal notification—were constitutional. But this time, the Court directly took up the question of whether to overturn *Roe v. Wade*. Internal documents released many years later showed that one month before the decision was issued, five justices were poised to discard *Roe*. For unknown reasons, Justice Anthony Kennedy changed his mind.[19] Although the Court preserved the right to an

TABLE 9.1   RESTRICTIONS ON ABORTION UPHELD BY THE U.S.
SUPREME COURT POST–*ROE V. WADE*

CASE AND YEAR	MARGIN	RESTRICTION
Harris v. McRae (1980)	5–4	• Court upheld a federal law that banned Medicaid funding for poor women seeking an abortion.
Webster v. Reproductive Health Services (1989)	5–4	• Court upheld a Missouri law that (1) banned the use of public facilities for all abortions except when the life of the mother was at stake, (2) required physicians to perform fetal viability tests, and (3) mandated counseling for all women seeking an abortion. • Court emphasized that it was not revisiting the essential decision in *Roe v. Wade*.
Planned Parenthood v. Casey (1992)	5–4	• Court upheld provisions of a Pennsylvania law that required (1) informed consent, (2) a 24-hour waiting period before an abortion, and (3) parental consent for minors seeking an abortion. • Justices imposed a new "undue burden" standard to determine the validity of laws restricting abortion. A restriction is unconstitutional only if it presents a "substantial obstacle in the path of a woman seeking an abortion before the fetus attains viability." For this reason, the Court declared unconstitutional a requirement for spousal consent.
Gonzalez v. Carhart (2007)	5–4	• Court upheld the federal ban on a late-term abortion procedure known as "partial birth abortion."

abortion, the decision allowed most of the provisions included in the Pennsylvania law, and made it easier to impose first trimester restrictions. As long as the restriction doesn't pose an "undue burden" on the woman, it's permissible.

That's not to say that all restrictions meet this test. In 2013, for example, Texas passed a statute that required doctors who perform abortions to have "admitting privileges at a hospital within 30 miles of where the abortion was performed." Another provision of the law required that "all abortion clinics comply with standards for ambulatory surgical centers." Because most abortion clinics in Texas do not meet these criteria, the law would have effectively closed the overwhelming majority of them. In 2016, the Supreme Court, in *Whole Women's Health v. Hellerstedt*, struck down the Texas law because it placed too substantial a burden on the fundamental abortion right.[20] This landmark decision made clear that seemingly neutral laws that result in dramatically curbed access to abortion are unconstitutional.

The Supreme Court's rulings surrounding abortion have remained quite stable since the early 1990s. This is largely because the Court has been comprised of five justices who support *Roe* and four who oppose it. The long-standing status quo could change, and the debate over abortion will certainly erupt, when a Supreme Court vacancy presents an opportunity to shift the balance of power.

A BIG MOVE TO THE RIGHT: ABORTION AND STATE LEGISLATIVE POLITICS

Public attitudes about abortion have not wavered much since the mid-1970s. And the Supreme Court has consistently voted to affirm the central holding in *Roe v. Wade*. But this hasn't diminished the political battle over reproductive rights. For the most part, abortion rights opponents have turned their attention to the states, which have proven to be fertile ground to advance their cause.

The focus on state abortion policies has been especially intense since the 2010 elections, when Republicans throughout the United States picked up 720 legislative seats. In what came to be described as a GOP electoral "tsunami," 22 state legislative chambers switched from Democratic to Republican control.[21] When the 2011 legislative session began, Republicans controlled 57 of the 99 legislative chambers across the country. (Nebraska has only one chamber.) In 25 states, the GOP controlled both chambers. The 2014 elections further bolstered GOP dominance. The Republicans saw a net gain of nearly 350 state legislative seats, which allowed them to flip an additional 11 chambers (for a total of 68), and thus control both chambers in 31 states.[22] And despite the expectation that the Democrats would take back some of these chambers in 2016, the Republicans held their ground. In fact, they picked up an additional three chambers.[23] When the 2017 legislative session began, the Republicans held more seats in state legislatures than at any time in modern history.

Republicans' victories had little to do with their positions on abortion. The overwhelming majority of voters in state legislative elections don't identify abortion as key to their voting decisions. Indeed, no pre-election polls rate abortion as a top issue. But the Supreme Court has made it clear that states can regulate women's access to the procedure. And Republicans seized the opportunity with their new majorities to do just that.

According to data compiled by the Guttmacher Institute, which tracks abortion-related legislation, states enacted a total of 334 new abortion restrictions from January 2011 to July 2016. During these five years, 31 states enacted at least one provision—from banning certain types of abortions, to limiting insurance coverage, to restricting who qualifies as a legal abortion provider. Ten states enacted at least 10 new restrictions. To put these numbers in perspective, more restrictions were enacted during this time period as in the 15 years prior to it (a total of 292). In fact, restrictions enacted between 2011 and 2016 account for more than 30 percent of the 1,120 abortion restrictions that have been passed at the state level since *Roe v. Wade*.[24]

This wave of new abortion legislation has culminated in more than three-quarters of states outlawing abortion once a fetus is viable, permitting individual health care providers and hospitals to opt out of performing abortions, mandating that abortions be carried out by a licensed physician, and requiring minors seeking the procedure to obtain parental consent or provide evidence of parental notification (see Table 9.2). The prohibition of state funding and 24-hour waiting periods are law in more than half the states. And measures that pro-choice advocates consider particularly extreme—such as restricting abortion coverage in private insurance plans or mandating that

TABLE 9.2   ABORTION RESTRICTIONS AT THE STATE LEVEL

	NUMBER OF STATES
General Restrictions	
Prohibit abortion after fetal viability except to protect the woman's life or health	43
Prohibit "partial birth" abortion	19
Funding	
No state funds except to protect a woman's life, or in cases of rape or incest	32
Restrict abortion coverage even in private insurance plans	11
Access	
Allow health care providers to refuse to participate in an abortion	45
Allow hospitals and medical institutions to refuse to perform abortions	42
Must be performed by a licensed physician	38
Must be performed in a hospital after a certain point in the pregnancy	18
Must involve a second physician after a certain point in the pregnancy	18
Counseling and Informed Consent	
Woman must be given information about the ability of a fetus to feel pain	12
Woman must receive counseling about long-term mental health consequences	7
Woman must be told of purported link between abortion and breast cancer	5
Waiting Periods	
Woman must wait at least 24 hours between counseling and having an abortion	27
Parental Consent	
One or both parents of a minor must consent to the abortion	25
One or both parents of a minor must be notified of decision to have an abortion	13

Data come from the Guttmacher Institute.[25]

women be informed of a fetus's alleged ability to feel pain—have passed in nearly one-quarter of the states. Whereas only five states in 2010 were classified by the Guttmacher Institute as "extremely hostile" toward abortion—that is, they restricted abortion in at least five ways—by 2014, that number had more than tripled to 18.[26]

Even with this recent flurry of legislation, there remains quite a bit of variation across states when it comes to restricting abortion access. Figure 9.3 presents a U.S. map that categorizes each state based on seven common abortion restrictions. Lighter states have fewer restrictions, and darker states have more. Washington, Oregon, Maine, and Vermont do not restrict access at all. California, New York, and Illinois are among those states with only one or two restrictions in place. But states such as Utah and Alabama, which have

FIGURE 9.3   THE PREVALENCE OF ABORTION RESTRICTIONS THROUGHOUT THE UNITED STATES

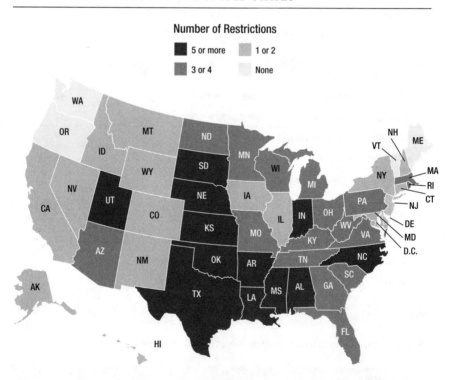

The seven restrictions on which this analysis is based are (1) 24-hour waiting period; (2) mandatory counseling; (3) mandatory ultrasound; (4) ban on all abortions after 24 weeks of pregnancy, unless the life of the woman is at risk; (5) parental consent; (6) clinic must meet conditions of a surgical center; and (7) provider must have hospital privileges. Data come from FiveThirtyEight.com and reflect the political landscape as of May 2014.[27]

regularly been controlled by Republican governors and state legislatures, have passed numerous regulations. Thirteen states have actually passed laws that ban abortion almost entirely. These laws are unconstitutional and cannot be enforced right now, but they will immediately go into effect if *Roe v. Wade* is ever overturned.[28]

In the meantime, as new restrictions are enacted, the number of clinics that provide abortions continue to decrease. Clinic closures are not systematically associated with a decline in a state's abortion incidence. But they do make it more onerous for women to access abortion providers.[29]

NO COMMON GROUND: ABORTION AND THE U.S. CONGRESS

Efforts in the U.S. Congress to enact federal legislation restricting abortion access have followed a similar pattern as in the states. After the Republicans gained control of the U.S. Congress in 2010, they introduced more than 125 bills that included anti-choice measures.[30] The Life at Conception Act, for example, would give constitutional rights and equal protection to a fetus from the moment of conception.[31] The Child Custody Protection Act would prohibit minors from crossing state lines to get around parental consent requirements.[32] The National Pro-Life Waiting Period Act would mandate that all abortion providers wait 24 hours between scheduling and performing an abortion.[33] Up through the end of 2016, Republicans had been much less successful than their state legislator counterparts enacting such restrictions. After all, Democratic President Barack Obama consistently threatened to veto such legislation. The election of Donald Trump, however, provides Republicans with an important ally for limiting abortion access.

Even prior to Trump's election, divided government in Washington, DC, didn't mean that the political struggle over abortion was absent in the nation's capital. Two high-profile incidents reveal just how deep and unyielding divisions over reproductive rights remain. First, consider the near government shutdown in 2015. What almost brought the federal government to a complete halt? Planned Parenthood. Because of their opposition to abortion, Republicans in the U.S. House and Senate sought to strip from government spending bills all support for Planned Parenthood (which amounted to roughly $500 million annually). Democrats fought to maintain the expenditure, arguing that federal spending guidelines already mandated that none of the government money Planned Parenthood received could be used for abortions.[34] Republican lawmakers were not persuaded. They were willing to shut down the federal government as a way to stop abortion providers. Democrats dug their heels in just as deep, and President Obama vowed to veto any spending bill that would defund the organization.[35] The debate was so heated and the potential of a government shutdown so real that Republican Speaker of the House John Boehner offered his resignation. Before leaving office, he worked on a budget compromise that maintained Planned Parenthood's funding and avoided a shutdown.[36]

The sudden death of conservative Supreme Court Justice Antonin Scalia in February 2016 marked another moment in which abortion politics exposed the fault lines in Washington. Within hours of the news of Scalia's death, Republican Senate Majority Leader Mitch McConnell announced that Republicans would not hold confirmation hearings for anyone President Obama appointed to fill the vacancy. According to McConnell, "This decision ought to be made by the next president, whoever is elected."[37] Although it's not unheard of to close down hearings on appointments late in a president's term, McConnell's decision was unprecedented. Obama would still be president for another 11 months, and the average length of time it has taken the U.S. Senate to vote on a Supreme Court nominee since 1980 has been just 66 days. The longest confirmation process ever was 125 days, still much less time than Obama would remain in the White House.[38] The reason for the obstructionism was clear: The next justice could sway the Court's balance of power on a number of key issues, including abortion.[39]

This reality, of course, was not lost on presidential candidates in 2016. Both Donald Trump and Hillary Clinton assured their supporters that they would appoint only the "right kind" of judges. Their position on abortion, in other words, would be an explicit litmus test. Pro-choice advocates were comforted by Clinton's promise to choose judges who believe *Roe v. Wade* is "settled law."[40] Trump, meanwhile, reminded those opposing abortion rights that, even if they didn't like him, they had to vote for him. "You know why?" he asked rhetorically. "Supreme Court judges, Supreme Court judges."[41] Indeed, according to Trump's running mate, Mike Pence, with Trump in the White House, "We'll see *Roe v. Wade* consigned to the ash heap of history where it belongs."[42] The importance of abortion and future Supreme Court justices didn't fall on deaf ears. Exit polls reveal that 21 percent of voters said that appointing justices to the Supreme Court was the most important factor in their vote. Trump won these voters by a hefty margin (56 percent cast ballots for Trump, compared to 41 percent who voted for Clinton). The U.S. Senate, therefore, will continue to wrestle with confirmation process showdowns over an issue on which politicians can find no common ground.

WHERE DO WE GO FROM HERE?

The abortion debate did not start with *Roe v. Wade*. Conflict over reproductive rights has been an enduring and contentious issue throughout time.[43] And there's no reason to expect that any future decision issued by the Supreme Court will end it. Both sides view the stakes as too sacred and fundamental. For abortion rights supporters, the battle over reproductive freedom bears directly on where we are as a culture when it comes to women's status, opportunities, and autonomy. According to feminist writer Katha Pollitt, "Legalizing abortion didn't just save women from death and injury and fear of arrest, it didn't just make it possible for women to commit to education and work . . . It changed how women saw themselves: as mothers by choice, not fate."[44] For opponents of abortion rights, the battle is about saving lives. Late Republican Congressman Henry Hyde, who spent much of the 1980s and 1990s fighting to restrict abortion, characterized the issue this way: "This is a debate about our understanding of human dignity, what it means to be a member of the human family, even though tiny, powerless, and unwanted."[45]

Not surprisingly, these differences in core beliefs have led each side to interpret national trends and abortion statistics differently, too—with each side confident that the data support its position and tactics. Abortion rights opponents argue that anti-abortion legislation effectively reduces the incidence of abortion. In 2011, the abortion rate in the United States hit its lowest point since the year *Roe v. Wade* was decided. The total number of abortions performed that year is estimated at around 1 million, down from more than 1.6 million in 1990. Abortion rights advocates, on the other hand, point out that the abortion rate had already been declining for 20 years prior to the onset of the post-2010 wave of legislation. They point to medical and health experts who cite comprehensive sex education in schools, along with the increased use of long-term birth control, for the decline in abortion rates.[46] A preliminary analysis of the impact of the new restrictions suggests that the new laws have not done much, in and of themselves, to diminish the number of abortions. When we compare the 2010 and 2012 abortion rates in each state, we see a drop of roughly the same magnitude in high and low restriction states.

Because of the deeply held convictions on both sides, reaching any sort of common ground is virtually impossible. Sociologist and legal scholar Kristin Luker, in an early study of post–*Roe v. Wade* politics, concluded: "The two sides share almost no common premises and very little common language."[47] Political scientist Karen O'Connor's analysis of the evolution of the abortion landscape roughly 10 years later led her to arrive at a similar judgment: compromise and common ground are unlikely.[48] And the 2016 Democratic and Republican party platforms illustrate that the battle lines today are as deep and intractable as ever. The Democratic Party believes unequivocally "that every woman should have access to quality reproductive health care services, including safe and legal abortion—regardless of where she lives, how much money she makes, or how she is insured."[49] The Republicans think that "the unborn child has a fundamental right to life which cannot be infringed."[50] For activists and party leaders, there is no room for compromise. The Supreme Court and the fight over potential justices will, therefore, remain ground zero in the struggle for control over abortion policy. But even with a dramatic shift in the composition of the Court, the two sides will continue to fight for what they're each sure is the only acceptable view.

QUESTIONS FOR REFLECTION AND DISCUSSION

1. There's a broad perception that women are more likely than men to support abortion rights. But public opinion polls show that men and women actually don't differ on the issue. What do you think explains their similar views? What accounts for the assumption that women are more pro-choice than men?

2. Although voters don't identify abortion as a top issue, presidential candidates often run campaign ads that highlight their position on reproductive rights. Visit www.livingroomcandidate.org and find campaign ads about abortion from the last three presidential elections. Assess how Democrats and Republicans differ in how they frame the issue and the language they use.

3. Do you think elected officials in state legislatures and in Congress should determine abortion policy? Or do you think the Supreme Court should continue to take the lead in establishing abortion policy? Explain your answer.

4. How does current U.S. abortion policy compare with other countries? Visit the Center for Reproductive Rights' website (http://worldabortionlaws.com) and choose 10 countries from different regions of the world. Describe the abortion laws in each.

5. Do you think abortion will always be an emotional and explosive issue in U.S. society? Or can you imagine a time when the intensity will dissipate? Explain your answer, and in doing so, consider whether abortion is controversial among your classmates and friends.

FOR FURTHER EXPLORATION

"An Overview of Abortion Laws." Guttmacher Institute, July 1, 2016, www.guttmacher.
org/state-policy/explore/overview-abortion-laws (accessed 7/26/16).

Dirty Dancing. 1987. Directed by Emile Ardolino. Los Angeles, CA: Vestron Pictures.

Irving, John. 1985. *The Cider House Rules*. New York: Ballantine Books.

Juno. 2008. Directed by Jason Reitmen. Los Angeles, CA: Fox Searchlight.

Knocked Up. 2007. Directed by Judd Apatow. Los Angeles, CA: Universal Studios.

Rohlinger, Deana. 2014. *Abortion Politics, Mass Media, and Social Movements in
America*. New York: Cambridge University Press.

Weddington, Sarah. 1992. *A Question of Choice*. New York: Penguin Books.

Wilson, Joshua. 2016. *The New States of Abortion Politics*. Stanford: Stanford
University Press.

Ziegler, Mary. 2015. *After Roe: The Lost History of the Abortion Debate*. Cambridge:
Harvard University Press.

Women now comprise one-third of federal judges throughout the United States, up from just 10 percent in the early 1990s. But women—even those who work in traditionally male-dominated fields—continue to shoulder most of the housework and child care. What does the future look like? Will the progress we've seen on the work front finally be matched on the home front?

CHAPTER 10

"FREE TO BE" OR STILL A BUMPY RIDE? GENDER EQUALITY IN THE UNITED STATES

Key Question: Do young women and men feel equally free to pursue their professional and personal dreams?

In 1956, Supreme Court Justice Ruth Bader Ginsburg entered Harvard Law School as one of only nine women in a class of 500 students. Shortly after the semester started, the dean of the school invited the women to dinner at his house. He asked them to go around the room and explain why they were at Harvard "occupying a seat that could be held by a man."[1] When Ginsburg graduated first in her class at Columbia Law School a few years later (she transferred from Harvard, where she also ranked first in her class), 14 law firms declined to offer her a job. And they made it clear why. "Employees were above board, open about it," explains Ginsburg. "They would say, 'We had a woman lawyer once and was she dreadful.'" At the time, 97 percent of practicing attorneys were men.[2] It was the early 1960s, after all, and women in the workforce were largely relegated to jobs as secretaries, bank tellers, teachers, sales clerks, and household workers.[3]

By the time Ginsburg's daughter, Jane, graduated from Harvard Law School in 1980, the legal profession was amid a sea change. Women comprised almost 30 percent of law students and had dramatically increased their numbers as practicing attorneys. When Ginsburg's granddaughter, Clara, entered Harvard Law School in 2014, close to 50 percent of her classmates were women, as was the dean.[4] The notion of asking women to justify their presence at a top law school had long since passed.

The same kind of progress also characterizes other traditionally male-dominated professions. In the business world, women now receive 37 percent of MBAs and occupy half of all high-level managerial positions.[5] The number of female medical students rose from only a handful in the 1950s and 1960s to nearly 50 percent by 2015.[6] More than one-third of practicing physicians in the United States are now women.[7] And for more than a decade, half of all doctoral degrees have been awarded to women, up from just 12 percent in the mid-1960s (see Figure 10.1). Name the profession, and it's easy to track progress. Major legal and political developments in the 1960s—including the Civil Rights Act, which banned employment discrimination, the Equal Pay Act, and the creation of the National Organization for Women (NOW)—transformed the workplace (see Chapter 1).[8]

Although there's little question that women have marched toward equality in the professional world, that's only part of the equation for gauging progress. Full equality also requires a fundamental shift in the division of labor on the

FIGURE 10.1 PERCENTAGE OF ADVANCED DEGREES AWARDED TO WOMEN

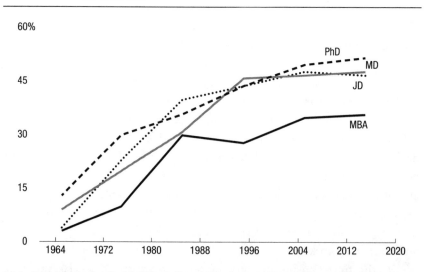

Sources: Catalyst, the American Bar Association, the Henry J. Kaiser Family Foundation, the American Medical Association, and the National Center for Education Statistics.

homefront. If women are disproportionately encumbered by household and family responsibilities, then they will have less freedom and flexibility to pursue their professional goals or climb the career ladders that have always been open to men. Along with passing laws and policies that help integrate the workforce, undoing the traditional power dynamics of the family—where women are the primary caregivers and men the primary breadwinners—is a key element of achieving political equality.

On this dimension, progress has been slower going than in the professional world. That's not to suggest that there hasn't been any. In 1967, almost 50 percent of women with children were "stay-at-home moms." A Gallup poll at that time revealed that an even higher percentage agreed that it was best for children when the mother stayed home and did not work.[9] Nowadays, there's broad acceptance that families with two working parents should share the household responsibilities,[10] and that working mothers and stay-at-home moms can be equally good parents.[11] But a full transition to egalitarian households has yet to materialize. Working women today are still roughly six times more likely than men (43 percent compared to 7 percent) to be responsible for the majority of household tasks. They're 10 times more likely (60 percent versus 6 percent) to be the primary child care provider.[12] Women continue to bear the brunt of the housework even when they are the family's primary breadwinner.[13] Today's households don't look like a portrait from the 1960s—approximately 40 percent of professionally successful women and men report an equal division of labor—but there hasn't been as much progress as we might expect.

Assessing prospects for full gender equality in the United States, therefore, demands that we examine the next generation's goals, both in terms of their professional and personal lives. A 2013 United Nations report about democracy and gender equality opens by making a similar argument: "Democratic ideals of inclusiveness, accountability, and transparency cannot be achieved without laws, policies, measures, and practices that address inequalities." The report goes on to state that we must then "weave these ideals into the social, political, and economic fabric of a society, so that girls and women can reach their potential on an equal basis with men, whatever they choose to do."[14] Justice Ginsburg made the same point in a 2012 interview, relying on lyrics from the Marlo Thomas song, "Free to Be You and Me":

> Free to be, if you were a girl—doctor, lawyer, Indian chief. Anything you want to be. And if you're a boy, and you like teaching, you like nursing, you would like to have a doll, that's okay too. That notion that we should each be free to develop our own talents, whatever they may be and not be held back by artificial barriers.[15]

A society, in essence, hasn't achieved equality of the sexes and can't claim democratic legitimacy if women and men don't believe that they're equally free to develop and pursue their professional goals—whatever they may be—and arrange their families and households in a way that makes their careers possible.

In this chapter, we gauge whether young people are "free to be" when thinking about their futures. The results of our national survey of thousands of high school and college students send mixed messages about the political progress we've made in achieving gender equality. On one hand, young women are quite open to bucking traditional gender norms when it comes to the professional sphere. And young people—male and female—accept women in many positions of professional leadership. On the other hand, when it comes to their personal lives and their attitudes about marriage and childrearing, many traditional ideas persist. Historian Estelle Freedman, in characterizing traditional gender roles, writes, "Women's domestic identities have proven to be quite tenacious."[16] That continues to be true for the next generation. The road to true gender equality is smoother than it was 50 years ago, but there are still lots of bumps to navigate along the way.

ANYTHING HE CAN DO, SHE CAN DO, TOO: YOUNG PEOPLE'S PROFESSIONAL GOALS AND ATTITUDES

In July 1943, *Mass Transportation Magazine* published an article titled "Eleven Tips on Getting More Efficiency Out of Women Employees."[17] Women had recently entered the workforce in large numbers—a result of men being deployed overseas during World War II—and male supervisors didn't quite know what to make of them or how to treat them. Among the "tips":

- If you can get them, pick young married women. . . . They're less likely to be flirtatious; as a rule, they need the work or they wouldn't be doing it.

- "Husky" girls—those who are just a little on the heavy side—are likely to be more even-tempered and efficient than their underweight sisters.

- Give every girl an adequate number of rest periods during the day. . . . A girl has more confidence and consequently is more efficient if she can keep her hair tidied, apply fresh lipstick, and wash her hands several times a day.

- Be tactful in issuing instructions or in making criticisms. Women are often sensitive; they can't shrug off harsh words the way that men do. Never ridicule a woman—it breaks her spirit and cuts her efficiency.

- Be reasonably considerate about using strong language around women. Even though a girl's husband or father may swear vociferously, she'll grow to dislike a place of business where she hears too much of this.

By the 1960s, attitudes toward women in the workplace had sufficiently evolved such that an article like this likely wouldn't have made it into print. Women rarely held powerful or prestigious positions, but they had come to comprise almost one-third of the labor force, and employers had grown accustomed to their presence. Fast-forward 50 years and readers of *Mass Transportation Magazine* might feel like they entered another universe. Almost 50 percent of full-time workers are women, many serving in top positions. And a bevy of state and federal laws prohibit gender discrimination in the workplace.[18] As evidence of the shift in attitudes, a 2011 Pew Center Survey of 18- to 34-year-olds found that, for the first time, women were more likely than men to report that succeeding in a high-paying profession ranked among their top life goals.[19] Women's entrance into the male-dominated professional world has been steady and swift.

There's more to professional gender equality than an equal proportion of women and men in the workforce and laws that bar overt gender discrimination and sexual harassment, though. Are women perceived as just as competent as men to hold the most prestigious jobs? Are women who reach the top tier of professional success just as likely as men to be admired and respected? Do young women express a broad range of professional aspirations? These questions serve as a barometer of how much progress society has made when it comes to professional equality, and how far we have to go. So these are the questions we posed to more than 4,000 high school and college students. Their answers indicate that there has indeed been substantial progress when it comes to gender equality in the professional world, including politics.

To start, we provided the high school and college students we surveyed with a list of several jobs. Some—such as doctor, lawyer, police officer, and president of the United States—are positions that have been historically held by men. Others—including teacher, nurse, and secretary—are jobs that women have been far more likely than men to occupy. We then asked a straightforward question: "For each of the jobs listed below, please tell us whether you think men or women would be better at the job, or whether men and women would do the job equally well." Across the board, whether in historically "male" or "female" positions, a majority of young people believed that women and men are equally capable (see Table 10.1). Given women's relatively recent entry into the legal and medical professions, it's remarkable that more than

TABLE 10.1   ARE WOMEN OR MEN BETTER SUITED FOR THE JOB?

	WOMEN AND MEN EQUALLY CAPABLE	WOMEN BETTER SUITED	MEN BETTER SUITED
Doctor	86%	5%	9%
Lawyer	83	5	12
U.S. Senator	82	4	14
Teacher	77	20	2
President of the United States	70	4	26
Nurse	62	37	1
Police Officer	56	2	43
Secretary	54	44	2

Responses based on a GfK survey of 4,229 high school and college students in October 2012.

eight out of 10 high school and college students expressed no doubts about women's suitability.

That's not to say, of course, that we find no vestiges of traditional attitudes about women's and men's professional strengths and weaknesses. Among those people who believed that either women or men would be better at a given job, the bias was always in a direction consistent with historic occupational segregation. This is particularly true of historically "female" jobs. More than one-third of young people thought, for example, that women were better suited than men to be nurses and secretaries. But we've seen substantial progress when it comes to women's perceived competence doing jobs traditionally held by men. This is true even for the most prestigious and competitive political positions.

Women's true equality in the workplace also requires that they are accepted and respected when they move into positions of authority and power. Accordingly, we asked the high school and college students whether they agreed or disagreed with a series of statements describing a hypothetical person who runs a company with 1,000 employees. Some of the statements had to do with the leader's effectiveness, while others pertained to personal background and characteristics. Before we asked these questions, we broke the sample into two.[20] Half were told that the head of the company they were evaluating was a man, and the other half were told that the company was run by a woman.

Figure 10.2 presents the results. The bars indicate the percentage of people who agreed that each statement applied to the hypothetical boss. Gray bars reflect responses from people who assessed a female boss; black bars represent responses from people who evaluated a male boss. In a nut-shell, nothing from our experiment suggests that women in leadership are viewed less favorably than men. In fact, women outperformed men when it came to perceptions of being an excellent leader and generating respect among employees. (This was the case for both male and female survey respondents.) There might still be a bit of gender stereotyping when consid-ering whether men or women are better suited for a position generally. But the young people we surveyed—regardless of their sex—didn't think twice about women's competence once they're serving in prestigious and powerful positions.

The one place where we do find gender differences has to do with assess-ments of the corporate leader's family life. The high school and college stu-dents we surveyed had the sense that a woman who runs a large company is less likely than a man in the same position to be married and have children. We don't want to make too much of this difference, though, because only a small subset of young people—less than one in six—thought it. And they didn't think that women were any worse than men at reconciling their career responsibilities with their family roles. But this perception is certainly con-sistent with a long-held and widespread belief that, for women, career success often comes at a price: giving up a "typical" family life.

FIGURE 10.2   YOUNG PEOPLE'S IMPRESSIONS OF FEMALE
                  AND MALE BOSSES

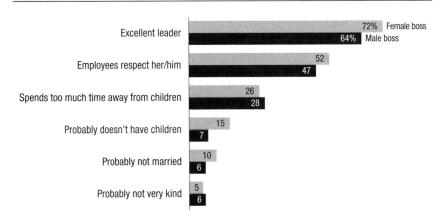

Bars indicate the percentage of respondents who thought that each statement described a typical female or male boss. Results are based on an experiment embedded into the GfK survey of high school and college students. We asked 2,121 people these questions about a female boss, and 2,159 people the same questions, but about a male boss.

Overall, these results represent a departure from previous research, much of which finds public discomfort with women holding top leadership roles. Indeed, research conducted by psychologists in the 1990s found that women were viewed more negatively and were judged more harshly when executing the typical responsibilities of leaders.[21] More recent research finds that women in positions of leadership are often considered just as effective as men, but are not viewed as favorably.[22] We don't need to look further than students' evaluations of their professors for evidence that today's young people sometimes still rate women in positions of authority more negatively than they do men.[23] An analysis of 14 million reviews on RateMyProfessor.com revealed that students are more likely to assess male professors as "brilliant," "knowledgeable," and "awesome" but to describe female professors as "bossy," "annoying," "beautiful," or "ugly."[24] It may be that the positive gender attitudes we uncovered in our questions about hypothetical bosses don't fully transfer when young people evaluate real leaders. There's no question, though, that they represent generational progress.

The ultimate test of professional gender equality, of course, is whether young women and men see a wide range of careers as open to them. We presented the high school and college students with a list of more than a dozen jobs—again, some historically "male" and others historically "female" (see Table 10.2). We then asked them to check off any—and as many—positions they might ever be interested in holding. Young women showed no hesitation expressing interest in many of the most respected, prestigious, and traditionally male-dominated professions. In fact, they were slightly more likely than young men to express interest in becoming a doctor, lawyer, or journalist. They were less likely than men to aspire to own a business or become a scientist, but the differences aren't very large.

We don't see a similar shift, though, when it comes to men's aspirations to pursue traditionally female-dominated jobs. Women were at least 50 percent more likely than men to report that they might want to work for a charitable cause, or be a teacher, nurse, or secretary. Survey responses about professions not listed in Table 10.2 reveal that men reported more interest in being a mechanic (12 percent), construction worker (10 percent), or plumber (5 percent) than a secretary or nurse. Gender differences also persist in what we consider two "fantasy jobs." Young men were more than three times as likely as young women to aspire to be a professional athlete (13 percent to 4 percent). Young women were twice as likely as young men to profess interest in being an artist (28 percent to 14 percent). These differences suggest that

TABLE 10.2   JOBS YOUNG PEOPLE ARE WILLING TO CONSIDER
FOR THE FUTURE

	WOMEN	MEN
Historically "Male" Jobs		
Business Owner	25%	31%
Doctor	20	14
Lawyer	15	14
Scientist	15	21
Journalist	15	10
Historically "Female" Jobs		
Teacher	32%	20
Nurse	22	4
Charity Work	22	11
Secretary	13	3
Salesperson	9	9

Results are based on a GfK survey of 2,139 female and 2,141 male high school and college students. Columns do not sum to 100% because respondents could choose as many jobs as they were open to considering. All gender differences are statistically significant except for lawyer and salesperson.

traditional gender socialization still affects many attitudes toward careers, although not the most prestigious, male-dominated professions from which women had long been excluded.

The occupational gender segregation that has dominated U.S. society may pose even greater challenges to women of color, as they are attempting to enter professions that have been devoid not only of women but also of racial minorities. For the most part, though, the results presented in Table 10.2 don't differ markedly across White, Black, and Latina women. And the handful of differences that do emerge don't give way to any particular pattern. Thirty-three percent of Black women, compared to 23 percent of White women, reported interest in owning a business. Black women (30 percent) were also more open than White women (17 percent) to the idea of becoming a doctor. The reverse was true for journalism and science—two other historically "male" professions; White women were more interested than Black women (by 6 and 7 percentage points, respectively).

Overall, the political and legal systems have made great strides establishing gender equality in the workplace. We're not all the way there yet, and debates over pay equity and sexual harassment will likely be on the radar screen for the foreseeable future. But explicit gender discrimination in the workplace is prohibited, legal recourse is available to employees who feel they suffered unfair treatment, and the environment working women faced in the 1960s is widely viewed as unacceptable. As laws and social norms that govern the workplace have changed, high school girls and college women have come to embrace the idea of entering historically male professions. Moreover, young women and men exhibit little reluctance when it comes to women's capabilities working in, or even leading, traditionally male fields. On the work front, young women are clearly "free to be."

BUSINESS OWNER, MOTHER, AND MAID: GENDER AND FAMILY ROLES IN THE MODERN ERA

Because political equality demands gender equity in both the professional and private spheres, the second dimension we must assess to determine where the United States is on the path to gender equality has to do with household dynamics and family arrangements. Up through the 1960s, part of the reason many women didn't even consider pursuing advanced degrees or top professional positions was because of the expectation that they prioritize their families. For most of human history, and still in many cultures around the world, it has been a given that women are the primary caretakers of the home and the children. It actually wasn't until 1975 that the U.S. Supreme Court discarded state laws that excused women from jury service on the grounds that it would interfere with their household responsibilities.[25] A woman's role as "wife and mother" was considered more important than her civic responsibility.

Norms have clearly changed in the last 50 years, as has the composition of a typical family. Most women are no longer expected to forgo their professional goals and ambitions to care for their spouses and children. And millions of households are run by single parents and same-sex couples. Yet the overwhelming majority of family units in the United States are still comprised of heterosexual couples with children.[26] In these families, women often find themselves balancing their careers and familial roles in a way that men don't. In families where two parents work, women take on a wider range of household tasks and perform them more often than men do.[27]

TABLE 10.3   YOUNG PEOPLE'S ATTITUDES ABOUT THE
WORK/LIFE BALANCE

	WOMEN	MEN
It will be most important to prioritize my career.	9%	13%
My career will be a little more important to me than family responsibilities.	5	8
I plan to balance my career and family responsibilities equally.	54	57
My family will be a little more important to me than my career.	19	12
It will be most important to prioritize my family.	15	10

Responses based on 2,116 female and 2,121 male high school and college students in an October 2012 GfK
national survey.

Little evidence suggests that this pattern will change dramatically anytime soon. Most of the young people we surveyed hoped to get married and
start a family. Roughly 80 percent of women and men said that getting married was an "important" or "very important" life goal; 74 percent of men and
79 percent of women felt the same way about having children. But even though
they want the same things in their personal lives, young women's and men's
priorities differ. We asked whether they thought that, once they have families and careers, they would prioritize their families, prioritize their careers,
or strike a balance between the two. Men were 50 percent more likely than
women (21 percent compared to 14 percent) to expect their career to be at
least a little more important than their family responsibilities (sum the top
two rows of Table 10.3). The opposite was true for women, 34 percent of whom
reported that their family responsibilities would likely take precedence over
their careers (just 22 percent of men felt the same way). Although more than
half the women and men planned to balance their career and family responsibilities equally—and that represents progress from previous generations—the
overall pattern is hardly egalitarian (see Chapter 8).

To assess young people's adherence to traditional gender roles, we also
asked five additional questions to get at whether they subscribed to conventional norms and expectations about women and men. Here, we uncovered
some evidence that traditional attitudes about women's and men's "proper"
roles persist, but also some evidence of a more progressive perspective.

Consider the top two questions presented in Figure 10.3. Nearly
three-quarters of women, compared to only about half of men, reported that
they plan to take time off from work to raise children. Moreover, a majority of

FIGURE 10.3   TRADITIONAL GENDER ROLES IN YOUNG WOMEN'S
AND MEN'S LIVES

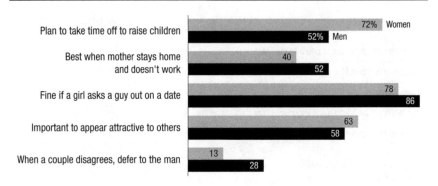

Bars indicate the percentage of male and female high school and college students who "agreed" or "strongly agreed" with each statement. Results are based on a GfK national survey. Gender differences are statistically significant in all comparisons except for the importance of appearing attractive to others.

young men still believe that it's better when a mother stays home and doesn't work. Women were less likely than men to subscribe to that view, but four in 10 still agreed with it.

When we move beyond parental roles, progress is more evident. An overwhelming majority of young people think it's "fine if a girl asks a guy out on a date" (in fact, men are even more likely than women to think so). Both women and men want to look attractive to people they hope to date. And there's little support for the idea that disagreements within a couple should be resolved by the woman deferring to the man. (Even though the overwhelming majority of young people don't hold this position, notice that nearly three out of every 10 men do. Men are more than twice as likely as women to fall into this category.) Overall, then, it's family roles that remain stickiest when it comes to movement toward gender equality beyond the professional sphere.

WHERE DO WE GO FROM HERE?

From 2007 to 2015, the popular television show *Mad Men* took viewers back to a 1960s New York City advertising agency. The series won praise for, among other things, its honest depiction of women in the workplace. Secretaries regularly endured lewd comments and harassment from their male superiors.

Women who tried to enter management were ridiculed and accused of sleeping their way to the top. And women who did manage to climb the corporate ladder—albeit very slowly—found themselves hitting one glass ceiling after the next.[28] Many of the workplace limitations, challenges, and expectations women faced in the 1960s have rapidly receded. Supervisors who pinch their secretaries on the bottom can now be fired for violating state and federal sexual harassment laws. Companies that pay women less than men can now face lawsuits and complaints filed with the Equal Employment Opportunity Commission (see Chapter 8). Compared to where we were just a few decades ago, we seem to be accelerating rapidly down the road to gender equality. Still, as we look to the future, three significant speed bumps slow the path to full political equality.

First, for all the advances women have made entering traditionally male-dominated fields, their integration into the top ranks of many of these professions has been slow going. And that's putting it lightly. Women account for only 20 percent of the partners in the nation's major law firms, compared to 17 percent a decade ago.[29] In 2016, only one of the 30 companies included in the Dow Jones industrial average had a female chief executive officer, and only 22 Fortune 500 companies had female CEOs.[30] Those numbers are no better than they were in 2005. Women also continue to hit career ceilings when they work at colleges and universities. Whereas women comprise more than half of all instructor positions (the least prestigious rank in academia), they represent less than a third of tenured full professors (the most prestigious rank).[31] Earning the degrees required to work in these fields is a necessary prerequisite to entering them, and on that dimension, progress has been significant. But we clearly have a long way to go before we achieve gender parity in the upper ranks of the professional sphere.

Part of the reason we see a gender gap in the highest levels of professional success has to do with the second speed bump: the lack of gender equity on the home front. The perpetuation of traditional family arrangements does more than simply contribute to inequity in the household. It also affects women's career choices and their ability to rise to the top of their chosen professions. A 2015 survey of working women with children found that 40 percent reported taking a significant amount of time off from work to care for their family.[32] A survey of corporate women found that the majority are not satisfied with having to balance their career and family responsibilities, so many take off several years to raise a family or pursue more "family friendly" work.[33] Indeed, trends in the fields of law, education, and business demonstrate that, for family reasons, many women either step away from their profession for a number of years or leave it altogether.[34] The tension between career and family remains a challenging balancing act for many women—a balancing act that most working men simply do not face.[35]

And that takes us to the final speed bump. Developing a legal framework or public policies to achieve equality in the household is nearly impossible. Feminist political theorists have argued that "family needs to be a just institution," one that "facilitate[s] the equal sharing by men and women of paid and unpaid work."[36] But as exhibited by the young people we surveyed, societal norms about family, motherhood, and the work/life balance are hard to change. Conversations about government policies that might shape the division of labor in a household are nonstarters, readily dismissed as social engineering of the family. The only policy area where there seems to be some sustained discussion is how to make child care more affordable. In the 2016 presidential election, Republican nominee Donald Trump advocated for a system of tax credits to subsidize child care.[37] Democratic nominee Hillary Clinton proposed subsidies for women who couldn't afford child care.[38] These proposals were noteworthy because they marked bipartisan recognition of the importance of expanding access to child care and, ostensibly, relieving the competing work and family responsibilities so many women face. Most analysts agree, however, that political debates about government spending and regulation make legislation that would ultimately provide subsidized child care unlikely. As a result, it will continue to fall on women to reconcile their dual roles. In fact, an entire multidisciplinary literature assesses the challenges the work/family balance poses for professional women and draws conclusions about the best ways for women with families to succeed.[39]

At the end of the day, it is clearly far more difficult to generate parity on the home front than in the workplace (the latter of which has been no small feat). But until we do, we'll never achieve complete political equality, as the professional and personal spheres are intertwined. The road to gender equality has certainly been paved since the 1960s, but the next generation will still encounter—and in some ways, even contribute to—several bumps that remain.

QUESTIONS FOR REFLECTION AND DISCUSSION

1. When you think about your career aspirations, do you think your sex hinders or helps you? Identify three jobs you think women have an advantage obtaining and three jobs where you think men have an edge. In comparing the lists, what conclusions can you draw about the workplace?

2. Throughout the last 50 years, women's integration into the workforce has not been matched by men taking on half the household and child care responsibilities. Are there any legal or policy changes that could lead to equality in the household? Or is the household division of labor outside the reach of what any public policy can address?

3. Societal attitudes toward working mothers have clearly changed. Is the same true when women with young children run for office? Go online and find some news coverage of the vice presidential candidacies of Geraldine Ferraro in 1984 and Sarah Palin in 2008. To what extent did the news media focus on each candidate's family and parental responsibilities?

4. Conduct an experiment about attitudes toward women and men in leadership. To do this, ask 10 fellow students to identify their five favorite and five least favorite professors. Ask them to provide a few adjectives for each professor. Make sure you note the sex of each professor. Compare the list of adjectives describing female professors to those describing men. Are there differences? If so, what types of differences?

5. The United States has never elected a female president, and typically, only about five states have female governors at any given time. To what degree do you think traditional gender role expectations about family and work explain women's political underrepresentation?

FOR FURTHER EXPLORATION

Freedman, Estelle. 2002. *No Turning Back*. New York: Ballantine Books.

Hidden Figures. 2016. Directed by Theodore Melfi. Atlanta, GA: Lavantine Films, Chernin Entertainment, and Fox 2000 Pictures.

Hirshman, Linda R. 2006. *Get to Work: A Manifesto for Women of the World*. New York: Viking.

Lawless, Jennifer L. 2014. "It's the Family, Stupid? Not Quite . . . How Traditional Gender Roles Do Not Affect Women's Political Ambition." *Governance Studies at Brookings*, Washington, DC: Brookings Institution.

Mad Men. 2007–2015. Los Angeles, CA: Lionsgate Television, Weiner Brothers, AMC.

Mr. Mom. 1983. Directed by Stan Dragoti. Los Angeles, CA: Aaron Spelling Productions.

Okin, Susan Moller. 1989. *Justice, Gender, and the Family*. New York: Basic Books.

Stone, Pamela. 2007. *Opting Out: Why Women Really Quit Careers and Head Home*. Berkeley: University of California.

Working Girl. 1988. Directed by Mike Nichols. New York, NY: Twentieth Century Fox.

ENDNOTES

CHAPTER 1: TRIUMPH AND DEFEAT

1. "Obama: Hillary Clinton Most Qualified Presidential Candidate Ever," *Chicago Tonight*, July 27, 2016, http://chicagotonight.wttw.com (accessed 12/17/16).

2. Lauren Carroll, "Rubio Says Hillary Clinton in Government Longer than Any Republican Running," *Politifact*, August 7, 2015, www.politifact.com (accessed 12/19/16).

3. "John and Abigail Adams," *PBS's American Experience*, www.pbs.org/wgbh/amex/adams/filmmore/ps_ladies.html (accessed 12/17/16).

4. For a detailed history of women's political involvement in U.S. history, see Evans, Sara M. 1997. *Born for Liberty: A History of Women in America*. New York: Free Press. For a discussion of how women's adherence to their "private sphere" roles served as an impetus for their participation in the temperance, moral reform, antislavery, and women's rights movements, see Alexander, Ruth M. 1988. "We Are Engaged as a Band of Sisters: Class and Domesticity in the Washingtonian Temperance Movement, 1840–1850." *Journal of American History* 75 (December): 763–85; and Ginzberg, Lori D. 1986. "Moral Suasion Is Moral Balderdash: Women, Politics, and Social Activism in the 1850s." *Journal of American History* 73(3): 601–22.

5. Friedan, Betty. 1963. *The Feminine Mystique*. New York: W. W. Norton & Company, p. 21.

6. This wasn't a new tactic; Alice Paul first drafted a similar ERA in 1923. She considered it the next logical step following suffrage. See "Equal Rights Amendment," *National Organization for Women*, http://now.org/resource/equal-rights-ammendment (accessed 12/17/16).

7. Just 35 state legislatures passed the ERA by the time of the 1982 deadline set by Congress. This was three short of the 38 required for ratification. For a detailed discussion of the history of the ERA and the political dynamics that prevented its ratification, see Mansbridge, Jane J. 1986. *Why We Lost the ERA*. Chicago: University of Chicago Press.

8. These women's quotes can all be found in Emily Crockett, "9 Prominent Feminists on What Hillary Clinton's Historic Candidacy Really Means," *Vox*, August 22, 2016, www.vox.com (accessed 12/17/16).

9. Suein Oh, "Hillary Clinton Fans Sport Pantsuits to the Polls," *ABC News*, November 8, 2016, http://abcnews.go.com (accessed 12/23/16).

10. Lucy Clarke-Billings, "Feminism Takes Massive Hit as Trump Celebrates Victory: Women's Group," *Newsweek*, November 9, 2016, www.newsweek.com (accessed 12/20/16).

11. "Women and Minorities React to Trump: 'I Feel Really Vulnerable'," *The 11th Hour with Brian Williams*, November 9, 2016, www.msnbc.com (accessed 12/17/16).

12. See Laura Geiser and Rozette Rago, "Women in Los Angeles React to Donald Trump's Election Victory," *Buzzfeed*, November 9, 2016, www.buzzfeed.com (accessed 12/17/16); and Mawra Eltagouri, Jodi S. Cohen, and Dawn Rhodes, "Some Illinois Women Worry about Message Trump Victory Sends," *Chicago Tribune*, November 9, 2016, www.chicagotribune.com (accessed 12/17/16).

13. Kristen Bellstrom, "Gloria Steinem: After Trump's Election, the U.S. Is Like a Victim of Domestic Abuse," *Fortune*, November 17, 2016, http://fortune.com (accessed 12/17/16).

14. Citizens are more ambivalent, in fact, than when asked to assess the other politically relevant groups included in the 2016 American National Election Study battery. More specifically, people's ratings for scientists (73), Whites (71), Blacks (67), Hispanics (66), the police (66), and gays and lesbians (57) were all significantly "warmer." Their attitudes toward Muslims (45) were a bit "cooler."

15. Emily Swanson, "Poll: Few Identify as Feminists, but Most Believe in Equality of the Sexes," *Huffington Post*, August 16, 2013, www.huffingtonpost.com (accessed 12/20/16).

16. See, for instance, Roth, Benita. 2003. *Separate Roads to Feminism: Black, Chicana, and White Feminist Movements in America's Second Wave*. New York: Cambridge University Press.

17. Smith, Barbara. 2000. *Home Girls: A Black Feminist Anthology*. New Brunswick, NJ: Rutgers University Press.

18. Similar results emerged from the March 2015 *Vox*/PerryUndem poll. Feminist self-identification was just 18 percent. But when the same people were asked if

they believe in "equality for women," 85 percent said yes. And when they were asked if they believe in "social, political, legal, and economic equality between the sexes," 78 percent said they did. The results from the 2013 *HuffPost/YouGov* poll revealed the same thing. Only 20 percent of people considered themselves feminists, but 82 percent of the same people believed that "women and men should be social, political, and economic equals."

19. See, for example, Roy, Robin E., Kristin S. Weibust, and Carol T. Miller. 2007. "Effects of Stereotypes about Feminists on Feminist Self-Identification." *Psychology of Women Quarterly* 31(2):146–56; Hymowitz, Kay S. 2002. "The End of Herstory." *City Journal* 12(3): 52–63; Douglas, Susan J. 1994. *Where the Girls Are: Growing Up Female with the Mass Media.* New York: Times Books; and Faludi, Susan. 1991. *Backlash: The Undeclared War against American Women.* New York: Crown.

20. Barakso, Maryann, and Brian Schaffner. 2006. "Winning Coverage: News Media Portrayals of the Women's Movement, 1969–2004." *Harvard International Journal of Press/Politics* 11(4): 22–44.

21. Jill Filipovic, "Why Don't More People Call Themselves Feminists?" *Cosmopolitan*, July 19, 2014, www.cosmopolitan.com (accessed 12/20/16).

22. "Here's Donald Trump's Presidential Announcement Speech," *Time*, June 16, 2015, http://time.com (accessed 12/20/16).

23. Deborah Orin, "Trump Toyz with Prez Run," *New York Post*, July 12, 1999, http://nypost.com (accessed 12/20/16).

24. Elisha Fieldstadt, "Donald Trump Consistently Made Lewd Comments on 'The Howard Stern Show'," *NBC News*, October 8, 2016, www.nbcnews.com (accessed 12/20/16).

25. Aaron Blake, "The First Trump-Clinton Presidential Debate Transcript, Annotated," *Washington Post*, September 26, 2016, www.washingtonpost.com (accessed 12/23/16).

26. Laura Bassett and Jonathan Cohn, "Female Trump Supporters Don't Really Care about His Sexism," *Huffington Post*, October 4, 2016, www.huffingtonpost.com (accessed 12/22/16).

27. *Fox News Sunday*, May 15, 2016, www.youtube.com/watch?v=z8YZY45sn2I (accessed 12/22/2016).

28. German Lopez, "Study: Racism and Sexism Predict Support for Trump Much More than Economic Dissatisfaction," *Vox*, January 4, 2017, www.vox.com (accessed 3/2/17).

29. Gregory Krieg, "White Males Dominate Trump's Top Cabinet Posts," *CNN.com*, December 15, 2016, www.cnn.com (accessed 12/23/16).

30. Russell Berman, "The Donald Trump Cabinet Tracker?" *The Atlantic*, March 1, 2017, www.theatlantic.com (accessed 3/2/17).

31. Matt Flegenheimer and Maggie Haberman, "Donald Trump, Abortion Foe, Eyes 'Punishment' for Women, Then Recants," *New York Times*, March 30, 2016, www.nytimes.com (accessed 12/23/16).

32. Charlotte Alter, "Here's What Donald Trump Thinks about Women's Issues," *Time*, August 5, 2016, http://time.com (accessed 12/24/16).

33. Jenna Johnson, "Donald Trump Says Companies Can 'Very Easily' Offer Childcare to Employees," *Washington Post*, November 19, 2015, www.washingtonpost.com (accessed 12/24/16).

34. Jill Filipovic, "What Does President Trump Mean for Feminists?" *Washington Post*, November 9, 2016, www.washingtonpost.com (accessed 12/23/16).

35. Emily Bazelon, "Bullying in the Age of Trump," *New York Times*, November 16, 2016, www.nytimes.com (accessed 12/23/16).

36. Katherine Stewart, "Donald Trump Has Unleashed a New Wave of Bullying in Schools," *The Nation*, November 7, 2016, www.thenation.com (accessed 12/23/16).

37. Katie Rogers, "Amid Division, a March in Washington Seeks to Bring Women Together," *New York Times*, November 18, 2016, www.nytimes.com (accessed 12/23/16).

38. Kaveh Waddell, "The Exhausting Work of Tallying America's Largest Protest," *The Atlantic*, January 23, 2017, www.theatlantic.com (accessed 3/2/17).

39. Niraj Chokshi, "Nonprofits Opposed to Trump's Ideology See a Surge in Donations," *New York Times*, November 17, 2016, www.nytimes.com (accessed 12/23/16).

40. Nicole Gaudiano, "Women Disappointed in 2016 Election Results Get Ready to Run," *USA Today*, November 20, 2016, www.usatoday.com (accessed 12/23/16).

41. Mahita Gajanan, "More than 4,500 Women Have Signed Up to Run for Office Since the Election," *Time*, December 8, 2016, http://time.com (accessed 12/23/16).

42. Clare Foran, "Will Hillary Clinton's Defeat Set Back Women in Politics?" *The Atlantic*, November 27, 2016, www.theatlantic.com (accessed 12/23/16). See also Hayes, Danny, and Jennifer L. Lawless. 2016. *Women on the Run: Gender, Media, and Political Campaigns in a Polarized Era*. New York: Cambridge University Press.

43. Political scientists have found, for example, that anger can motivate people to vote and engage in other forms of political activism (Valentino, Nicholas A., Ted Brader, Eric W. Groenendyk, Krysha Gregorowicz, and Vincent L. Hutchings. 2011. "Election Night's Alright for Fighting: The Role of Emotions in Political Participation." *Journal of Politics* 73[1]:156–70; see also Albertson, Bethany, and Shana Kushner Gadarian. 2015. *Anxious Politics: Democratic Citizenship in a Threatening World*. New York: Cambridge University Press).

44. Leigh Hornbeck, "Why Would Feminists Vote for Donald Trump?" *Times Union*, December 20, 2016, www.timesunion.com (accessed 12/23/16).

CHAPTER 2: FALLING FURTHER BEHIND

1. For current and historical data on women's representation, see the Center for American Women and Politics website, www.cawp.rutgers.edu (accessed 4/4/16).

2. Men and women have performed equally well in elections since the 1980s. Female incumbents are reelected at comparable rates to male incumbents. The same is true of challengers. And women seeking open seats have just as good a shot at winning as do the men against whom they compete. For a review of the literature about women's electoral fortunes over time, see Lawless, Jennifer L., and Richard L. Fox. 2010. *It Still Takes a Candidate: Why Women Don't Run for Office*. New York: Cambridge University Press; and Palmer, Barbara, and Dennis Simon. 2008. *Breaking the Political Glass Ceiling: Women and Congressional Elections*, 2nd edition. New York: Routledge.

3. Information on various types of quotas, thresholds, and countries' adoption of them is available through the QuotaProject: A Global Database of Quotas for Women, www.quotaproject.org/ (accessed 4/5/16).

4. When they examine variation in women's representation more systematically, political scientists conclude that nations with quotas tend to see a greater proportion of women in politics than nations without them. See, for example, Dahlerup, Drude. 2012. *The Impact of Gender Quotas*. New York: Oxford University Press; Krook, Mona Lena. 2009. *Quotas for Women in Politics: Gender and Candidate Selection Reform Worldwide*. New York: Oxford University Press; McDonagh, Eileen. 2010. "It Takes a State: A Policy Feedback Model of Women's Political Representation." *Perspectives on Politics* 8(1):69–91. Even without quotas, though, democracies tend to see a greater proportion of women in politics when they use proportional party list electoral systems (see Rosen, Jennifer. 2013. "The Effects of Political Institutions on Women's Political Representation: A Comparative Analysis of 168 Countries from 1992 to 2010." *Political Research Quarterly* 66[2]: 306–21; Tremblay, Marion. 2012. *Women and Legislative Representation: Electoral Systems, Political Parties, and Sex Quotas*. Basingstoke: Palgrave Macmillan).

5. In Washington, California, and Louisiana, all candidates—regardless of party—compete in the same primary election. The top two vote-getters advance to the general election, even if they're of the same party.

6. Jacobson, Gary C., and Jamie L. Carson. 2015. *The Politics of Congressional Elections*, 9th edition. New York: Roman and Littlefield.

7. See, for example, Freidenvall, Lenita, and Drude Dahlerup. 2013. "Electoral Gender Quota Systems and Their Implementation in Europe." *European Parliament Think Tank*, www.europarl.europa.eu/thinktank/en/document.html?reference=IPOL-FEMM_NT(2013)493011 (accessed 12/30/16).

8. Htun, Mala. 2016. *Inclusion without Representation in Latin America: Gender Quotas and Ethnic Reservations.* New York: Cambridge University Press.

9. Freedman, Estelle. 2002. *No Turning Back.* New York: Ballantine Books; Stone, Pamela. 2007. *Opting Out: Why Women Really Quit Careers and Head Home.* Berkeley: University of California.

10. Duerst-Lahti, Georgia. 2006. "Presidential Elections: Gendered Space and the Case of 2004." In Susan J. Carroll and Richard L. Fox (eds.), *Gender and Elections: Shaping the Future of American Politics.* New York: Cambridge University Press; Duerst-Lahti, Georgia, and Rita Mae Kelly. 1995. *Gender, Power, Leadership and Governance.* Ann Arbor: University of Michigan Press; Enloe, Cynthia. 2004. *The Curious Feminist.* Berkeley: University of California Press.

11. For a discussion of how cultural attitudes toward women as political leaders continue to leave this kind of gendered imprint, see Enloe, Cynthia. 2004. *The Curious Feminist.* Berkeley: University of California Press; Flammang, Janet. 1997. *Women's Political Voice: How Women Are Transforming the Practice and Study of Politics.* Philadelphia: Temple University Press.

12. Lawless, Jennifer L., and Richard L. Fox. 2010. *It Still Takes a Candidate: Why Women Don't Run for Office.* New York: Cambridge University Press; and Lawless, Jennifer L., and Richard L. Fox. 2012. *Men Rule: The Continued Under-Representation of Women in U.S. Politics.* Washington, DC: Women & Politics Institute.

13. For a discussion of the intersection of race and gender in political recruitment, which strongly affects political ambition, see Lawless, Jennifer L. 2012. *Becoming a Candidate: Political Ambition and the Decision to Run for Office.* New York: Cambridge University Press.

14. Public Policy Polling, "Congress Less Popular than Cockroaches, Traffic Jams," January 8, 2013, www.publicpolicypolling.com (accessed 4/5/16).

15. "Women and Leadership." *Pew Research Center*, January 14, 2015, www.pewsocialtrends.org (accessed 4/6/16).

16. Lauren Rankin, "A Libertarian Man's Surprising Goal: Gender Quotas!" *Salon.com*, December 8, 2013, www.salon.com (accessed 4/3/16).

17. U.S. Senate, "Measures Proposed to Amend the Constitution," www.senate.gov (accessed 12/30/16).

18. Paul Herrnson and Kathleen Weldon, "The Public and Proposed Constitutional Amendments: We Love You, You're Perfect, Now Change," *Huffington Post*, September 15, 2014, www.huffingtonpost.com (accessed 12/30/16).

19. Theriault, Sean M. 2005. *The Power of the People: Congressional Competition, Public Attention, and Voter Retribution.* Columbus: Ohio State University Press.

20. The 1992 5–4 U.S. Supreme Court decision in *U.S. v. Thornton* ruled that the power granted to each House of Congress to judge the "Qualifications of its own Members," Art. I, §5, cl. 1, does not include the power to alter or add to the qualifications set forth in the Constitution's text.

21. Twenty-one states have passed legislative term limits at some point, but since the late 1990s, six states have repealed them on the grounds that they are unconstitutional. For more, see the National Conference of State Legislatures website: www.ncsl.org (accessed 4/4/16).

22. Kousser, Thad. 2005. *Term Limits and the Dismantling of State Legislative Professionalism*. New York: Cambridge University Press.

CHAPTER 3: GIRL POWER ISN'T POLITICAL POWER

1. Partisanship is a much more powerful force in shaping policy than whether a legislator is a man or a woman, but the policy-making process is no doubt affected by gender diversity among office holders. For an overview of this body of research, see Lawless, Jennifer L. 2015. "Female Candidates and Legislators." *Annual Review of Political Science* 18: 349–66; and Mansbridge, Jane. 1999. "Should Blacks Represent Blacks and Women Represent Women? A Contingent 'Yes.'" *Journal of Politics* 61(3): 628–57.

2. Leila Butt, "Women's Economic Opportunity," *The Economist*, June 2010, http://graphics.eiu.com (accessed 2/21/16).

3. Amber Phillips, "One Election Bright Spot for Democrats: Women of Color," *Washington Post*, November 10, 2016, www.washingtonpost.com (accessed 1/6/17).

4. Clinton, Bill. 2004. *My Life*. New York: Alfred A. Knopf, p. 63.

5. Throughout the last 20 years, researchers have tracked high school and college students' professional aspirations with the careers they ultimately pursue. These studies reveal a strong correlation between specific job aspirations at age 16 with those attained by age 35. For a recent study in this vein, see Schoon, Ingrid, and Elzbieta Polek. 2011. "Teenage Career Aspirations and Adult Career Attainment: The Role of Gender, Social Background and General Cognitive Ability." *International Journal of Behavioral Development* 35(3): 210–7.

6. All statistically significant differences meet the $p < .05$ threshold.

7. Our survey, conducted by GfK, classified all respondents as women and men. In no case did a survey respondent skip the question or indicate that a non-binary gender classification was preferred.

8. Jeffrey M. Jones, "Atheists, Muslims See Most Bias as Presidential Candidates," *Gallup*, June 21, 2012, www.gallup.com (accessed 2/21/16).

9. For a discussion of how cultural attitudes toward women as political leaders continue to leave this kind of gendered imprint, see Enloe, Cynthia. 2004. *The Curious Feminist.* Berkeley: University of California Press; and Flammang, Janet. 1997. *Women's Political Voice: How Women Are Transforming the Practice and Study of Politics.* Philadelphia: Temple University Press.

10. Pajares, Frank. 2002. "Gender and Perceived Self-Efficacy in Self-Regulated Learning." *Theory into Practice* 41(2): 116–25; Wigfield, Allan, Jacquelynne S. Eccles, and Paul R. Pintrich. 1996. "Development between the Ages of 11 and 25." In D. C. Berliner and R. C. Calfee (eds.), *Handbook of Educational Psychology.* New York: Macmillan.

11. "Report of the Steering Committee on Undergraduate Women's Leadership," Princeton University, March 2011, www.princeton.edu/reports/2011/leadership/documents/SCUWL_Report_Final.pdf (accessed 2/22/16).

12. Liz Dannerlein, "Study: Females Lose Self-Confidence throughout College," *USA Today,* September 26, 2013, www.usatoday.com (accessed 2/24/16).

13. In 2001 and 2011, we surveyed thousands of male and female "potential candidates"—lawyers, business leaders, educators, and political activists, all of whom were well-situated to pursue a political candidacy. We found that women were less likely than men ever to have considered running for office; and even when they had considered a candidacy, women were less likely than men actually to seek an elected position. The two largest contributors to this gender gap in political ambition were gender differences in political recruitment and in perceptions of being "qualified." See Lawless, Jennifer L., and Richard L. Fox. 2010. *It Still Takes a Candidate: Why Women Don't Run for Office.* New York: Cambridge University Press; and Lawless, Jennifer L., and Richard L. Fox. 2012. *Men Rule: The Continued Under-Representation of Women in U.S. Politics.* Washington, DC: Women & Politics Institute.

14. For details about IGNITE's programs and outcomes, visit the organization's website: http://ignitenational.org (accessed 12/28/16).

15. For details about Running Start, visit the organization's website: http://running startonline.org (accessed 12/28/16).

CHAPTER 4: INTO THE FRYING PAN

1. Alana Horowitz Satlin, "MSNBC Interrupts Hillary Clinton's Speech to Complain about Her Voice," *Huffington Post,* March 7, 2016, www.huffingtonpost.com (accessed 4/23/16).

2. "Woodward: Clinton Has to Get Off Screaming Stuff," *Morning Joe,* February 3, 2016, www.msnbc.com (accessed 4/23/16).

3. Alana Horowitz Satlin, "MSNBC Interrupts Hillary Clinton's Speech to Complain about Her Voice," *Huffington Post*, March 7, 2016.

4. Peggy Noonan, "The High Cost of a Bad Reputation," *Wall Street Journal*, January 14, 2016, www.wsj.com (accessed 4/23/16).

5. Eric Bradner, "Sanders: I Am Not Shouting at Hillary Clinton," *CNN.com*, October 25, 2015, www.cnn.com (accessed 4/23/16).

6. "Hannity" transcript, *Fox News*, February 3, 2016, www.foxnews.com/transcript/2016/02/03/rubio-rejects-establishment-label-trump-supporter-cruz-campaign-acted (accessed 4/23/16).

7. Willa Frej, "Bob Woodward's Problems with Hillary Clinton Definitely Aren't Sexist, No Sir," *Huffington Post*, February 2, 2016, www.huffingtonpost.com (accessed 4/23/16).

8. A Google search (conducted on January 5, 2017) of "Donald Trump yells" turned up 18,200 hits, more than nine times as many as "Hillary Clinton yells." Clinton's 1,960 hits also paled in comparison to the 5,860 results from a "Bernie Sanders yells" search.

9. Lawless, Jennifer L., and Richard L. Fox. 2010. *It Still Takes a Candidate: Why Women Don't Run for Office*. New York: Cambridge University Press.

10. Hayes, Danny, and Jennifer L. Lawless. 2016. *Women on the Run: Gender, Media, and Political Campaigns in a Polarized Era*. New York: Cambridge University Press, Chapter 1.

11. See Lawless, Jennifer L., and Richard L. Fox. 2012. *Men Rule: The Continued Under-Representation of Women in U.S. Politics*. Washington, DC: Women & Politics Institute. More than half the female potential candidates we surveyed did not believe that women who run for office fare as well as men. Seven out of 10 doubted that women can raise as much money as men. And the majority thought that the local and congressional election landscapes they'd have to navigate were "highly competitive." This last point is particularly telling because male potential candidates who lived in the same places and were exposed to the same political environments were about 25 percent less likely than women to assess the electoral terrain this way.

12. For a review of this research, see Hayes, Danny, and Jennifer L. Lawless. 2016. *Women on the Run: Gender, Media, and Political Campaigns in a Polarized Era*. New York: Cambridge University Press.

13. See Duerst-Lahti, Georgia. 2006. "Presidential Elections: Gendered Space and the Case of 2004." In Susan J. Carroll and Richard L. Fox (eds.), *Gender and Elections: Shaping the Future of American Politics*. New York: Cambridge University Press; and Miller, Melissa K., and Jeffrey S. Peake. 2013. "Press Effects, Public Opinion, and Gender: Coverage of Sarah Palin's Vice-Presidential Campaign." *International Journal of Press/Politics* 18(4): 482–507.

14. Bystrom, Dianne G., Mary Christine Banwart, Lynda Lee Kaid, and Terry A. Robertson. 2004. *Gender and Candidate Communication.* New York: Routledge; Kahn, Kim Fridkin. 1996. *The Political Consequences of Being a Woman.* New York: Columbia University Press.

15. See, for example, Kittilson, Miki Caul, and Kim Fridkin. 2008. "Gender, Candidate Portrayals, and Election Campaigns: A Comparative Perspective." *Politics & Gender* 4(3): 371–92; Lawless, Jennifer L. 2004. "Women, War, and Winning Elections: Gender Stereotyping in the Post September 11th Era." *Political Research Quarterly* 57(3): 479–90; Mo, Cecilia Hyunjung. 2015. "The Consequences of Explicit and Implicit Gender Attitudes and Candidate Quality in the Calculations of Voters." *Political Behavior* 37(2): 357–95.

16. Graber, Doris A. 2010. *Mass Media and American Politics*, 8th edition. Washington, DC: Congressional Quarterly Press.

17. We rely on the 2014 news data collected by Danny Hayes and Jennifer L. Lawless and presented in Chapter 4 of *Women on the Run: Gender, Media, and Political Campaigns in a Polarized Era.* New York: Cambridge University Press.

18. A content analysis of a sample of congressional races uncovers a similar pattern. See Ward, Orlanda. 2016. "Seeing Double: Race, Gender, and Coverage of Minority Women's Campaigns for the U.S. House of Representatives." *Politics & Gender* 12(3): 317–43.

19. Hayes, Danny, and Jennifer L. Lawless. 2015. "A Non-Gendered Lens? Media, Voters, and Female Candidates in Contemporary Congressional Elections." *Perspectives on Politics* 13(1): 95–118.

20. See Hayes, Danny, and Jennifer L. Lawless. 2016. *Women on the Run: Gender, Media, and Political Campaigns in a Polarized Era.* New York: Cambridge University Press.

21. Bruni, Frank. 2002. *Ambling into History: The Unlikely Odyssey of George W. Bush.* New York: Harper Collins; Graber, Doris A., and Johanna Dunaway. 2014. *Mass Media and American Politics*, 9th edition. Washington, DC: Congressional Quarterly Press; Hayes, Danny, and Jennifer L. Lawless. 2015. "As Local News Goes, So Goes Citizen Engagement: Media, Knowledge, and Participation in U.S. House Elections." *Journal of Politics* 77(2): 447–62.

22. For evidence of gender stereotyping in the 1990s and early 2000s, see Huddy, Leonie, and Nayda Terkildsen. 1993. "Gender Stereotypes and the Perception of Male and Female Candidates." *American Journal of Political Science* 37(1): 119–47; Lawless, Jennifer L. 2004. "Women, War, and Winning Elections: Gender Stereotyping in the Post September 11th Era." *Political Research Quarterly* 57(3): 479–90.

23. Jacobson, Gary. 2015. "It's Nothing Personal: The Decline of the Incumbency Advantage in U.S. House Elections." *Journal of Politics* 77(3): 861–73.

24. Bartels, Larry M. 2002. "Beyond the Running Tally: Partisan Bias in Political Perceptions." *Political Behavior* 24(2): 117–50; Cohen, Geoffrey L. 2003. "Party over Policy: The Dominating Impact of Group Influence on Political Beliefs." *Journal of Personality and Social Psychology* 85(5): 808–22; Sides, John, and Lynn Vavreck. 2013. *The Gamble: Choice and Chance in the 2012 Presidential Election.* Princeton: Princeton University Press.

25. Githens, Marianne, and Jewel L. Prestage. 1977. *A Portrait of Marginality: The Political Behavior of the American Woman.* New York: Longman; Kirkpatrick, Jeanne J. 1974. *Political Woman.* New York: Basic Books.

26. Boxer, Barbara. 1994. *Politics and the New Revolution of Women in America.* Washington, DC: National Press Books; Schroeder, Patricia. 1998. *Twenty-Four Years of Housework … and the Place Is Still a Mess.* Kansas City: Andrews McMeel.

27. Barbara Burrell. 1994. *A Woman's Place Is in the House.* Ann Arbor: University of Michigan Press.

28. For evidence of gender-neutral outcomes in congressional primaries, see Burrell, Barbara. 1992. "Women Candidates in Open Seat Primaries for the U.S. House of Representatives, 1968–1990." *Legislative Studies Quarterly* 17(4): 493–508; Lawless, Jennifer L., and Kathryn Pearson. 2008. "The Primary Reason for Women's Under-Representation: Re-Evaluating the Conventional Wisdom." *Journal of Politics* 70(1): 67–82. For more on women's and men's performance in general elections, see Burrell, Barbara. 2014. *Gender in Campaigns for the U.S. House of Representatives.* Ann Arbor: University of Michigan Press; Dolan, Kathleen. 2004. *Voting for Women: How the Public Evaluates Women Candidates.* Boulder: Westview Press.

29. "House Election Results: GOP Keeps Control," *New York Times,* www.nytimes.com/elections/results/house (accessed 1/5/17).

30. Russ Choma, "Money Won on Tuesday, but Rules of the Game Changed," *OpenSecrets.org,* November 5, 2014, www.opensecrets.org (accessed 4/26/16).

31. Paul Farhi, "Why Does Bernie Sanders Dress Like That? Because He Can," *Washington Post,* October 13, 2015, www.washingtonpost.com (accessed 1/4/17).

32. "Is the Political Media Biased against Women?" *Politico,* June 26, 2012, www.politico.com (accessed 1/4/17).

33. "Trump 'Not Responsible' for Tweet," *TeaParty.org,* April 18, 2015, www.teaparty.org (accessed 5/16/16).

34. Paul Solotaroff, "Trump Seriously: On the Trail with the GOP's Tough Guy," *Rolling Stone,* September 9, 2015, www.rollingstone.com (accessed 5/16/16).

35. Ruth Sherlock, "Carly Fiorina Faces Down Donald Trump over Sexist Remarks in Republican Debate," *The Telegraph,* September 17, 2015, www.telegraph.co.uk (accessed 5/16/16).

36. Alan Rappeport, "Donald Trump Keeps Playing 'Woman's Card' against Hillary Clinton," *New York Times*, April 27, 2016, www.nytimes.com (accessed 5/16/16).

37. Sandy Fitzgerald, "Trump: Hillary Wouldn't Run for City Council without 'Woman Card'," *Newsmax*, April 28, 2016, www.newsmax.com (accessed 5/16/16).

38. Claire Cohen, "Donald Trump Is Sexist and He Doesn't Care. Period," *The Telegraph*, August 8, 2015, www.telegraph.co.uk (accessed 5/16/16).

39. Ben Cohen, "Donald Trump Is a Sexist Monster and Republicans Who Cheer Him Are Pigs," *The Daily Banter*, August 6, 2015, http://thedailybanter.com (accessed 5/16/16).

40. Dylan Byers, "Fox News Hits Donald Trump for 'Sexist Verbal Assaults' on Megyn Kelly," *CNN.com*, March 18, 2016, http://money.cnn.com (accessed 5/16/16).

41. Dylan Matthews, "Read Every Horrible Thing Donald Trump Has Said about Women and Tell Me He's Not a Sexist," *Vox*, May 16, 2016, www.vox.com (accessed 5/17/16).

CHAPTER 5: SHOW ME THE MONEY

1. Sara Fischer, "White House Stumbles Explaining Soap Opera Producer as Ambassador," *CNN.com*, December 3, 2014, www.cnn.com (accessed 6/23/16).

2. Tamara Keith, "When Big Money Leads to Diplomatic Posts," *NPR*, December 3, 2014, www.npr.org (accessed 6/20/16).

3. "Noah Mamet Nominated as U.S. Ambassador," *Buenos Aires Herald*, August 1, 2013, www.buenosairesherald.com (accessed 6/20/16).

4. "Obama Fundraiser Noah Mamet Appointed U.S. Envoy to Argentina," *Haaretz*, December 3, 2014, www.haaretz.com (accessed 6/20/16).

5. Samantha Lachman, "Obama Nominee for Ambassador to Argentina Has Never Actually Been There," *Huffington Post*, February 7, 2014, www.huffingtonpost.com (accessed 6/7/17).

6. Andy Kroll, "The White House Is for Sale under Barack Obama, Too," *Mother Jones*, March 12, 2013, www.motherjones.com (accessed 6/20/16).

7. Alice Baghdjian, "Marc Rich, 'King of Oil,' Pardoned by Clinton, Dies at 78," *Reuters*, June 26, 2013, www.reuters.com (accessed 6/20/16).

8. Peter Schweizer, "Bill Clinton's Pardon of Fugitive Marc Rich Continues to Pay Big," *New York Post*, January 17, 2016, http://nypost.com (accessed 6/20/16).

9. Issac Arnsdorf, "Trump Rewards Big Donors with Jobs and Access," *Politico*, December 27, 2016, www.politico.com (accessed 1/1/17).

10. Brian Greene, "Rod Blagojevich Begins 14 Year Prison Sentence," *U.S. News & World Report*, March 15, 2012, www.usnews.com (accessed 6/20/16).

11. Bill Chappell, "Former Rep. 'Duke' Cunningham Freed after Bribery Sentence," *NPR*, June 4, 2013, www.npr.org (accessed 6/20/16).

12. West, Darrell M. 2014. *Billionaires: Reflections on the Upper Crust.* Washington, DC: Brookings Institution Press.

13. Meyer, Jane. 2016. *Dark Money: The Hidden History of the Billionaires behind the Rise of the Radical Right.* New York: Doubleday.

14. "Americans' Views on Money in Politics," *New York Times*/CBS News Poll, June 2, 2015, www.nytimes.com (accessed 6/20/16).

15. See, for example, Ansolabehere, Stephen, John M. de Figueiredo, and James M. Snyder. 2003. "Why Is There So Little Money in U.S. Politics?" *Journal of Economic Perspectives* 17: 105–30. A recent study of state legislators, however, does find that buying influence is prevalent, though it varies from state to state (Powell, Lynda W. 2012. *The Influence of Campaign Contributions in State Legislatures.* Ann Arbor: University of Michigan Press).

16. Kalla, Joshua, and David E. Broockman. 2015. "Campaign Contributions Facilitate Access to Congressional Officials: A Randomized Field Experiment." *American Journal of Political Science* 60(3): 545–58.

17. Epstein, David, and Peter Zemsky. 1995. "Money Talks: Deterring Quality Challengers in Congressional Elections." *American Political Science Review* 89(2): 295–308; Gerber, Alan. 1998. "Estimating the Effect of Campaign Spending on Senate Election Outcomes Using Instrumental Variables." *American Political Science Review* 92(2): 401–11.

18. Mark Uhlig, "Jesse Unruh, a California Political Power, Dies," *New York Times*, August 6, 1987, www.nytimes.com (accessed 6/23/16).

19. Lynn Vavreck, "Why Fundraising Is Important, Even If You Are Trump," *New York Times*, September 3, 2015, www.nytimes.com (accessed 1/3/17).

20. Philip Bump, "Bernie Sanders Keeps Saying His Average Donation is $27, but His Own Numbers Contradict That," *Washington Post*, April 18, 2016, www.washingtonpost.com (accessed 1/6/17).

21. "Contributions." *Federal Election Commission*, www.fec.gov/pages/brochures/contrib.shtml (accessed 6/22/16).

22. Aaron Smith and Maeve Duggan, "Presidential Campaign Donations in the Digital Age," *Pew Research Center*, October 25, 2102, www.pewinternet.org (accessed 6/26/16).

23. Josh Dunbar, "The 'Citizens United' Decision and Why It Matters," *Center for Public Integrity*, October 18, 2012, www.publicintegrity.org (accessed 6/23/16).

24. Doyle McManus, "For the GOP, It's the Billionaires' Primary," *Los Angeles Times*, April 21, 2015, www.latimes.com (accessed 6/19/16).

25. Michael Isikoff, "Millions at Stake, the 'Adelson Primary' Is Neck and Neck," *Yahoo News*, December 2, 2015, www.yahoo.com (accessed 6/19/16).

26. "'Forbes 400 List of Wealthiest Americans Only 13 Percent Women," *New York Times*, September 30, 2015, http://nytlive.nytimes.com (accessed 6/19/16).

27. "Top Individual Contributors." *OpenSecrets.org*, December 9, 2016, www.opensecrets.org (accessed 1/3/17).

28. Elizabeth Winkler, "Women's Political Donations Are Rising Fast, but Men Are Still Way Out-Donating Them," *Quartz.com*, September 23, 2016, http://qz.com (accessed 1/3/17).

29. Will Tucker, "Clinton Raises Historic Share—and Amount—of Campaign Cash from Women," *OpenSecrets.org*, June 9, 2016, www.opensecrets.org (accessed 6/25/16).

30. Crespin, Michael H., and Janna L. Deitz. 2010. "If You Can't Join 'Em, Beat 'Em: The Gender Gap in Individual Donations to Congressional Candidates." *Political Research Quarterly* 63(3): 581–93; Francia, Peter L. 2001. "Early Fundraising by Nonincumbent Female Congressional Candidates." *Women & Politics* 23(1-2): 7–20; Hannagan, Rebecca J., Jaimie P. Pimlott, and Levente Littvay. 2010. "Does an EMILY's List Endorsement Predict Electoral Success, or Does EMILY Pick the Winners?" *PS: Political Science & Politics* 43(3): 503–8.

31. Bonica, Adam. "Database on Ideology, Money in Politics, and Elections." Public version 1.0, http://data.stanford.edu/dime (accessed 6/24/16).

32. See Burrell, Barbara. 1994. *A Woman's Place Is in the House*. Ann Arbor: University of Michigan Press; Thomas, Sue, and Clyde Wilcox (eds.). 2014. *Women and Elective Office: Past, Present, and Future*, 3rd edition. New York: Oxford University Press; and Uhlaner, Carole, and Kay Lehman Schlozman. 1986. "Candidate Gender and Congressional Campaign Receipts." *Journal of Politics* 48(1): 30–50.

33. If women constituted an even greater share of the donor pool, then female candidates would likely see their fundraising numbers surpass men's and they might outperform the men against whom they compete.

34. Public version 1.0, http://data.stanford.edu/dime (accessed 6/24/16).

35. Ian Vandewalker and Lawrence Norden, "Small Donors Still Aren't as Important as Wealthy Ones," *The Atlantic*, October 18, 2016, www.theatlantic.com (accessed 1/3/17).

36. Nicholas Confessore, Sarah Cohen, and Karen Yourish, "The Families Funding the 2016 Presidential Election," *New York Times*, October 10, 2015, www.nytimes.com (accessed 1/3/17).

37. Catherine Dunn, "The 1 Percent: How Women and Men Compare in the Top Income Brackets," *International Business Times*, October 6, 2014, www.ibtimes.com (accessed 6/26/16).

38. "Women's Earnings and Income," *Catalyst*, April 8, 2016, www.catalyst.org (accessed 6/24/16).

39. Lilly Ledbetter Fair Pay Act, *National Women's Law Center*, January 29, 2013, www.nwlc.org (accessed 3/21/15).

40. Debra Mesch, "The Gender Gap in Charitable Giving," *Wall Street Journal*, February 1, 2016, www.wsj.com (accessed 6/26/16).

41. "Women and Wealth." *U.S. Trust's Insights on Wealth and Worth*, www.ustrust.com (accessed 6/26/16).

42. Mesch, Debra J., Melissa S. Brown, Zachary I. Moore, and Amir Daniel Hayay. 2011. "Gender Differences in Charitable Giving," *International Journal of Nonprofit and Voluntary Sector Marketing* 16: 342–55.

43. Lawless, Jennifer L., and Richard L. Fox. 2013. *Girls Just Wanna Not Run: The Gender Gap in Young Americans' Political Ambition*. Washington, DC: Women & Politics Institute.

44. For a discussion of the differences in resources women and men can devote to politics, see Schlozman, Kay Lehman, Nancy Burns, and Sidney Verba. 1994. "Gender and the Pathways to Participation: The Role of Resources." *Journal of Politics* 56(4): 963–90.

CHAPTER 6: HIS AND HER POLITICS

1. Anna Palmer and John Bresnahan, "GOP Men Told How to Talk to Women," *Politico*, December 5, 2013, www.politico.com (access 5/23/16).

2. Jennifer Steinhauer, "Senate Races Expose Extent of Republicans' Gender Gap," *New York Times*, November 7, 2012, www.nytimes.com (accessed 5/25/16).

3. Halimah Abdullah, "How Women Ruled the 2012 Election and Where the GOP Went Wrong," *CNN.com*, November 8, 2012, www.cnn.com (accessed 5/25/16).

4. Kirsten Powers, "GOP: Respect Women or Keep Losing," *Daily Beast,* November 8, 2012, www.thedailybeast.com (accessed 5/25/16).

5. "Rush Limbaugh vs. Sandra Fluke: A Timeline," *The Week*, March 9, 2012, http://theweek.com (accessed 3/19/15).

6. David Cohen, "Todd Akin: Legitimate Rape Victims Rarely Get Pregnant," *Politico*, August 19, 2012, www.politico.com (accessed 3/17/15).

7. Michael McAuliff, "Richard Mourdock on Abortion: Pregnancy from Rape Is Something God Intended," *Huffington Post*, October 23, 2012, www.huffingtonpost.com (accessed 3/17/15).

8. Editorial Board, "The Campaign against Women," *New York Times*, May 19, 2012, www.nytimes.com (accessed 5/30/16).

9. Stephanie Condon, "Boehner: Republicans Need to Be 'A Bit More Sensitive' to Women," *CBS News*, December 5, 2013, www.cbsnews.com (accessed 5/19/16).

10. Mike Allen, "Men Tutored in Running against Women," *Politico*, December 5, 2012, www.politico.com (accessed 5/19/16).

11. Deirdre Walsh and Dana Bash, "GOP Tries to Deal with Damage Done with Women," *CNN.com*, December 6, 2013, www.cnn.com (accessed 5/20/16).

12. Katie McDonough, "Republicans Are Trying to Learn How to Talk to Women (Again)," *Salon.com*, December 5, 2013, www.salon.com (accessed 5/17/16).

13. Dahlia Lithwick, "How to Talk to Republican Congressmen: A Guide for Women," *Slate.com*, December 10, 2013, www.slate.com (accessed 5/17/16).

14. Erin Gloria Ryan, "Republicans Offer Class on How to Talk to Women without Being a Dick," *Jezebel*, December 5, 2013, http://jezebel.com (accessed 6/5/16).

15. Kathleen Parker, "Teaching Republicans How to Talk to Women," *Washington Post*, December 10, 2013, www.washingtonpost.com (accessed 5/21/16).

16. Jocelyn Kiley, "As GOP Celebrates Win, No Sign of Narrowing Gender, Age Gaps," *Pew Research Center*, November 5, 2014, www.pewresearch.org (accessed 5/25/16).

17. Dozens of scholarly articles use Gilligan's work as the basis for exploring gender differences. See, for example, Brown-Kruse, Jamie, and David Hummels. 1993. "Gender Effects in Laboratory Public Goods Contribution." *Journal of Economic Behavior & Organization* 22(3): 255–67; Chaney, Carole Kennedy, R. Michael Alvarez, and Jonathan Nagler. 1988. "Explaining the Gender Gap in U.S. Presidential Elections, 1980–1992." *Political Research Quarterly* 51(2): 311–39; and Fox, Richard L., and Robert A. Schuhmann. 1999. "Gender and Local Government: A Comparison of Women and Men City Managers." *Public Administration Review* 59(3): 231–42.

18. Frank Newport, "Americans Prefer Boys to Girls, Just as They Did in 1941," *Gallup Organization*, June 23, 2011, www.gallup.com (accessed 5/23/16).

19. "The Gender Gap in Religion around the World," *Pew Research Center*, March 22, 2016, www.pewforum.org (accessed 5/25/16).

20. "Attitudes toward Work," *Pew Research Center*, September 3, 2009, www.pewsocialtrends.org (accessed 5/24/16).

21. Kevin Roderick, "Now That's a Gender Gap," *LA Observed*, November 12, 2012, www.laobserved.com (accessed 5/23/16).

22. Data drawn from Pew Research Center polls conducted between 2011 and 2016, and a compilation of polls available from the Center for American Women and Politics. See "The Gender Gap: Attitudes on Public Policy Issues," www.cawp.rutgers.edu/sites/default/files/resources/gg_issuesattitudes-2012.pdf (accessed 5/19/16).

23. "Republican Platform 2016," *GOP.com*, www.gop.com (accessed 12/29/16).

24. "2016 Democratic Party Platform," *Democrats.org*, www.presidency.ucsb.edu/papers_pdf/117717.pdf (accessed 12/29/16).

25. "2016 Party Identification Detailed Tables," *Pew Research Center*, September 13, 2016, http://assets.pewresearch.org/wp-content/uploads/sites/5/2016/09/09-13-16-Party-ID-Combined-Detailed-Tables.pdf (accessed 12/29/16).

26. Amy Walter, "The Myth of the Independent Voter," *Cook Political Report*, January 15, 2014, http://cookpolitical.com (accessed 5/29/16). See also Keith, Bruce E., David B. Magleby, Candice J. Nelson, Elizabeth A. Orr, Mark C. Westlye, and Raymond E. Wolfinger. 1992. *The Myth of the Independent Voter*. Berkeley: University of California Press.

27. "Election Polls—Presidential Vote by Groups," *Gallup*, www.gallup.com (accessed 5/28/16); and "Exit Polls," *CNN.com*, http://edition.cnn.com/election/results/exit-polls (accessed 1/4/17).

28. Bartels, Larry M. 2000. "Partisanship and Voting Behavior, 1956–1996." *American Journal of Political Science* 44(1): 35–50; Cohen, Geoffrey L. 2003. "Party over Policy: The Dominating Impact of Group Influence on Political Beliefs." *Journal of Personality and Social Psychology* 85(5): 808–22; King, David C., and Richard E. Matland. 2003. "Sex and the Grand Old Party: An Experimental Investigation of the Effect of Candidate Sex on Support for a Republican Candidate." *American Politics Research* 31(6): 595–612; Sides, John, and Lynn Vavreck. 2013. *The Gamble: Choice and Chance in the 2012 Presidential Election*. Princeton: Princeton University Press.

29. "Party Identification Trends," *Pew Research Center*, April 7, 2015, www.people-press.org (accessed 5/28/16); and "2016 Party Identification Detailed Tables," *Pew Research Center*, September 13, 2016.

30. The overall gender gap of 13 points is actually slightly larger than the gender gap among Whites, Blacks, and Latinos. This disparity can be accounted for by the 6 percent of voters who do not identify as White, Black, or Latino. The exit polls did not break this group down by sex, but it is sizeable enough to bring the overall gap to 13 percent.

31. For a discussion of the importance of focusing not only on differences, but also similarities, between men and women, see Ridgeway, Ceceila L. 2011. *Framed by Gender: How Gender Inequality Persists in the Modern World*. New York: Oxford University Press.

32. Jelen, Ted, Sue Thomas, and Clyde Wilcox. 1994. "The Gender Gap in Comparative Perspective." *European Journal of Political Science* 25: 171–86.

33. Goldberg, Gertrude Schaffner, and Eleanor Kremen. 1994. "The Feminization of Poverty: Not Only in America." In Marianne Githens, Pippa Norris, and Joni Lovenduski (eds.), *Different Roles, Different Voices*. New York: HarperCollins.

34. Herek, Gregory M. 2002. "Gender Gaps in Public Opinion about Lesbians and Gay Men." *Public Opinion Quarterly* 66: 40–67; "The Gender Gap: Three Decades

Old and as Big as Ever," *Pew Research Center*, March 29, 2012, www.people-press.org (accessed 5/30/16).

35. Freeman, Jo. 1999. "Gender Gaps in Presidential Elections." *PS: Political Science and Politics* 32(2): 191–2; Huddy, Leonie, Francis K. Neely, and Marilyn R. Lafay. 2000. "The Polls—Trends: Support for the Women's Movement." *Public Opinion Quarterly* 64: 309–50.

36. Greenberg, Anna M. 2000. "Why Men Leave: Gender and Partisanship in the 1990s," http://citeseerx.ist.psu.edu/viewdoc/summary?doi=10.1.1.508.4768 (accessed 6/4/16); Kaufmann, Karen M., and John R. Petrocik. 1999. "The Changing Politics of American Men: Understanding the Sources of the Gender Gap." *American Journal of Political Science* 43(3): 864–87; Wirls, Daniel. 1986. "Reinterpreting the Gender Gap." *Public Opinion Quarterly* 50(3): 316–30.

37. Dan Cassino, "Thought of a Woman President Rattles Male Voters in New Jersey," *Public Mind Poll*, March 23, 2016, http://view2.fdu.edu/publicmind/2016/160323/ (accessed 6/5/16).

38. Hannah Hartig, John Lapinski, and Stephanie Psyllos, "Hillary Clinton Holds Slim National Lead over Donald Trump: Poll," *NBCNews.com*, May 15, 2016, www.nbcnews.com (accessed 6/5/16).

39. Michael Tesler, "The Striking Decline in Women's Support for Donald Trump (in Two Graphs)," *The Monkey Cage*, May 9, 2016, www.washingtonpost.com (accessed 6/7/16).

CHAPTER 7: HE'S A PARTISAN, SHE'S A PARTISAN

1. Allison Pearson, "Margaret Thatcher Dies: We Must Show Men that We're Better Than They Are," *The Telegraph*, April 8, 2013, www.telegraph.co.uk (accessed 10/4/16).

2. John Haltiwanger, "Youngest Congresswoman Ever Explains Why We Need More Female Leaders," *Elite Daily*, March 8, 2016, http://elitedaily.com (accessed 5/18/17).

3. John Cookson, "Why Women Make Better Politicians," *BigThink.com*, http://bigthink.com (accessed 10/4/16).

4. Kim Parker, Juliana Menasce Horowitz, and Molly Rohal. "Chapter 2: What Makes a Good Leader and Does Gender Matter?" in "Women and Leadership: Public Says Women Are Equally Qualified, but Barriers Persist," *Pew Research Center*, January 14, 2015, www.pewsocialtrends.org (accessed 10/22/16).

5. Jay Newton-Small, "Women Are the Only Adults Left in Washington," *Time*, October 16, 2013, http://swampland.time.com (accessed 10/4/16).

6. Laura Bassett, "Men Got Us into this Shutdown, Women Got Us Out," *Huffington Post*, October 16, 2013, www.huffingtonpost.com (accessed 10/4/16).

7. Jay Newton-Small, "Women Are the Only Adults Left in Washington," *Time*, October 16, 2013.

8. Laura Bassett, "Men Got Us into this Shutdown, Women Got Us Out," *Huffington Post*, October 16, 2013.

9. Jay Newton-Small, "Women Are the Only Adults Left in Washington," *Time*, October 16, 2013.

10. Jonathan Weisman and Jennifer Steinhauer, "Senate Women Lead in Effort to Find Accord," *New York Times*, October 14, 2013, www.nytimes.com (accessed 10/4/16).

11. See Granovetter, Mark. 1985. "Economic Action and Social Structure: The Problem of Embeddedness." *American Journal of Sociology* 91(3): 481–510; and Shah, Pri Pradhan, and Karen A. Jehn. 1993. "Do Friends Perform Better than Acquaintances? The Interaction of Friendship, Conflict, and Task." *Group Decision and Negotiation* 2(2): 149–65.

12. Jordain Carney, "Senators Give Candy, Adele Albums in Secret Santa Gift Swap," *The Hill*, December 8, 2015, http://thehill.com (accessed 3/10/16).

13. U.S. Senate. "Seersucker Thursday," www.senate.gov/artandhistory/history/common/generic/SeersuckerThursday.htm (accessed 3/10/16).

14. "The Congressional Baseball Game for Charity," www.congressionalbaseball.org (accessed 5/9/16).

15. "Take 5: Rep. Ed Perlmutter," *Roll Call*, March 16, 2015, www.rollcall.com (accessed 5/9/16).

16. For details about these social engagement data, and year-by-year gender comparisons, see Lawless, Jennifer L., and Sean M. Theriault. 2016. "Mean Girls (and Boys)? Sex, Bipartisanship, and Collaboration in the U.S Congress." Paper presented at the spring meeting of the National Capital Area Political Science Association, Washington, DC: June 8, www.dannyhayes.org/uploads/6/9/8/5/69858539/lawless_theriault_workshop_june2016.pdf (accessed 10/22/16).

17. Men's lower rates of participation are not simply because they can field a team with a smaller fraction of men in Congress. For both games, the number of participants exceeds the number of players required, and everyone gets to play for at least part of the game. The rules are flexible enough to accommodate and encourage broad participation.

18. This is also true of corporate boards (see Konrad, Alison M., Vicki Kramer, and Sumru Erkut. 2008. "The Impact of Three or More Women on Corporate Boards." *Organizational Dynamics* 37[2]: 145–64) and local and state-level elected officials (see Epstein, Michael J., Richard G. Niemi, and Lynda W. Powell. 2005. "Do Women

and Men State Legislators Differ?" In Sue Thomas and Clyde Wilcox [eds.], *Women and Elective Office: Past, Present, and Future*, 2nd edition. New York: Oxford University Press; Richardson, Lilliard E., Jr., and Patricia K. Freeman. 1995. "Gender Differences in Constituency Service among State Legislators." *Political Research Quarterly* 48[1]: 169–79; Tolleson Rinehart, Sue. 1991. "Do Women Leaders Make a Difference? Substance, Style, and Perceptions." In Debra Dodson [ed.], *Gender and Policymaking: Studies of Women in Office*. New Brunswick: Rutgers University; Weikart, Lynne A., Greg Chen, Daniel W. Williams, and Haris Hromic. 2007. "The Democratic Sex: Gender Differences and the Exercise of Power." *Journal of Women, Politics & Policy* 28[1]: 119–40).

19. Kessler, Daniel, and Keith Krehbiel. 1996. "Dynamics of Cosponsorship." *American Political Science Review* 90(3): 555–66; Krehbiel, Keith. 1995. "Cosponsors and Wafflers from A to Z." *American Journal of Political Science* 39(4): 906–23; Woon, Jonathan. 2008. "Bill Sponsorship in Congress: The Moderating Effect of Agenda Positions on Legislative Proposals." *Journal of Politics* 70(1): 201–16.

20. The Center, which is "committed to thoughtful analysis and civil dialogue that facilitates bipartisan governance," uses sponsorship and cosponsorship data to create a measure of members' abilities to work across the aisle. See "Mission": www.thelugarcenter.org/about.html (accessed 5/9/16).

21. The Lugar Center has also computed the Bipartisan Index for members of the House of Representatives in the 113th Congress. Those results mirror the multi-year Senate results displayed in Figure 7.2.

22. See Dodson, Debra L. 1998. "Representing Women's Interests in the U.S. House of Representatives." In Sue Thomas and Clyde Wilcox (eds.), *Women and Elective Office*. New York: Oxford University Press; Paolino, Phillip. 1995. "Group-Salient Issues and Group Representation: Support for Women Candidates in the 1992 Senate Elections." *American Journal of Political Science* 39(2): 294–313; Swers, Michele L. 2002. *The Difference Women Make*. Chicago: University of Chicago Press.

23. It is actually procedural votes where the rise of congressional partisanship has been the most dramatic. See Roberts, Jason M., and Steven S. Smith. 2003. "Procedural Contexts, Party Strategy, and Conditional Party Voting in the U.S. House of Representatives, 1971–2000." *American Journal of Political Science* 47(1): 305–17; Sinclair, Barbara. 2006. *Party Wars: Polarization and the Politics of National Policy Making*. Norman: University of Oklahoma Press; Theriault, Sean M. 2008. *Party Polarization in the Congress*. New York: Cambridge University Press.

24. The algorithm does not standardize scores across time, so a dip in mean scores from one Congress to the next cannot necessarily be interpreted as a shift in mean procedural vote scores. Hence, the dotted lines in the figure.

25. We conducted a similar analysis in the Senate. Never have more than 21 women served in the U.S. Senate, and Republicans have never had more than six at any one time. But even with a limited number of cases, the pattern is similar.

26. See, for example, Dodson, Debra L. 1998. "Representing Women's Interests in the U.S. House of Representatives." In Sue Thomas and Clyde Wilcox (eds.), *Women and Elective Office*. New York: Oxford University Press; Frederick, Brian. 2011. "Gender Turnover and Roll Call Voting in the U.S. Senate." *Journal of Women, Politics & Policy* 32(3): 193–210; MacDonald, Jason A. and Erin E. O'Brien. 2011. "Quasi-Experimental Design, Constituency, and Advancing Women's Interests: Reexamining the Influence of Gender on Substantive Representation." *Political Research Quarterly* 4(2): 472–86; Swers, Michele L. 2002. *The Difference Women Make*. Chicago: University of Chicago Press.

27. In the Senate, for example, the stark differences between the parties on issues pertaining to women, families, and children now far exceed any gender differences on these issues (Swers, Michele L. 2013. *Women in the Club: Gender and Policy Making in the Senate*. Chicago: University of Chicago Press). Other scholars find that, controlling for party and constituency influences, member sex does not predict the "liberalness" of roll call behavior in the House (see Schwindt-Bayer, Leslie A., and Renato Corbetta. 2004. "Gender Turnover and Roll-Call Voting in the U.S. House of Representatives." *Legislative Studies Quarterly* 29[2]: 215–29; Frederick, Brian. 2009. "Are Female House Members Still More Liberal in a Polarized Era?" *Congress & the Presidency* 36[2]: 181–202).

28. For a summary of research on gendered leadership styles, see Leire-Gartzia, Marloes van Engen. 2008. "Are (Male) Leaders 'Feminine' Enough?: Gendered Traits of Identity as Mediators of Sex Differences in Leadership Styles." *Gender in Management: An International Journal* 27(5): 296–314.

29. Wesley Lowery, "How Congress Became So Partisan, in Four Charts," *Washington Post*, April 14, 2014, www.washingtonpost.com (accessed 10/7/16).

30. Elahe Izade, *National Journal*, February 3, 2014, "Congress Sets Record for Voting along Party Lines," www.nationaljournal.com (accessed 10/7/16).

31. Hayes, Danny, and Jennifer L. Lawless. 2016. *Women on the Run: Gender, Media, and Political Campaigns in a Polarized Era*. New York: Cambridge University Press.

32. Cox, Gary W., and Matthew D. McCubbins. 1993. *Legislative Leviathan: Party Government in the House*. Berkeley: University of California Press; Rohde, David W. 1991. *Parties and Leaders in the Postreform House*. Chicago: University of Chicago Press.

33. Anzia, Sarah F., and Christopher R. Berry. 2011. "The Jackie (and Jill) Robinson Effect: Why Do Congresswomen Outperform Congressmen?" *American Journal of Political Science* 55(3): 478–93.

34. Volden, Craig, Alan E. Wiseman, and Dana E. Wittmer. 2013. "When Are Women More Effective Lawmakers than Men?" *American Journal of Political Science* 57(2): 326–41.

35. Pearson, Kathryn, and Logan Dancey. 2011. "Speaking for the Underrepresented in the House of Representatives: Voicing Women's Interests in a Partisan Chamber." *Politics & Gender* 7(4): 493–519.

36. Burns, Nancy, Kay Lehman Schlozman, and Sidney Verba. 2001. *The Private Roots of Public Action: Gender, Equality, and Political Participation.* Cambridge: Harvard University Press; Hansen, Susan B. 1997. "Talking about Politics: Gender and Contextual Effects on Political Proselytizing." *Journal of Politics* 59(1): 73–103.

37. Jones, Philip E. 2014. "Does the Descriptive Representation of Gender Influence Accountability for Substantive Representation?" *Politics & Gender* 10(2): 175–99.

38. Campbell, David E., and Christina Wolbrecht. 2006. "See Jane Run: Women Politicians as Role Models for Adolescents." *Journal of Politics* 68(2): 233–47.

39. Jaclyn Friedman, "Why Hillary Clinton Being the 'First Woman' President Matters," *Time*, June 13, 2016, http://time.com (accessed 10/12/16).

40. Prachi Gupta, "19 Women Who Will Make History If Elected to Congress This Year," *Cosmopolitan*, August 16, 2016, www.cosmopolitan.com (accessed 10/12/16).

CHAPTER 8: HE EARNS, SHE EARNS (LESS)

1. Kate Pickert, "2-Minute Bio: Lilly Ledbetter," *Time*, January 29, 2009, http://content.time.com (accessed 10/28/16).

2. *Ledbetter v. Goodyear Tire and Rubber Company*, 550 U.S. 618 (2007).

3. "Pay Equity Pioneer Lilly Ledbetter Addresses the DNC," *PBS Newshour*, August 26, 2008, www.pbs.org (accessed 11/11/16).

4. Glenn Kessler, "Lilly Ledbetter, Barack Obama, and the Famous 'Anonymous Note'," *Washington Post*, May 14, 2015, www.washingtonpost.com (accessed 11/11/16).

5. Title VII of the Civil Rights Act, www.eeoc.gov/laws/statutes/titlevii.cfm (accessed 11/26/16).

6. "Justice Ginsburg Dissent." *Ledbetter v. Goodyear Tire and Rubber Company*, 550 U.S. 618 (2007), www.law.cornell.edu/supct/pdf/05-1074P.ZD (accessed 11/23/16).

7. Robert Barnes, "Over Ginsburg's Dissent, Court Limits Bias Suits," *Washington Post*, May 30, 2007, www.washingtonpost.com (accessed 11/1/16).

8. See Bernie Sanders's presidential campaign website, http://feelthebern.org/bernie-sanders-on-equal-pay (accessed 11/14/16).

9. "Hillary Clinton Takes on the Gender Pay Gap: 'There's No Discount for Being a Woman'," *AOL News*, April 12, 2016, www.aol.com (accessed 11/3/16).

10. Bryce Covert, "Where the Presidential Candidates Stand on Equal Pay," *ThinkProgress*, April 14, 2015, https://thinkprogress.org (accessed 10/28/16).

11. Jessica Militare, "This Is What Donald Trump Thinks about Equal Pay," *Glamour*, August 21, 2015, www.glamour.com (accessed 11/14/16).

12. "Celebrate Equal Pay Day with AAUW on Twitter," April 12, 2016, www.aauw.org/event/2016/04/equal-pay-day-on-twitter (accessed 11/16/16).

13. "Equal Pay and the Wage Gap," *National Women's Law Center*, https://nwlc.org/issue/equal-pay-and-the-wage-gap (accessed 11/16/16).

14. For instance, see Kevin Cochrane, "Why Is There a Gender Pay Gap?" *Weekly Standard*, May 20, 2016, www.weeklystandard.com (accessed 10/30/16).

15. "Whoops! Vox Just Disproved the Gender Pay Gap by Accident," *Breitbart.com*, August 2, 2016, www.breitbart.com (accessed 11/16/16).

16. "On Pay Gap, Millennial Women Near Parity for Now," *Pew Research Center*, December 11, 2013, www.pewsocialtrends.org (accessed 11/17/16).

17. Lapidus, Jane, and Deborah M. Figart. 1998. "Remedying Unfair Acts: U.S. Pay Equity by Race and Gender." *Feminist Economics* 4(3): 7–28.

18. The racial double disadvantage is also affected by region, the influx of immigrants and job opportunities, and cultures specific to particular groups. See McCall, Leslie. 2001. "Sources of Racial Wage Inequality in Metropolitan Labor Markets: Racial, Ethnic, and Gender Differences." *American Sociological Review* 66(4): 520–41.

19. See, for example, Fukuda-Parr, Sakiko. 1999. "What Does Feminization of Poverty Mean? It Isn't Just Lack of Income." *Feminist Economics* 5(2): 99–103; Goldberg, Gertrude Schaffner, and Eleanor Kremen. 1990. *The Feminization of Poverty: Only in America?* Westport, CT: Praeger; Jones, John Paul, and Janet E. Kodras. 1990. "Restructured Regions and Families: The Feminization of Poverty in the U.S." *Annals of the Association of American Geographers* 80(2): 163–83; Pressman, Steven. 2003. "Feminist Explanations for the Feminization of Poverty." *Journal of Economic Issues* 37(2): 353–61.

20. *Goesart et al. v. Cleary et al.*, 335 U.S. 464 (1948).

21. For an image of the job announcement, see http://file.vintageadbrowser.com/l-9fyd87orjhfme9.jpg (accessed 11/21/16). For a more detailed account of airlines' hiring practices, see Vantoch, Victoria. 2013. *The Jet Sex: Airline Stewardesses and the Making of an American Icon.* Philadelphia: University of Pennsylvania Press.

22. Ariante Hegewisch and Heidi Hartman, "Occupational Segregation and the Gender Wage Gap: A Job Half Done," *Institute for Women's Policy Research*, January 2014, www.iwpr.org (accessed 11/20/16).

23. Shane Ferro, "There's a Gender Pay Gap at Every Age, and It Only Gets Worse as Workers Get Older," *Business Insider*, January 28, 2015, www.businessinsider.com (accessed 11/23/16).

24. Leibbrant, Andreas, and John A. List. 2012. "Do Women Avoid Salary Negotiations?: Evidence from a Large-Scale Field Experiment." NBER Working Paper 18511.

25. Small, Deborah A., Michele Gelfand, Linda Babcock, and Hilary Gettman. 2007. "Who Goes to the Bargaining Table? The Influence of Gender and Framing on the Initiation of Negotiation." *Journal of Personality and Social Psychology* 93(4): 600–13.

26. Bowles, Hannah Riley, Linda C. Babcock, and Kathleen McGinn. 2005. "Constraints and Triggers: Situational Mechanics of Gender in Negotiation." *Journal of Personality and Social Psychology* 89(6): 951–65.

27. Babcock, Linda, and Sarah Laschever. 2003. *Women Don't Ask: Negotiation and the Gender Divide*. Princeton, NJ: Princeton University Press.

28. "Salary Stats: Women versus Men." *Washington Post*, November 7, 2008, www.washingtonpost.com (accessed 11/19/16).

29. "Attorney/Lawyer Salary." Pay Scale Human Capital, www.payscale.com/research/US/Job=Attorney_%2F_Lawyer/Salary (accessed 11/19/16).

30. "Salary Stats: Women versus Men." *Washington Post*, November 7, 2008.

31. Jeremy C. Fox, "Elizabeth Warren Slams Donald Trump's Economic Plan," *Boston Globe*, August 9, 2016, www.bostonglobe.com (accessed 11/23/16).

32. People may also use the Family and Medical Leave Act to take time off to care for a sick relative or to tend to an illness of their own.

33. "Family and Medical Leave Act." Department of Labor, Wages and Hours Division, www.dol.gov/whd/fmla (accessed 11/28/16).

34. Overall, the law is quite limited. It applies only to employees of public agencies, elementary and secondary schools, and businesses with at least 50 employees. Moreover, employees qualify only if they've worked for the company, school, or agency for at least a year and at a minimum of 24 hours per week. Employees at small businesses, as well as part-time workers, are not covered by the law.

35. Alexis Boncy, "Paid Family Leave, Explained," *The Week*, August 2, 2016, http://theweek.com (accessed 11/28/16).

36. Margaret Talbot, "America's Family Leave Disgrace," *The New Yorker*, January 22, 2015, www.newyorker.com (accessed 1/7/17).

37. Josh Levs, "Paid Family Leave Could Be a Reality in Trump's America," *Time*, November 14, 2016, http://time.com (accessed 11/28/16).

38. Kling, Kristen C., Janet Hyde, Carolin Showers, and Brenda N. Buswell. 1999. "Gender Differences in Self-Esteem: A Meta-Analysis." *Psychological Bulletin* 125(4): 470–500.

39. Wigfield, Allan, Jacquelynne S. Eccles, and Paul R. Pintrich. 1996. "Development Between the Ages of 11 and 25." In D. C. Berliner and R. C. Calfee (eds.), *Handbook of Educational Psychology*. New York: Macmillan.

40. Furnham, Adrian, and Richard Rawles. 1995. "Sex Differences in the Estimation of Intelligence." *Journal of Social Behavior and Personality* 10: 741–48; Beloff, Halla. 1992. "Mother, Father and Me: Our IQ." *Psychologist* 5: 309–11.

41. See, for example, S. 84, Paycheck Fairness Act, 113th Congress (2013–2014), www.congress.gov/bill/113th-congress/senate-bill/84 (accessed 11/23/16).

42. Sarah Portlock, "Gender Wage Gap in Eight Charts," *Wall Street Journal*, April 14, 2015, http://blogs.wsj.com (accessed 11/16/16).

CHAPTER 9: THE PAST, PRESENT, AND FUTURE OF REPRODUCTIVE RIGHTS IN THE UNITED STATES

1. Liam Stack, "A Brief History of Deadly Attacks on Abortion Providers," *New York Times*, November 29, 2015, www.nytimes.com (accessed 7/24/16).

2. These allegations resulted in congressional hearings, an audit of Planned Parenthood's medical and financial records, and countless calls—from activists, elected officials, and Republican presidential candidates during the 2016 GOP primary—to shut down Planned Parenthood. Still today, no evidence exists to support these claims. See Tamar Lewin, "Planned Parenthood Won't Accept Money for Fetal Tissue," *New York Times*, October 13, 2015, www.nytimes.com (accessed 7/24/16).

3. "2015 Violence and Disruption Statistics." *National Abortion Federation*, April 2016, 5aa1b2xfmfh2e2mk03kk8rsx.wpengine.netdna-cdn.com/wp-content/uploads/2015-NAF-Violence-Disruption-Stats.pdf (accessed 7/25/16).

4. For overviews on the changing tactics of the anti-choice movement, see Wilson, Joshua C. 2013. *The Street Politics of Abortion: Speech, Violence, and America's Culture Wars*. Stanford: Stanford University Press; and Williams, Daniel K. 2016. *Defenders of the Unborn: The Pro-Life Movement before* Roe v. Wade. New York: Oxford University Press.

5. This ruling launched the contentious debate over an issue that had been percolating at a lower profile for many years. Indeed, in the second half of the nineteenth century—more than 100 years before *Roe v. Wade*—early feminists, the American Medical Association, and anti-obscenity advocates fought to outlaw abortion. And they were largely successful. It wasn't until the 1960s that a new wave of feminists working with health care professionals began pushing for more lenient abortion policies. That movement was making headway—13 states between 1967 and 1972 legalized therapeutic abortions and three states removed all restrictions—when the *Roe v. Wade* ruling hit.

6. The Court argued that a "zone of privacy" is found in the First, Fourth, Ninth, and Fourteenth Amendments and that it was "broad enough to encompass a woman's decision whether or not to terminate her pregnancy."

7. *Roe v. Wade*, 410 U.S. 113 (1973). To listen to the oral arguments in the case, visit www.oyez.org/cases/1971/70-18 (accessed 7/19/16).

8. "Abortion." *National Women's Law Center*, https://nwlc.org/issue/abortion (accessed 7/19/16).

9. "Abortion." *Family Research Council*, www.frc.org/abortion (accessed 7/10/16).

10. "Who We Are." *Operation Rescue*, www.operationrescue.org/about-us/who-we-are (accessed 7/19/16).

11. For an overview of the legal, medical, religious, and political aspects of the abortion debate, see Solinger, Rickie. 2013. *Reproductive Politics: What Everyone Needs to Know*. New York: Oxford University Press. And for a discussion of the tactics employed by both sides of the debate, including when and how to use media to further their cause, see Rohlinger, Deana A. 2014. *Abortion Politics, Mass Media, and Social Movements in America*. New York: Cambridge University Press.

12. Somewhat surprisingly, 54 percent of Catholics say that abortion should be legal in all or most circumstances, which is roughly the same as Black Protestants (52 percent), but quite a bit lower than White Mainline Protestants (66 percent) and people with no religious affiliation (78 percent). See "Public Opinion on Abortion, 1995–2016," *Pew Research Center*, April 8, 2016, www.pewforum.org (accessed 7/31/16).

13. See Roberts, Dorothy. 1997. *Killing the Black Body: Race, Reproduction, and the Meaning of Liberty*. New York: Vintage Books.

14. Pew Research Center poll, conducted from March 17–27, 2016.

15. In an additional four states, abortion restrictions were proposed, but they failed to garner sufficient support to make their way onto the ballot.

16. Toobin, Jeffrey. 2007. *The Nine: Inside the Secret World of the Supreme Court*. New York: Anchor Books.

17. Seth Stern, "Brennan's Rule of Five as Campaign Mantra," *The Justice Brennan Blog*, September 20, 2010, http://justicebrennan.com/blog/?p=130 (accessed 7/19/16).

18. "A History of Key Abortion Rulings of the Supreme Court." *Pew Research Center*, January 13, 2016, www.pewforum.org (accessed 7/24/16).

19. "Justices Almost Overturned *Roe versus Wade* in 1992," *USA Today*, March 4, 2004, http://usatoday30.usatoday.com (accessed 7/24/16).

20. *Whole Woman's Health v. Hellerstedt*, 579 U.S. (2016), www.oyez.org/cases/2015/15-274 (accessed 7/24/16).

21. Tim Storey, "GOP Makes Historic State Legislative Gains in 2010," *Rasmussen Reports*, December 10, 2010, www.rasmussenreports.com (accessed 7/20/16).

22. Tim Storey, "StateVote: 2014 Election Results," *National Conference of State Legislatures*, November 19, 2014, www.ncsl.org/research/elections-and-campaigns/statevote-2014-post-election-analysis635508614.aspx (accessed 7/20/16).

23. Alan Greenblatt, "Republicans Add to Their Dominance of State Legislatures," *Governing*, November 9, 2016, www.governing.com (accessed 12/28/16).

24. "The 334 abortion restrictions enacted by states from 2011 to July 2016 account for 30% of all abortion restrictions since *Roe v. Wade*," *Guttmacher Institute*, July 21, 2016, www.guttmacher.org/infographic/2016/334-abortion-restrictions-enacted-states-2011-july-2016-account-30-all-abortion (accessed 8/1/16).

25. "An Overview of Abortion Laws," *Guttmacher Institute*, July 1, 2016, www.guttmacher.org/state-policy/explore/overview-abortion-laws (accessed 7/20/16).

26. "Extremely hostile" states restrict abortion in at least five ways. See "The number of states considered hostile to abortion skyrocketed between 2000 and 2014," *Guttmacher Institute*, January 5, 2015, www.guttmacher.org/sites/default/files/infographic_attachment/2000-2014-maps-states.pdf (accessed 8/1/16).

27. Allison McCann, "Maps of Access to Abortion by State," *FiveThirtyEight*, May 14, 2014, http://fivethirtyeight.com (accessed 8/1/16).

28. "*Roe v. Wade* and the Right to Choose." *NARAL Pro-Choice America,* www.prochoiceamerica.org/media/fact-sheets/government-federal-courts-scotus-roe.pdf (accessed 7/24/16).

29. Rachel K. Jones and Jemma Jerman, "Abortion Incidence and Service Availability in the United States, 2014," *Guttmacher Institute*, January 17, 2017, www.guttmacher.org/journals/psrh/2017/01/abortion-incidence-and-service-availability-united-states-2014 (accessed 3/3/17).

30. Data compiled from GovTrack for the 112th, 113th, and 114th Congress, using "abortion" as a keyword, www.govtrack.us/congress/bills/subjects/abortion/5897#congress=112 (accessed 7/22/16).

31. H.R. 1091 (113th), Life at Conception Act. Sponsored by Jim Jordan (R-OH4) and introduced on March 12, 2013.

32. S. 32 (113th), Child Custody Protection Act. Sponsored by Rob Portman (R-OH) and introduced on January 22, 2013.

33. H.R. 3802 (112th), National Pro-Life Waiting Period Act of 2012. Sponsored by Jeff Duncan (R-SC3) and introduced on January 23, 2012.

34. David M. Herszenhorn, "House Republicans Vote to Stop Funding Planned Parenthood," *New York Times*, September 18, 2015, www.nytimes.com (accessed 7/24/16).

35. Deirdre Walsh, "Senate Vote to Defund Planned Parenthood Fails," *CNN.com*, August 3, 2015, www.cnn.com (accessed 7/24/16).

36. Benjamin Siegel, "Boehner: Promises No Government Shutdown over Planned Parenthood," *ABC News*, September 27, 2015, http://abcnews.go.com (accessed 7/24/16).

37. Manu Raju, Ted Barrett, and Tom LoBianco, "Senate GOP: No Hearings for Supreme Court Nominee," *CNN.com*, February 23, 2016, www.cnn.com (accessed 7/24/16).

38. "How Long Does It Take to Confirm a Supreme Court Nominee?" *New York Times*, February 13, 2016, www.nytimes.com (accessed 7/24/16).

39. Politico Pro Staff, "Scalia's Death Could Change Court on Abortion, Race, Climate," *Politico*, February 13, 2016, www.politico.com (accessed 7/24/16).

40. Steve Ertelt, "Hillary Clinton: I Would Not Appoint Someone to the Supreme Court Who Did Not Support Abortion," *LifeNews.com*, March 29, 2016, www.lifenews.com (accessed 7/24/16).

41. Jesse Byrnes, "Republicans Have 'No Choice' but to Vote for Me," *The Hill*, July 28, 2016, http://thehill.com (accessed 8/1/16).

42. Matthew Facciani, "Pence Says Abortions Will Become Illegal if Trump Wins," *Patheos*, June 29, 2016, www.patheos.com (accessed 8/1/16).

43. Gordon, Linda. 2002. *The Moral Property of Women: A History of Birth Control Politics in America*. Chicago: University of Illinois Press.

44. Pollitt, Katha. 2014. *Pro: Reclaiming Abortion Rights*. New York: Picador, p. 4.

45. "National Right to Life Committee Mourns the Death of Former Congressman Henry J. Hyde," *NRLC.com*, November 29, 2007, www.nrlc.org/archive/press_releases_new/Mourns%20Henry%20Hyde.htm (accessed 8/3/16).

46. Sandhya Somashekhar, "Study: Abortion Rate at Lowest Point since 1973," *Washington Post*, February 2, 2014, www.washingtonpost.com (accessed 8/2/16).

47. Luker, Kristin. 1984. *Abortion and the Politics of Motherhood*. Berkeley: University of California Press.

48. O'Connor, Karen. 1996. *No Neutral Ground? Abortion Politics in an Age of Absolutes*. Boulder: Westview Press.

49. "2016 Democratic Party Platform," www.demconvention.com/wp-content/uploads/2016/07/Democratic-Party-Platform-7.21.16-no-lines.pdf (accessed 7/26/16).

50. "Republican Platform 2016," https://prod-static-ngop-pbl.s3.amazonaws.com/media/documents/DRAFT_12_FINAL[1]-ben_1468872234.pdf (accessed 7/26/16).

CHAPTER 10: "FREE TO BE" OR STILL A BUMPY RIDE?

1. "Makers Profile: Ruth Bader Ginsburg," www.makers.com/ruth-bader-ginsburg (accessed 8/23/16).

2. "The 1960s–1970s American Feminist Movement: Breaking Down Barriers for Women," https://tavaana.org/en/content/1960s-70s-american-feminist-movement-breaking-down-barriers-women (accessed 8/23/16).

3. Ginsburg persevered, though, and it paid off. She landed a district court clerkship in 1963 and went on to become the first tenured female law professor at Columbia. In 1980, President Jimmy Carter appointed Ginsburg to the U.S. Court of Appeals for the District of Columbia. Thirteen years later, President Bill Clinton appointed her a justice to the U.S. Supreme Court.

4. "Women in Law in Canada and the U.S." *Catalyst*, March 3, 2015, www.catalyst.org (accessed 8/23/16).

5. "Statistical Overview of Women in the Workforce." *Catalyst*, April 6, 2016, www.catalyst.org (accessed 8/23/16).

6. Philip Cohen, "More Women Are Doctors and Lawyers than Ever—But Progress Is Stalling," *The Atlantic*, December 11, 2012, www.theatlantic.com (accessed 8/23/16).

7. "Distribution of Physicians by Gender." *Henry J. Kaiser Family Foundation,* April 2016, http://kff.org/other/state-indicator/physicians-by-gender (accessed 8/23/16).

8. Kenneth T. Walsh, "The 1960s: A Decade of Change for Women," *U.S. News & World Report*, March 12, 2010, www.usnews.com (accessed 9/5/16).

9. Elizabeth Barber, "Stay-at-Home Moms: A Rising Trend, Fueled by Immigration and a Weak Economy," *Christian Science Monitor,* April 9, 2014, www.csmonitor.com (accessed 8/23/16).

10. Kim Parker and Wendy Wang, "Modern Parenthood," *Pew Research Center*, March 14, 2013, www.pewsocialtrends.org (accessed 8/18/16).

11. D'Vera Cohn, Gretchen Livingston, and Wendy Wang, "Chapter 4: Public Views on Staying at Home Versus Working," *Pew Research Center*, April 8, 2014, www.pewsocialtrends.org (accessed 8/18/16).

12. Or think about how these successful women and men filled a typical 24 hours. Women and men, on average, spent similar amounts of time working (9 hours) and sleeping (7 hours) every day. But women reported spending about 30 percent more of their remaining time than men did on household tasks, and 64 percent more time on child care. See Fox, Richard L., and Jennifer L. Lawless. 2014. "Reconciling Family Roles with Political Ambition: The New Normal for Women in 21st Century U.S. Politics." *Journal of Politics* 76(2): 398–414; Lawless, Jennifer L., and Richard L. Fox. 2012. *Men Rule: The Continued Under-Representation of Women in U.S. Politics*. Washington, DC: Women & Politics Institute.

13. Taryn Hillin, "Women Are Literally Expected to Do All the Chores, Depressing Study Finds," *Fusion*, August 23, 2016, http://fusion.net (accessed 8/28/16).

14. Massimo Tommasoli (ed.), "Democracy and Gender Equality: The Role of the U.N.," Report from the International Roundtable on Democracy and Gender Equality, September 2013, www.idea.int/publications/democracy-and-gender-equality/loader.cfm?csModule=security/getfile&pageid=59108 (accessed 9/5/16).

15. "Makers Profile: Ruth Bader Ginsburg," www.makers.com/ruth-bader-ginsburg (accessed 8/23/16).

16. Freedman, Estelle. 2002. *No Turning Back*. New York: Ballantine Books.

17. L. H. Sanders, "1943 Guide to Hiring Women," *Mass Transportation Magazine*, July, pp. 244–57, www.snopes.com/language/graphics/women2.jpg (accessed 8/26/16).

18. See "Federal Laws Prohibiting Job Discrimination Questions and Answers," *Equal Employment Opportunity Commission*, www.eeoc.gov/facts/qanda.html (accessed 9/5/16).

19. Eileen Patten and Kim Parker, "A Gender Reversal on Career Aspirations," *Pew Research Center*, April 19, 2012, www.pewsocialtrends.org (accessed 8/27/16).

20. We embedded this simple experiment in the GfK survey and used random assignment to determine which respondents evaluated a male versus a female boss.

21. Eagly, Alice H., and Steven J. Karay. 2002. "Role Congruity Theory of Prejudice toward Female Leaders." *Psychological Review* 109(3): 573–98.

22. Eagly, Alice H. 2007. "Female Leadership Advantage and Disadvantage: Resolving the Contradictions." *Psychology of Women Quarterly* 31(1): 1–12.

23. Scott Jaschik, "Rate My Word Choice," *Inside Higher Education*, February 9, 2015, www.insidehighered.com (accessed 12/28/16).

24. Clair Cain Miller, "Is the Professor Bossy or Brilliant? Much Depends on Gender," *New York Times*, February 6, 2015, www.nytimes.com (accessed 12/28/16).

25. Kerber, Linda. 1998. *No Constitutional Right to Be Ladies*. New York: Hill and Wang.

26. D'Vera Cohn, "How Many Same-Sex Married Couples in the United States? Maybe 170,000," *Pew Research Center*, June 24, 2015, www.pewresearch.org (accessed 8/29/16).

27. Wendy Klein, Carolina Izquierdo, and Thomas N. Bradbury, "The Difference between a Happy Marriage and a Miserable One: Chores," *The Atlantic*, March 1, 2013, www.theatlantic.com (accessed 8/30/16).

28. Amanda Marcotte, "What *Mad Men* Says about Women," *The Guardian*, April 5, 2013, www.theguardian.com (accessed 8/28/16).

29. "A Current Glance at Women and the Law." *American Bar Association*, May 2016, www.americanbar.org/content/dam/aba/marketing/women/current_glance_statistics_may2016.authcheckdam.pdf (accessed 8/23/16).

30. "Women CEOs of the S&P 500." *Catalyst*, July 26, 2016, www.catalyst.org (accessed 8/23/16).

31. "Women in Academia." *Catalyst*, July 9, 2015, www.catalyst.org (accessed 8/23/16). For a full breakdown of all faculty positions by sex, see Table 11 of the American Association of University Professors 2013–14 report, www.aaup.org/sites/default/files/files/2014%20salary%20report/Table11.pdf (accessed 9/6/16).

32. Eileen Patten, "On Equal Pay Day, Key Facts about the Gender Pay Gap," *Pew Research Center*, April 14, 2015, www.pewresearch.org (accessed 9/3/16).

33. Lisa McKenzie, "Are Women Opting Out of Corporate Careers?" www.prweb.com/releases/2004/06/prweb130800.htm (accessed 9/3/16).

34. See Lisa Belkin, "The Opt-Out Revolution," *New York Times Magazine*, October 26, 2003, www.nytimes.com (accessed 9/3/16); and Hirshman, Linda. 2006. *Get to Work: A Manifesto for Women of the World*. New York: Viking.

35. Pamela Stone provides a more authoritative account of this phenomenon. She concludes that many of the women who "opt-out" are actually responding to significant private and professional pressures that ultimately force them out of the workplace (Stone, Pamela. 2007. *Opting Out: Why Women Really Quit Careers and Head Home*. Berkeley: University of California). For a broader historical discussion of how women struggle to strike a balance between their competing private and public sphere roles, see Jamieson, Kathleen Hall. 1995. *Beyond the Double Bind*. New York: Oxford University Press.

36. Okin, Susan Moller. 1989. *Justice, Gender, and the Family*. New York: Basic Books, pp. 170–1.

37. "Child Care Reforms That Will Make America Great Again," www.donaldjtrump.com (accessed 9/26/16).

38. Danielle Paquette, "The Enormous Ambition of Hillary Clinton's Child Care Plan," *Washington Post*, May 12, 2016, www.washingtonpost.com (accessed 9/26/16).

39. See, for example, Halpern, Diane F., and Fanny M. Cheung. 2008. *Women at the Top: Powerful Women Leaders Tell Us How to Combine Work and Family*. Malden: Wiley-Blackwell; and van Steenbergen, Elianne F., Naomi Ellemers, and Ab Mooijaart. 2007. "How Work and Family Can Facilitate Each Other: Distinct Types of Work-Family Facilitation and Outcomes for Women and Men." *Journal of Occupational Health Psychology* 12(3): 279–300. A recent review of research pertaining to balancing family and professional life identifies more than 150 studies that address the types of programs and policies that work best for women to navigate their dual roles (Kelly, Erin L., Ellen Emst Kossek, Leslie B. Hammer, Mary Durham, Jeremy Bray, Kelly Chermack, Lauren A. Murphy, and Dan Kaskubar. 2008. "Chapter 7: Getting There from Here: Research on the Effects of Work-Family Initiatives on Work-Family Conflict and Business Outcomes." *The Academy of Management Annals* 2[1]: 305–49.

CREDITS

INDEX

In this index, page locators in **bold** indicate illustrative material.